PHILOSOPHY OF EDUCATION AND THE CURRICULUM

A

PHILOSOPHY OF EDUCATION AND THE CURRICULUM

EDITED BY

KEITH DIXON
DEPARTMENT OF SOCIOLOGY
UNIVERSITY OF YORK

PERGAMON PRESS
OXFORD · NEW YORK · TORONTO
SYDNEY · BRAUNSCHWEIG

Pergamon Press Ltd., Headington Hill Hall, Oxford

Pergamon Press Inc., Maxwell House, Fairview Park, Elmsford,
New York 10523

Pergamon of Canada Ltd., 207 Queen's Quay West, Toronto 1

Pergamon Press (Aust.) Pty. Ltd., 19a Boundary Street,
Rushcutters Bay, N.S.W. 2011, Australia

Vieweg & Sohn GmbH, Burgplatz 1, Braunschweig

First edition 1972

Library of Congress Catalog Card No. 70-171837

Printed in Great Britain by A. Wheaton & Co., Exeter

CONTENTS

INTRODUCTION

EDITORIAL responsibility carries with it both obligations and opportunities. I have, in general, neglected my obligations and seized my opportunities.

In determining the format of the book I have chosen to include mathematics, science and history as examples of disciplines which are dissimilar in subject matter but which are clearly all forms, though not necessarily autonomous forms, of knowledge. These activities or discourses I have distinguished from moral education which is not concerned with knowledge but with the more or less consistent and 'rational' sets of *decisions* we take in evaluating human conduct in a total context. I have also chosen to include a section on learning theory which both implicitly and explicitly raises questions relevant to the philosophy of mind and the philosophy of action, and which at the same time provides an account of some important theoretical and empirical issues in learning theory.

I have omitted philosophical analyses of 'aesthetic' education – not because I think these areas unimportant – but because the scope of aesthetics, covering as it does literature, music, art and physical education, dictates separate and more lengthy treatment than I could justifiably allow. Furthermore, the criteria involved in the justification of aesthetic judgements are notoriously difficult to adumbrate and to relate firmly to teaching and curriculum construction.

But perhaps the most serious criticism that might be levelled at my editorial selection is the neglect of religious education. I want to say more about this in what follows.

The Forms of Knowledge Argument and Religious Education

Two of the contributors – Colin Holroyd and Peter Rogers – have explicitly stated their dissatisfaction with some of Paul Hirst's arguments concerning the existence of 'forms of knowledge' which may be identified and justified as curriculum subjects in view of the fact that they exhibit 'conceptual autonomy' or their own coherent internal logic and are tested by 'experience'. The relevant quotations, cited elsewhere in this book, are by this time pretty familiar to most students of education. Hirst includes as distinct disciplines or forms of knowledge: mathematics, the physical sciences; the human sciences, history, religion, literature, the fine arts, philosophy and moral knowledge. These represent the ways we have of understanding and organising our experience according to him.

Now as I have argued in my contribution to this symposium, morality is *not* a form of knowledge even though it employs a range of concepts which distinguish it from, say, sociology. But one counter-example is not enough. The case for teaching religion as a body of knowledge derives from a certain interpretation of some of the darker sayings of Wittgenstein and his disciples — a case characterised by Kai Nielsen in an article in the journal *Philosophy* (July 1967) as 'Wittgensteinian Fideism'.

Nielsen argues that Malcolm, Winch, and D. Z. Phillips[1] derive their key conclusions from a 'cluster of dark sayings'.
Among these are as follows:

1. The forms of language are the forms of life.
2. What is given (i.e. experienced) are the forms of life.
3. Ordinary language is all right as it is.
4. The different modes of discourse which are distinctive forms of life all have a logic of their own.
5. Forms of life taken as a whole are not amenable to criticism — each form having its own criteria of intelligibility, rationality, and reality.

Let us examine these assumptions with respect to religion. Briefly, the argument runs as follows. Religious discourse reflects a particular form of life or mode of behaviour which has its own internal rationale, logic, and concepts. As such, religion cannot be understood or criticised except in its own terms. Each of the forms of knowledge has a conceptual self-sufficiency and this is what qualifies them as *knowledge*. Their uniqueness and autonomy is in a sense unassailable from without. To know about

1   See D. Z. Phillips, Philosophy and Religious Education, *British Journal of Educational Studies*, Vol. 18, No. 1 (Feb. 1970)
Also: P. H. Hirst, A reply to D. Z. Phillips, *B. J. E. S.* Vol. 18, No. 2. (June 1970).
(The latter is a repudiation by Hirst of Fideism.)

religion, for example, is to participate in a particular and irreducible aspect of human understanding. Thus, aesthetic, scientific, moral or religious experience is *sui generis* and self-justifying. To test the religious concept of sin *'against* experience' is *to* experience sin in a religious context.

Now clearly there is a truth contained in the contention that one cannot be critical of religion without understanding what is involved in religious discourse. Nevertheless, to understand religion in its traditional context is not necessarily to accept or believe in the religion in question. As Nielsen points out, witchcraft and astrology were once widely practised in Britain. Both discourses reflected real forms of behaviour and possessed their own internal concepts and 'logic'. Yet these activities and discourses were challenged by sceptics operating within a social framework which gave partial credence to such activities. Internal conceptual self-sufficiency was not a sufficient criterion to safeguard witch-talk and astrological mumbo-jumbo as forms of knowledge. Astrologers and witches issued statements which claimed to be empirical or looked to have predictable consequences for the empirical world. In this sense, therefore, astrology and witch-talk, like religion, shared a number of key categories with other discourses — notably scientific and empirical discourse. And it was the manifest failure of the superstitious to justify the apparent contradictions in their discourse within the empirical world that led to a decay in their belief-system.

Of course, many Christians of a liberal and 'modernist' persuasion would argue that traditional Christian claims must be read, not as empirically falsifiable statements, but as 'moral poetry'. In this case, the argument would turn to a consideration of whether 'moral poetry' could be treated as a form of knowledge.

I have indicated both that conceptual self-sufficiency cannot be treated as a sufficient criterion to establish a claim to be a form of knowledge and that the claim to conceptual self-sufficiency of religion is false unless the religionist retreats into the realm of moral poetry. The essence of my argument is, however, that where religion, science and commonsense knowledge are concerned there exists a *common conceptual area* which enables the unbeliever to raise questions about the intelligibility and truth or falsity of religious claims. Whether religion is a form of knowledge seems to me to turn on the intelligibility and coherence of its concepts and upon its empirical truth or falsity. As Nielsen remarks: "Perhaps God-talk is not as incoherent and irrational as witch-talk; perhaps there is an intelligible concept of the reality of God, and perhaps there is a God, but the fact that there is a form of life in which God-talk is embedded does not preclude our asking these questions or our giving, quite intelligibly, though perhaps mistakenly the same negative answer we gave to witch-talk."

Even if it can be established then that a discourse contains within it unique sets of categories or concepts this does not in itself justify a claim that the discourse is a form of knowledge and hence justify its inclusion in the curriculum. The only 'form of *knowledge*' which is conceptually autonomous is perhaps mathematics. Religion, history and physical science – all may make claims to knowledge – but they share common elements in their methodology and concepts through which we can evaluate their claims. Most educated men grant the status of knowledge (whatever the philosophical problems associated with claiming this status) to the work of competent historians and scientists. A great many of us would jib at the subject-label 'Religious knowledge' and raise questions about the relation of the concept of 'education' in the phrase 'Religious education' to the concept of education in such phrases as 'Scientific education' or 'Historical education'. Education is not one thing. And if we are to recommend the education of the emotions, moral education, historical education and the like, it is vital to understand the differences concealed by the application of that common word. If we can establish that a discipline gives us *knowledge*, then there is a *prima facie* case for teaching it, although we may not wish to do so. If the teaching of 'moral poetry' attracts us then we have to make out a case on other grounds. Religious education has either *to be defended* as a form of knowledge or as an aesthetic experience that ought to be conveyed to others. The claim that it has 'central concepts which are peculiar in character' and thus is a form of knowledge simply won't do. Otherwise, we had better start considering applications to teach from astrologers and magicians.

Philosophy and the Curriculum

Everyone who teaches, at whatever level, is forced on occasion to reflect upon the process in which he or she is engaged. This is not to say that teaching cannot become a nearly mechanical process, but simply to note that even the most stereotyped form of teaching raises questions which must be answered to the satisfaction of the practitioner if for no other reason than giving him peace of mind and security in the performance of his job. Philosophising about education begins when such reflections are made general. That is, when the issue becomes not, for example, what is the point of teaching the differential calculus to these particular children but what is the point of teaching mathematics at all, or what is it to teach mathematics as distinct from mechanical numerical operations.

Philosophy impinges upon education in a variety of different and sometimes subtle ways. It is not concerned solely to examine the way in which a man's view of the world, his moral code or his assumptions about the nature of man in general may affect his teaching; neither is its task to provide except by accident, as it were, such a world view.

Philosophy is primarily *analysis* — but analysis of a particular type directed towards the answering of certain kinds of general questions and meeting certain kinds of challenges. Examine the following questions and comments for examples:

(a) Why should I teach mathematics?

(b) I feel I am not really teaching *science* at all.

(c) Moral and religious education is just indoctrination.

These three questions or challenges raise philosophical issues although many of them could be answered in a non-philosophical way — for example, attempts might be made to justify the teaching of mathematics by arguing that a minimal ability in handling relationships between numbers is a necessary condition of leading a successful life in a complex culture such as our own — and this argument at its own level might be perfectly adequate as James Fearnley points out. But philosophy always raises *further* questions about the justification and nature both of the subject matter of education and the teaching process. Implicit in distinctively philosophical reflection about education are such questions as: What is the nature of knowledge?; What is to count as knowledge and what mere belief?; What is the justification for treating knowledge in separate compartments labelled 'subjects'?; Are all subjects similar in their logical structure and if not what are the differences and how are they to be accounted for?; What is the relation between the 'form' of a subject and the process by which it is taught and learnt?

The essays in this symposium are directed towards answering some of the questions raised above. But our central concern is to examine the relationship which exists between those characteristics of a discipline which allegedly make it 'what it is and not another thing' and the demands of the teaching situation. Thus, for example, mathematical propositions may very well be regarded as part of a 'self-generative' *deductive* scheme independent of the nature of the empirical world and yet be best taught through a process of *induction* which enables children to see exemplified in 'real' terms the kinds of relationship which are defined as arithmetical for example. In history teaching too, there may very well be a tension exhibited between what is counted as history by practising historians and what is taught to children in schools by 'history' teachers. The intervention of psychological and sociological considerations into the teaching situation inevitably creates problems for the teacher – not only involving differences of ability and cultural background – but problems which directly affect the definition of what he or she is doing *qua* subject teacher.

All the contributors to this symposium although currently teaching in universities or colleges of education have extensive teaching experience in schools. Some have had formal philosophical training; others have 'reflected philosophically' on their disciplines in relation to teaching. As a result of a diversity of background and training, differences of emphasis, style, and opinion are inevitable. What divides us is of course philosophically and pedagogically important, but what unites us is perhaps more important. It is the desire to demonstrate that reasonably demanding philosophical analysis is not incompatible with relevance to class-room teaching and to the wider professional concerns of educationists in general. It is upon the twin criteria of rigour and relevance that I hope the book will be judged; for rigour without relevance is pointless and relevance without rigour is simply unintelligent.

MATHEMATICS

JAMES D. FEARNLEY

1. Introduction

There are several things wrong with the teaching of mathematics in this country and I suspect, on the basis of minimal evidence, elsewhere. I do not expect this statement to surprise anyone. Some of these things are:

(i)   There are not enough teachers.

(ii)   Too many people who are teaching the subject know too little maths themselves.

(iii)   People's views of mathematics are too narrow.

(iv)   The subject is still taught in a very rigid way.

(v)   The subject is still made boring for the majority.

(vi)   Not enough teachers are prepared to bother about the psychology of learning.

(vii) There is too much unconsidered dabbling with 'experimental' approaches.

(viii) Rigid examination requirements still govern many schools' mathematics syllabuses.

I think these eight observations are true. They are also, by this time, fairly commonplace. I want to propose another, which often goes unmentioned and which would not necessarily be put right if the first eight were, but which itself encompasses some of the eight:

(ix)   Too many people teach mathematics as something static instead of something dynamic.

Now that needs some explanation. What are a teacher's terms of reference with respect to the teaching of mathematics? Too often he is limited to a syllabus, which itself is invariably simply a list of topics or narrowly circumscribed areas of the subject. So the only guide most teachers have encourages them to think of the teaching of mathematics in terms of ticking items off on a list; having 'done' long multiplication of money, we must now 'do' areas of rectangles. Even with the changes that are taking place in many schools in the way mathematics is being approached, it is still possible to level the same criticism, although the items in the list may fit together better and what is demanded in the way of an approach to the items by the children may be different, that is to say, not purely traditional. Indeed, I have heard 'modern' approaches to mathematics teaching criticised by established teachers (of the 'old school'?) on the grounds that there is less sense and cohesion in the list of things 'done', that the result is a less coherent 'product' than is obtained by traditional means. I shall return to this later; what interests me at the moment is that both traditional and non-traditional approaches tend to be presented to the teacher (who far more often than not is a non-specialist) in terms of a list of items and nothing else, and this does not seem to me to be good enough.

If you regard the syllabus as the only document or set of considerations of any kind to be of any importance to the mathematics teacher, this is rather like viewing the mathematics which one wants the pupil to acquire as being like the set of equipment one must acquire before going off on a camping holiday — you start off with a list and pack the items in one by one. Or perhaps more like building a house, since some orders of assembling the parts will do and some will not. And this analogy is better, too, because it allows for different plans, from which to produce different kinds of houses in just the same way as there might be different kinds of syllabuses for producing different kinds of mathematical products; think of secondary syllabuses in agricultural or technical mathematics. Once the plan has been executed, the syllabus 'covered', the house can be lived in, the mathematical body of knowledge used. And that all seems very neat and useful.

However, to state the obvious, there are ways in which mathematics is not like an edifice. Chiefly, there is the fact that mathematics is not the static dead thing that a house is; it has a self-generative character which a house does not, and it is my contention that it is the communication of this self-generative character of mathematics and of the way in which the self-generation takes place that is the most important, though one of the most difficult, of the tasks of the teacher of mathematics.

Some objections which could be made at this point are:

(i) It is not clear what "the self-generative character of mathematics" means,

(ii) It is clear what "the self-generative character of mathematics" means, but it is not true that this is the most important characteristic of mathematics,

(iii) It may be important to some to be introduced to this characteristic of mathematics, but it is irrelevant for the majority.

I ought to try to answer the first of these objections, at any rate briefly, right away. I shall be going into greater detail elsewhere and also saying something in response to the second and third.

Mathematics has for centuries been awarded a position of high standing in the realms of knowledge, higher normally than any other area of knowledge except logic. If you could have certain knowledge at all, you could have it in logic and mathematics. Why? Because of the independence of mathematics: because mathematics does not depend upon the world (in the way that physics and history do) but only on its own definitions and the laws of logic. This is what I mean by the "self-generative character of mathematics"; in mathematics, one thing follows logically from something else. At one level, if you have learned to solve problems, do calculations of one kind, more or less as a matter of routine, then there is a further class of problems whose solutions should be accessible to you, even though not quite so readily, through the extension of what you know already. The logical steps will not be great: the question will simply be whether *in fact* in your case they are (psychologically) possible. At another level, 'old' (existing) mathematics leads to new; not in the sense that the new will unfold itself unbidden, but in the sense that it will have a logical dependence on the old and no dependence on anything else. Subjectively, these two levels need scarcely be distinguished; objectively, they are not so much discrete levels as points on a continuum. It is this connectedness of one thing in mathematics with another which I think it is important for us as teachers to try to communicate and the further along the continuum we can bring our pupils the better.

2. On the Nature of Mathematics

Abstract vs. Concrete

There are times when the abstract nature of mathematics seems to be a liability in terms of its rating in the popularity polls. There are many teachers who would rather it were· less abstract. But it is at least agreed that by its nature it *is* abstract — notwithstanding frequent attempts to pretend otherwise.

History is about events and states of affairs and trends; metallurgy is about real metals; physics is about forces and fields and particles; all these are objects about which observations — fairly direct in some cases, very indirect in others — have to be made. But mathematics is about such abstractions as numbers, algebraic identities, ideal shapes, operations, and the like; observations of real things are not much help here!

True, mathematics is used to solve practical problems, but between the translation into some kind of symbolic form that takes place at the beginning, and the reverse translation that takes place at the end, there is likely to be an expanse of stuff that can quite fairly be characterised as abstract. It consists in making use of identities, recognising patterns, applying 'appropriate operations', recalling established relationships: this is what people call 'working in the abstract'. The steps in the calculation, the moves in the solution of the differential equation, the steps in the logical simplification, all take place 'in the abstract' without reference to the 'real' situation which provided the problem; otherwise often a solution would be impossible. One relies upon seeing that a given situation has a structure which resembles that of a system with which one is familiar; it would be very inconvenient if there were no such resemblances in the world. (Suppose that five books plus four books came to nine books, but five cups plus four cups came to something other than nine cups! It is hard to imagine that; if you try, the concept of counting seems to crumble away.) And it is the existence of such resemblances that makes it possible to talk of abstract concepts and abstract systems.

If you could choose to solve a problem 'in the concrete' then either it would be a rather simple problem or it would be a cumbersome solution or it would be quite impossible to find a solution at all. Think of finding out how many small cubes would make a 10 x 10 x 10 cube without doing anything abstract; or finding the length of the diagonal of a square. Here, in the first case, I suppose doing a multiplication sum would count as using an abstract process, and building the cube out of small ones, counting the while, would do as the concrete approach. This, anyway, is what is meant by a 'concrete' approach to such a problem, and there are occasions when an approach like this, though cumbersome, is useful as a step in the learning sequence. In the second case, the abstract approach would be to use the Theorem of Pythagoras, a square-rooting method, rudimentary knowledge of irrational numbers and an approximation. Any concrete approach would run into difficulties over checking the result, for attempts to do this without calculation (for that, within the defined terms, would be to work in the abstract) would be very complicated and tedious. But if we reserve the embargo on calculation, while otherwise keeping things as concrete as possible (cutting up cards, and using rulers) then we have about as concrete a way of introducing the *highly* abstract concept of irrational numbers as we are likely to find.

The extent to which you can avoid the abstract in mathematics is relative to the complexity of the concepts involved; they do not have to be very complex before it becomes more confusing to try to avoid the abstract than to come to terms with it. Working in the abstract is what mathematics is all about.

Why all this talk then about making things concrete, sticking to the concrete, teaching arithmetic by concrete analogy?[1] This in itself makes perfect sense as long as the object is to engender understanding, to lead to the ability to 'work in the abstract', to make sense of certain abstract concepts or processes. But not everyone seems to understand that 'the abstract' in mathematics is a good thing. Our object in teaching people mathematics should include getting them actually to *like* it for its abstract nature; certainly the last thing we want is people metaphorically (or even literally!) counting on their fingers and proud of it.

Proof

I have already mentioned that it is characteristic of mathematics that one bit develops from another, that there are logical connections between

1.   J. D. Williams, Teaching arithmetic by concrete analogy *British Journal of Educational Psychology*, 1961/62.

pieces of mathematics. In fact, of course, no-one needs to be told this; everyone has some acquaintance with the axioms and theorems of Euclid — happy or otherwise. I think it may be worthwhile pointing out, though, that mathematics seems, in the way it develops, to be like an inverted pyramid: starting from very little, it grows into a great deal. Think of the simple operation of counting: from there we develop addition of whole numbers; then subtraction and multiplication; then division; from subtraction to negative numbers; from division to fractions; and so on and so on, developing algebra, calculus, complex number theory, etc., etc. And always the new layer rests on the old, in the logical sense that it can be shown incontrovertibly to be entailed by the old — and thus by the very 'earliest' pieces of mathematics. All theorems are traceable back logically to the axioms of the system. As a matter of historical fact, a particular theorem, a particular relationship, may have been arrived at intuitively but that does not matter; the story does not end when the theorem is formulated; it has to have its credentials verified; its logical indubitability must be established. The theorem, in fact, has to be proved.

This is what mathematics is like and it is to an appreciation of this that a pupil must be brought if he is to know mathematics. But having said that, I shall be giving the impression of being totally out of touch with the real 'teaching situation', so I had better say that I do not really believe, of course, that Euclid and axiomatic set theory are essentials for every reception class. And I do understand that the development of manipulative skill takes time and can only occur in due order anyway. Finally, I concede that some children are 'less able'. But what I would still like to contend is that the teaching of mathematics can nevertheless be carried out with the intention of communicating the idea of logical con- nectedness, at many, many levels and stages — not strict proof at all stages, but certainly connectedness. As I said earlier, it might just be a matter of tackling a problem that falls outside the current stereotype and as a result making some small advances; not of course once, but whenever possible. But it was not my intention here to go into detail about how the teaching should be approached; here I want to establish what we are trying to get at and what sort of things ought to be borne in mind. And the first essential is to have some agreement as to what mathematics is like.

3. Assumptions and Prejudices

One can appreciate mathematics for its own sake, for the elegance that can be found in it; or one can use it as a tool for solving problems in agriculture or engineering or bathroom decoration. Either way, one uses an abstract system of rules; one uses formulae that have a logical dependence on the most elementary principles; one uses theorems that have the axioms of the system as their logical pedigree. There is no necessary reason why the rules used in the two sorts of cases should not be the same. A proof is not a calculation, but some of the same sorts of moves may be made in the process of a calculation as are made in the process of a proof. I may use the difference of two squares identity to help me calculate how many tiles I shall need to cover the bathroom wall round the washbasin; and I may use the same identity to help me to prove that 1 has four complex roots in addition to its two real ones. There is a closer resemblance between the use of rules in calculations and their use in developing formulae and using theorems than many people will admit. I am thinking partly of those teachers who insist that to them mathematics is just a tool and it is as a tool that it should be taught. This is a view common in technical education and in some areas of secondary education. It arises, obviously, from the fact that certain kinds of calculation are currently associated with certain jobs. The result is often that 'teaching mathematics' is interpreted as introducing the students to an unconnected selection of mathematical moves, with accompanying stereotyped exercises. This is, for some teachers, "keeping away from the abstract", which they feel they must do because:

(a)   They only understand if it is kept practical;
(b)   They only *need* certain bits of maths for their calculations;
(c)   There is not time to get them to understand what it is all about;
(d)   They must learn to use the technique before they can come to understand what it is based upon.[2]

And it is not only in technical colleges that these attitudes are met. The primary school head who says that "These modern approaches are all very well but there isn't time", or the infant school teacher who has her

2.   The City and Guilds of London Institute syllabus for General Engineering Mathematics, Stage 1, specifies that the use of logarithms should be taught merely as an aid to calculation: the theory should be taught at the next stage.

6-year-olds chanting tables are subscribing to (b), (c) and (d): post-primary, (a) is used mostly, I think, to justify subjecting 'non-academic' pupils to a fragmentary course of 'real-life' sums.

(a) to (d) above represent for me a depressing set of opinions. I think they are depressing for two reasons: firstly, because they are so narrow and so short-sighted at the same time; and secondly, because even from the purely practical point of view, starting from the same instrumental position, they seem to me to be mistaken. I think they represent a narrow view of education: education is not just preparing for a job. I think they are short-sighted in the way they exclude generality and the possibility of further development by catering specifically and only for today's (or even yesterday afternoon's) calculations. Finally, it seems to me that even if you just want your students to be able to cope with the calculations of their trade, these four 'principles' function more like four millstones. (They are all more or less quotations from life, by the way.)

How do you keep the solution of linear equations practical for a group of steel fabricators? Answer: write the word 'tons' after every item! This requirement is a stumbling block. The only sensible thing to do is to embark on a course of action designed to show that this quasi-concreteness is just a nuisance; the whole point of learning to solve linear equations is to have the benefit of an abstract, more or less mechanical technique. Secondly, to limit the choice of topics to those that are in use *now* precludes both the possibility of developing some understanding of the important areas and also the possibility of making a reasonable stab at the solution of a hitherto unforeseen problem in the future. (c) and (d) are related and are possibly the worst of all, since they suggest that understanding is a kind of bonus, an optional extra. What *are* we aiming at, if not understanding? Back comes the answer, reverberating down the Victorian staircases: "they have these exams to pass". It does not matter what exams – they can be 'A', 'O', 11-plus, Common entrance, or not even an exam at all, simply what the Junior Head expects of new entrants – they can be drilled for with a fair degree of immediate success.

Actually, I do not think this view is so downrightly expressed in connection with 'O' and 'A' levels. Here we are at the other pole, the academic one. Here the treatment is to give the fully logical development – and to assume that understanding then follows. It is an unfortunate but indubitable fact that this is not necessarily so: you can 'achieve' without understanding, but the achievement is then a cul-de-sac. Again, the effect is long-term; you need understanding for insight to develop. Imaginative, creative mathematics without understanding is inconceivable.

The traditional approach in the primary school starts from the belief that there are certain computational skills which children need to know because they are useful, and proceeds by a process of presentation and drill. The stress is upon the separate processes *as* processes and their interconnection is seen as a *merely factual* one, rather than treated as something which itself has to be taught or shown to the children because it is important. ('Factual' in the sense that you cannot *in fact* tackle, say, multiplication until the children can add, though even facts like this are not universally accepted – I have already commented on the existence of teachers who drill classes of 6-year-olds in their tables!)

The cohesion of the parts of elementary mathematics into a whole, the dependence of one process upon another, the *development* from simple to more complex, is not considered; or it is considered to be outside the scope of the work, or is seen as being beyond the capacity of the children. Attention is focused solely on the exercise, the practice, of each individual process: attention is not focused, while the process is being learned, on the nature of the process in terms of its relation to the other, already known processes. Yet the usefulness of any process in the future may well depend on the extent to which it can be related to other processes.

We have to remember that we do not want children to be able to operate in the future only in contexts *exactly* like those that have been seen before.[3] They ought to be able to assess situations and choose systems and processes that fit; this is going to be made more difficult if they do not recognise *any* connections – any similarities and differences – between situations and processes they are familiar with.

I know that in practice many of these connections *are* made, but my point is that we should be making it easier by teaching for that kind of

3.   Z. P. Dienes, *The Power of Mathematics*, 1964: "In the conventional method of learning mathematics, a great deal of attention is devoted to symbol-manipulations. . . . It is seldom that such manipulation learning forms part of a larger and more purposeful pattern. . . . 'Knowing' resulting from such drill-teaching only means the establishing of stimulus-response patterns. . . ."

appraisal, and I do not think we are. We have all heard children say, "I can't do this problem! Is it an add or a multiply?"

There is not much, if anything at all, that is new about this attack. The word 'understanding' has been given a great deal of attention in recent times and many different moves have been made in the direction of getting children to understand what they are doing rather than simply learning mechanically how to do it. There has been a flood of structural material and associated theories, a good deal of enterprise and a swing in the direction of 'child-centredness'. The whole complex of thinking, writing, investigating and experimenting was needed. It still is needed, for no-one has reached the stage of knowing all the answers. I think a great many children have been helped towards an understanding of some part of mathematics as a result of the joint but unco-ordinated efforts of the researchers, experimenters and teachers who have been tackling these problems in the past few years. If a few less people go rigid at the mention of maths than would have done without the upheaval, that alone would make it worthwhile even if there was nothing else to show for it.

But novel approaches and rooms full of apparatus cannot succeed on their own, and it is my fear that a great many teachers act as if they thought otherwise. You have to *use* apparatus; as a teacher you have to know the apparatus and its potential inside-out; you have to know what kinds of concepts it is useful for exploring and what questions may be good openers for certain directions of enquiry. You have to be sufficiently familiar with the whole business to be able to respond in original but useful ways to unexpected queries and departures. Conversation and questioning is not just an optional extra; it is as important as the material itself, if not more so. This is much harder than teaching by the traditional approach!

Concurrent with changes of approach there are also moves in the direction of widening the scope of mathematics, both in primary and secondary education by delving into such areas as sets, elementary geometry, and graphical work, at the primary level, and logic, vectors, and statistics at the secondary level. There is a strong case to be made out for this, but I want to avoid going into syllabus details here. For the moment I simply want to comment that even teaching a 'modern' syllabus, using a 'modern' approach it remains possible that one might be guilty of propagating a fragmentary and static view of mathematics. If one is to avoid doing this, one must be conscious of what it is one is trying to achieve, other than the teaching of specific pieces of mathematics.

The problem does not only exist for teachers who are struggling on with an inadequate grasp of the subject themselves; even a teacher who knows a great deal of mathematics can easily do his pupils a disservice by emphasising the pieces of mathematics rather than the processes of development, the established routines rather than the pattern-finding probings. (This is related to the contrast Professor Geoffrey Matthews pointed to in his Inaugural Lecture at the Chelsea College of Science and Technology in May 1970. He called his lecture "Hailstones and Folkweave"; the hailstones are discrete packets of mathematics as traditionally used for the bombarding of pupils. "Folkweave" stresses interconnectedness.)

4. Why Should Anyone Learn Mathematics?
And What Should They Learn?

The short answer to the question, "Why should anyone learn mathematics?" is, "Because no-one has any choice". Mathematics is part of our way of life in this advanced and complex society. Some degree of mathematical skill is taken for granted, just as reading is; without it a measure of independence is lost. This is an artificial question in the sense that we are not, in point of fact, considering whether or not to do without it. Mathematics is not in the position of a piece of decoration in a house; it is more nearly on a par with the plumbing.

It could be argued that the mathematics we have just been talking about is pretty low-level stuff; we all deal with simple arithmetic but people do not, in the normal course of day-to-day affairs solve quadratic equations or tussle with geometrical puzzles. This, of course, is true. Yet this higher level mathematics *is* very much a part of our world; there is no branch of industry or commerce that does not make use of it. Moreover, the mathematics that is used in this realm tends to become more sophisticated almost day by day. So it is some kind of preparation for the world to have a grasp of mathematics above the level of shoppers' arithmetic. I suppose that if the general level of mathematics (unquantifiable though that might be!) had been lower over the past fifty years than it in fact was in the civilised world, then technological development just could not have reached the stage it has reached. (This is not the place for arguing whether this would have been a good or a bad thing.) And the technological stage of development being what it is now, it makes certain demands in terms of required mathematics.

It would be foolish to deny that usefulness does have something to do with the choice of what we teach. The danger of saying that it does rightfully have something to do with what we teach is that one can be misconstrued as saying that (a) everything that someone learns should be something that he knows he is going to use, and (b) there are no criteria other than usefulness. I would deny both of these constructions emphatically. The first is clearly absurd; it *could* only make sense *vis-à-vis* vocational training. In the second case, there are other subjects which are normally included in the curriculum which are much less useful than mathematics; no-one queries whether singing or painting are useful enough to be included. Art and music are included because they are associated with forms of experience which on the whole cannot occur without encouragement; the experience a music lover has on hearing a particular piece of music is of a different order from the experience a musical philistine has on hearing the same piece. The musical education of the music-lover contributes to the quality of the experience; he is constantly making comparisons, noting balance, pitch, tone and so on, and it is the fact that he is constantly on the *qui vive* in this particular way, and has the background of previous experience for comparison, that singles him out as musically aware.

In addition to the fact that mathematics also has its uses, could not mathematics be looked at in a rather similar sort of way to this? We just have to say that we want to give people the chance to become mathematically aware, as we want them to have the chance to become musically or artistically aware. When is someone mathematically aware? When he can appreciate a particular piece of mathematics; when he understands the terms, the processes; when his background is such that different moves in the game make sense to him; when he can sometimes anticipate moves correctly; and when he takes pleasure in all this.

The parallel with art or music is not exact, of course. In music, one does not have to be a practitioner at all to be able to appreciate a piece;

similarly in respect of art. But one must have some sort of expertise in mathematics or one cannot *follow* moves; but one may not be creative in the sense of producing new mathematics.

What mathematics should people learn? If one of the points of teaching mathematics in schools is to introduce children to the procedures, concepts and preoccupations of the subject, then one should clearly try to communicate the diversity that exists within the subject. But, of course, there is such diversity that it may often be a matter of making an arbitrary choice between two alternatives. Does this matter?

5. The Case for Stressing Mathematics as a Field of Experience

Need one say more than that children *can* become interested in finding patterns and rules? Scepticism about this may arise from thinking in terms of fairly sophisticated algebra and calculus, and finding this incongruous in the context of the class of 6-year-olds. One needs to think in simple terms. I have seen 6-year-olds delighted with the discovery that there are as many odd as even numbers in the series 1—100. Think of things at this level. The child for whom this new field of experience is opening up looks for opportunities of using the dexterity of mathematical processes that he has so far acquired; he looks deliberately for puzzles and problems in just the same way as he may decide to paint a picture; he notices things in terms of mathematics that are not necessarily being presented to him in those terms — that are not, indeed, being 'presented' to him at all. (For example, symmetries in pictures, speed estimates on a motorway, elementary topological problems on a toy railway, cost calculations . . .) This is how you recognise a possible initiate. (You cannot, of course, hope for a 100% conversion, any more than 100% of the population are musical. But if you set out to initiate children in this way, if you look out for signs and then, recognising them, act accordingly, the bag might be bigger than you expect!)

These are the small beginnings; but even at this stage, there is an enrichment of the child's total experience; the number and quality of possible individual mathematical experiences is increased by every successful spontaneous eruption of mathematical awareness. Finding that there are as many odd as even numbers in the series 1—100 was significant in several ways:

(i)   It was satisfying to find out something what was not known before; and satisfaction is addictive.

(ii) The *pattern* was striking: it was *the same number*. Now in the future these children might be looking, in similar situations, for patterns of this sort — and if they only ask: "Are the two numbers the same?" that future experience will have acquired a dimension it might not have had.

(iii) It might possibly have 'stuck' as a piece of information, to be drawn on on a future occasion.

If I am making heavy weather of this it is because I am anxious to establish that it does make some sense to bracket mathematics with art and music. The differences do have to be borne in mind, though: mathematics is a cognitive business, which art and music (*despite* Herbert Read) are not. At the level of my example it was sufficient to find something out empirically about a specific case — but ultimately proving that it could not be otherwise is what one is concerned about in maths. But one's experience of the world is affected by one's commitment to mathematics just as by commitment to art or music; one continually sees the world in mathematical terms, sees things of mathematical interest or that are puzzling, just as artistically committed people will tend to emphasise aesthetic considerations. The artistically committed person leads his special life in terms of pictures while the mathematically committed man lives his special life in terms of theorems, proofs, diagrams, and manipulations.

One other point needs to be made before moving on to the question of how, if at all, the splendid state of affairs envisaged here might be achieved. One ought to temper one's enthusiasm with realism and recognise that the mathematically committed person might have a functioning ceiling at any level. Mathematics is no different from art or music in that respect. Tastes differ; and people can function at different levels of appreciation with equal degrees of enthusiasm. Criticism of pop can be detailed and technical but enthusiasm for this form of music does not necessarily lead later to enthusiasm for some other form. It might be argued that pop, jazz, folk, classical music, etc., do not form a hierarchy; I think I can side-step that issue by claiming that this illustration will not suffer if they are not thought of hierarchically — either way there are mathematical parallels. A Beethoven enthusiast may get enormous pleasure from listening to the symphonies over a number of years and yet may never develop the acutely technical discernment which another man might acquire in a relatively short time. If a middle-aged man gets satisfaction from doing rather simple calculations, we might be sorry that he will never experience the greater subtlety of some more high-flown piece of mathematics, but we ought not to be snide about the way he takes his pleasure, any more than we ought to sneer at the lover of Gilbert and Sullivan.

But in school, we hope to be able to take advantage of the enthusiasm and make the enthusiast's initiation into mathematics as complete as possible. No doubt the musicians have the same kind of idea; and like them, even when we know what we are doing, we shall sometimes fail. But the first thing is to know what we are doing.

6. Modus Operandi

As teachers, we have to introduce children to the concepts and procedures of mathematics. I have already argued that we ought to do this in such a way that the children see the way in which one part of mathematics depends on another. I have also argued that we want the concept of elementary mathematics to be acquired in such a way that the children can *use* the mathematics they are learning, and in such a way that they can select the procedure to suit the problem, instead of having to be told which one to use. We want the learning to be a pleasurable process. As I argued in the last section, we want the mathematical concepts to become part of each child's intellectual make-up to the extent that he begins quite early to see the world in mathematical terms outside the classroom; to find absorbing bits of mathematics cropping up in the normal course of his life.

Two possible counters that might occur at this point are:

(i)   It is just a pipe dream. Children are not interested in mathematics. Mathematics is hard.

(ii)   There already *are* children like this without our doing anything about it.

What could I say to (i) except flatly contradict it? Many children find mathematics absorbing at the earliest stages but are then steadily turned against it by the ignorance and laziness of their teachers and the evil persuasive influence of the rest of the world outside the classroom. (Some day I am going to prepare a volume of the anti-mathematics sayings to which children are subjected from the day they can first hear.)

(ii) is true but what follows? It is no commendation of falling off cliffs that one or two people have survived the experience. Our object is to increase the output of numerate persons.

And how is this increased productivity to be achieved? The central principle is not to answer questions unless absolutely necessary, but to get the children to answer themselves. As far as possible they should then check to see if the answer is right. I am making no claim for the patent on this principle. I only want to emphasise it, because it is not used sufficiently widely or sufficiently rigorously, and to offer a justification of it.

Suppose a boy asks "What are nine sevens?" If I say, "Sixty-three", the fact drops into a bottomless pit and I shall have to tell him again tomorrow and every day he wants to know. If I say, "What do you think?" he will either make a serious attempt to find out or he will make a guess. If he makes a guess we can discuss whether it is likely to be right. (Will it be bigger or smaller than ten sevens?") If he makes a serious attempt to find out he will be doing some learning; not only will he be more likely to remember the product once he has established it but also he will have acquired a little more insight into relationships between numbers. As a bonus, he will also have experienced the excitement of finding something out. Whether he made a guess or at once made a serious attempt to work it out, learning was going on. And teaching was going on — which would only be true in a very inferior sort of way if I merely told the answer. I think this is interesting: it is more or less the opposite of the traditional view, which has the teacher always in the position of handing out information — be it facts or methods.

To ask a boy to find out for himself is to ask him to make use of his own resources. It is to ask him to draw on facts, patterns and procedures which he already possesses; he has to make a selection of what seems to him to be relevant to the problem in hand. Now this is all material he already possesses and he is *supposed* to be able to use it. (Isn't this why he has learned it?) This is giving him a chance to use it in a non-stereotyped way, since he is not *expecting* to have to use any particular piece of material, as he would be expecting if he were doing a routine exercise. And this is good for his understanding; no-one can be sure he understands unless he has had the chance of making mistakes. I do not particularly mean a factual mistake, a mistake of simple arithmetic. I mean a mistake relating to the structure of the problem. An example in this context of the sort of mistake I mean would be this:

Suppose a boy has done a little exercise consisting of noting that 9 x 1 is 1 less than 10, that 9 x 2 is 2 less than 20, that 9 x 3 is 3 less than 30, and so on. Some days later, he needs to work out 9 x 55; he gets it right by a long method (instead of say 550 less 55), although later questioning shows that the relevant exercise is still fresh in his memory. He has not made a mistake in the sense of having got the wrong answer. But he missed the trick. He made a mistake in the sense that he failed to recognise 9 x 55 as an instance of this recent addition to his stock of patterns and so in a sense showed less understanding than he might have of the pattern of his problem and/or the pattern embodied in that exercise.

I have been discussing an approach at an elementary level that seems to me to make a genuine contribution to mathematical education. It is not all there is to mathematical education, but it represents at least one thread. Whether in simple calculation, in problem solving or in proof-finding, the same kind of thing must go on: the task has to be made sense of in terms of patterns and procedures that one already possesses. If these patterns and procedures have been merely learned and practised as things in their own right, mechanically, then the job of finding the right ones for a particular given situation is a hard one. Choosing the approach to a solution must not be a special kind of exercise that is used for a change once every term: it must be a staple diet. An important aspect of understanding anything is seeing relationships between that and other things one knows. So let us give people plenty of opportunity to look for such relationships. We must arrange for them to build up their mathematical knowledge and expertise in this active way, by making use of what is already there to build a new procedure for tackling a new level of problem.

The approach I have just described needs to be complemented by another one. The first approach copes adequately with the concept of development and is specially useful in so far as the possibility of developing B from A functions as a measure of the understanding of A. The other approach needs to establish the concept of proof. Here it seems to me one needs to think in terms of a gradual progression from purely empirical fact-finding to the generalisation of these facts into a law and then later to a proof of that law. Here is an example:

The game called "The Tower of Hanoi" is played like this: Start with a number of graded discs on a rod, and two other empty rods. Moving them one at a time and never putting a larger on a smaller, move all the discs onto another rod.

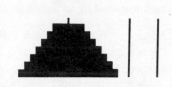

That is the game – a sort of patience, I suppose. The problem is to find the law or formula which enables one to calculate the number of moves required for any given number of discs. The solution could go like this:

(i)   Do it for 1, 2, 3, 4, etc., discs and record the number of moves. The "finding of facts" stage.

(ii) Look at the results and form a generalisation from them; the formula: number of moves = $2^n - 1$, where n is the number of discs, fits.

The query "Will all the cases we haven't looked at fit the formula too?" leads to a further look at the process involved and the discovery that this *must* be the formula – i.e. to the finding of a proof. I have included this rather long-winded example because I wanted to show the sort of consideration that can, I think, lead children to *look* for proofs; it is the kind of situation which gives sense to the concept of proof. Other people, notably Piaget, have issued warnings against trying to get children to carry out proofs too early. But it is important I think to know not only when proofs would be inappropriate but also what kind of considerations make the concept of proof a viable one.

8. Finale

If we could all convince ourselves that the purpose of teaching people mathematics is to give them pleasure, the release of pressure would increase the output of numerate people phenomenally! For then we should have the time, which we foolishly believe we have not now, to ask questions instead of giving answers.

I know I have been advocating a hard approach, particularly for anyone who is insecure in the subject already. However, I am convinced it is not possible to improve the learning of mathematics without involving the learners much more actively in the way I have described – and this is bound to place an extra burden on the teacher. But I think there may be remarkable compensations in the way of far greater intellectual independence on the part of the pupils and hence much greater satisfaction in the job.

Furthermore, it is impossible to teach in this way without being constantly enlightened oneself. This applies to the experienced, mathematically-orientated teacher as well as to the less numerate novice and to the hardened philistine. Anyone who commits himself *seriously* to teaching mathematics as I have tried to describe it, will find himself involved in a process which tends to deepen his own understanding of mathematics along with the children's.

Understanding in mathematics is more complicated than people generally allow. (I think one might generalise that comment to cover the understanding of *any* subject-matter!) It is difficult to define, with respect to any particular topic, and difficult to legislate for. An approach which brings A to a certain level of understanding of, say, the geometry of the circle, may be less successful for B, who may nevertheless respond well to a different approach. Understanding involves fitting the new phenomenon into the network of knowledge one already possesses. An imperfectly understood phenomenon only fits partially. I don't mean it only fits partially because it is imperfectly understood, but that it is *said to be* imperfectly understood because it only fits partially.

On the other hand, I do not mean to suggest that 'perfect understanding' of any phenomenon or concept can be defined (in a specific case) or is even a viable concept in general. Indeed it may be possible to prove (though not by me, now) that complete understanding of a phenomenon is logically impossible. It certainly seems clear that in many cases the understanding of a phenomenon can be deepened by successive degrees. This may happen as the relation of the phenomenon to patterns already known, but newly recognised as relevant, takes place. It may also happen as further new phenomena are seen to be related or as implications of the phenomenon under consideration are gradually worked out. Notice that it is insufficient that the phenomenon under discussion should *in fact* be related in a certain way to something one knows. The relation has to be *seen* − and being told that it exists is not always enough.

I do not want to make this whole business sound mystical. One can plan sequences of work to bring out certain relations and so hope to develop understanding of certain ideas. One can plan unexpected juxtapositions of problem situations to provide the possibility of imaginative pattern-spotting of the sort which, as I have suggested earlier, provides evidence of understanding. But one cannot assume that every mind works in the same way. The most challenging thing about serious teaching is the necessity of finding out what makes sense to an individual. This is challenging because what makes sense to an individual, apropos of certain subject-matter, is unfortunately not a function of subject-matter. The planned sequences one uses *may* work on their own, but unless one is constantly probing to find out what kind of *sense* is being made of the material, these sequences may remain exercises at a relatively superficial level. It is hard to avoid seeing examples of this kind of abortive 'teaching for understanding' or 'modern maths' in schools. The planned sequences designed to lead to 'understanding of concepts' become themselves stereotyped exercises. The structural apparatus becomes material that simply has to be used because it's there. Often a kind of mathematical limbo is created in which there is no sense of direction or of development, and this is in its way just as bad as the traditional unadulterated diet of rote-learning and practice.

It is a pity to replace one form of rigidity by another. In the teaching of mathematics as a mode and field of enquiry (not a body of routines and facts) anything goes if it makes something make sense. This applies to methods, to the timing of mathematically-loaded comment, to the use of concrete aids and to anything else relevant whatever. We want to introduce our pupils to mathematics as an organic body of connected parts, growing and full of fascination. But it is not any use our just telling them about it; each time, at each stage, with each person, we have to find out what makes sense to him. We have to lead him to see patterns, in terms of what he

knows already. *He* has to take each step, make each connection, and we
can only *help* by preparing, prodding, questioning. If we do not believe
this, we might as well do it the army way: "But I *ordered* you to understand!"

NATURAL SCIENCE

COLIN HOLROYD

IT would be satisfying to have answers to three questions: Is science a developed and distinct form of knowledge? What is scientific method? How, if at all, can answers to these first two questions affect our thinking on the content and methods of school science? In this section an attempt will be made to explore some of the fields in which tentative answers lie buried; the intention is as modest as this — any greater claim would be naïve, arrogant or both.

Science — a Form of Knowledge?

Paul Hirst has made clear on several occasions the distinguishing features ascribed to the forms of knowledge. The different forms are characterised by distinct type of concepts; these concepts form a network of possible relationships in which experience can be understood; different types of tests have been developed to assess the expressions and propositions of the several forms (Hirst, 1965, 1966). An examination of the legitimacy of describing science as a developed form of knowledge requires three things:

(a) that the concepts and structure of science and its tests for validity be described;

(b) that the concepts, structure and tests be shown to be distinct from those in other areas of human enquiry; and

(c) that science be shown to be so homogeneous that a sub-division into component disciplines is unnecessary.

THE CONCEPTS, STRUCTURE AND TESTS OF SCIENCE

"Concept" is a messy rag bag of a word in that semantic sifting through its usages tends to produce confusion rather than clarification; from the vagueness of some currently fashionable usage (the 'concept' of educational technology, the 'concept' of a university) where the word means little more than a "general notion", one can move through a spectrum of definitions to the precise, but limited, usage of learning theorists – for them, a concept is simply a class of stimuli with common characteristics.

Hirst lists the following examples of concepts: gravity, acceleration, hydrogen, photosynthesis, atom, magnetic field (science), ought, good, wrong, virtue (moral concepts), God, sin, heaven and predestination (religious concepts). It is not immediately clear from the list what definition of 'concept' would be sufficiently comprehensive as to cover all the examples; it would seem that in considering a variety of phenomena and verbal expressions one becomes aware of a distillation, a general notion, which has to be given a name to be further handled – this distillation or generalised abstraction is a concept. It is a little disconcerting to find *hydrogen* in the scientific list. Was it chosen because having no colour, taste or smell it is not in any ordinary sense observable and is to that extent more notional? If it is simply included as an example of an element we need a somewhat unusual view of concept in order to admit the *other* elements; in what sense is, say, sulphur a concept?

For any verbal manipulation of the concepts of science we need names or terms with which to refer to them. How do we specify the meaning of scientific term and thus characterise the concept? "Define your terms" sounds an appropriately scientific imperative; it is impossible to give precise definition to every term in a given area of science by means of other 'scientific' terms without lapsing into circularity. Some theoretical terms can be defined by others: acceleration may be defined as the second derivative of position as a function of time – although we note in passing that acceleration (one of Hirst's concepts of science) is defined partly in terms of derivative (a mathematical concept). It is necessary for the others to use pre-theoretical terms which help to specify the meaning of theoretical terms with the help of previously understood expressions.

The operationist school of thought has provided a clear conception of the way in which scientific terms may be related to an antecedently available vocabulary; the central requirement is that the meaning of every term is specifiable in such a way that it prescribes a "definite testing operation that provides a criterion for its application" (Hempel, 1966). An example should make this clear; an acid may, at an early stage of chemical knowledge, be operationally defined as any liquid which turns blue litmus paper red; here we have implied a testing operation (insert blue litmus paper into the liquid) and a test result (the litmus paper turns red) which can be used to discriminate between examples and non-examples of acids. The operationist principle also extends to the characterisation of terms which stand for quantitative concepts such as mass, length, and temperature; here the definition indicates a procedure for ascribing a numerical value. It provides rules of measurement.

This school of thought has had considerable importance in the development of both the natural sciences, and, as we shall see later, the social sciences; on its own it is, however, inadequate. The arguments to support this contention are not easy to summarise but let us start from a sentence in *The Logic of Modern Physics* (Bridgman, 1927): "The concept is synonymous with the corresponding set of operations." Thus the concept of temperature may be operationally defined by describing how the temperature of something can be measured using a mercury thermometer. The determination could then be carried out with an alcohol thermometer and as different operational criteria characterise different concepts we have arrived, essentially, not at the concept of temperature but at the two concepts of mercury — temperature and alcohol-temperature.

As the field of knowledge is cultivated its concepts become linked to each other and to other concepts already available. These linkages can provide new criteria and new testing instruments and procedures; when a law links the resistance of a wire to temperature a resistance thermometer is possible and can be used to measure temperature. The operationist position thus leads to a pullulation of concepts, endless in theory and unmanageable in practice; a simple, unified, systematic account of the material world is unattainable.

This unhappy position is avoided by giving due place to the systematic import of concepts; concepts are diversely connected to one another by laws and theoretical principles — they form the "knots in a network of systematic interrelationships". Thus, the more threads leading to and coming from a conceptual knot the greater is the systematising power of that concept. The development of the theoretical framework, moreover, regularly leads to an adjustment of the original operational definitions of the concepts; one can begin measuring time by regularities in the apparent movements of sun and stars, but a heliocentric theory, Newtonian theory, and the theory that the rotation of the earth is slowing down, demand recognition that the original procedures for time measurement are only approximate and that more accurate time scales, for example from atomic clocks, should be adopted.

"The process might be compared to building a bridge by putting it first on temporary supports into the river bottom, then using the bridge as a platform for improving and even shifting the foundations, and then again adjusting and expanding the superstructure in order to develop an increasingly well-grounded and structurally sound total system" (Hempel, 1966). In this situation the answer to the question, "Which came first, the concept or the principle?" can only be — "A simpler, and perhaps operationally defined, concept."

There are two conclusions from this. Firstly, the empirical emphasis of operationism is necessary, but not sufficient, for scientific concepts — systematic import is indispensable. Secondly, the idea that scientific concepts can be *individually* characterised by a number of operational criteria gives way to the more sophisticated idea that the principles which link the concepts indicate a variety of situations which will both test the principles and modify the concepts.

It is the aim of science to provide some explanatory insight into the phenomena of the physical world. Concepts which denote, in however complex a way, some aspect of that world do not have, of themselves, explanatory power; they are the prerequisite tools of explanation. Implicit in explanation is the relating of different aspects of experience and that relationship is expressed by the linking of concepts in what we have already called (without adequate definition) principles. Any one concept can, of course, occur in many such principles — there necessarily emerges the network previously referred to in which concepts are the knots and principles are the 'nomic threads'. This is one, possibly simplistic, view of the *structure* of science (Holroyd, 1969). It would be as well to comment on the dangers of adopting misleading metaphors to describe the structure. It is, for example, too easy to suggest that concepts are building bricks which, when appropriately arranged, give rise to the scientific edifice; this architectural analogy is far to static and final — science does not start with the bricks, put them together and leave a finished article. The structure of science is a more dynamic and unfinished thing; the concepts provide the unifying principles, but the testing of the principles – and indeed a developing technology which makes different testing procedures possible – changes the concepts.

The ability of science to 'explain' needs a little closer scrutiny and as a by-product some clarification should emerge on the nature and role of laws and theories in science. We have already used 'principle' to cover any relationship between concepts; the nature of the concepts and of the linkages determines the character of laws and theories.

A boy holds two balloons by the string which joins them; one balloon has a dog painted on it and the other a cat; the two balloons do not hang together but seem to be pushing each other apart. How is this phenomenon to be explained? If we receive the answer that just as dogs dislike cats so the balloons dislike each other and get out of each other's way, we rightly reject it – and for at least two reasons: the answer fails to meet the requirement of explanatory relevance (despite the "just as . . . so", the behaviour of cats and dogs is totally unconnected with the behaviour of balloons) and the requirement of testability (the concept of antipathy between balloons yields no test implications, no empirical finding could corroborate or refute it). A more satisfactory 'scientific' explanation is that the balloons have similar electrical charges in their surfaces which repel each other; this explanation follows from the statement of particular facts and general laws:

1. The boy rubbed both ballons on his hair. (*Fact.*)
2. Whenever a balloon is rubbed on the hair an electrical charge is produced on the surface of the balloon and this charge is always of the same kind. (*'Law'.*)
3. Like charges repel. (*'Law'.*)

Explanations like this, by deductive subsumption under general laws, are properly called deductive – nomological explanations. The laws invoked are statements of universal form, which assert that whenever and wherever some set of specified conditions occur then so always will certain conditions of another kind. Many, but not all, scientific laws are of this type. [It is unfortunate if the word 'law' should suggest some perfect and permanent truth, for two reasons; firstly being an empirical generalisation, there is always an element of accident or convention (or perhaps of scientific enthusiasm) in the decision that the evidence has become good enough to dignify a statement with the name 'law'; and secondly, many laws can be shown to hold only approximately and this for reasons which theory can explain.]

Scientific laws, however, may not claim universality but be content with probability. Examples of probabilistic laws may be thought more common in the biological and medical sciences (because of the inherent variability in and between living organisms) but they are also of great importance in the physical sciences: the reader will be able to identify the probabilistic laws of radio-chemistry and classical thermodynamics.

It might seem that all the laws of science should be described as probabilistic, as all laws are supported by a finite and logically inconclusive body of empirical evidence, but this is to confuse the evidential support for the laws with the nature of the claim they make. No matter how good or bad the evidence for a universal law it claims that "whenever and wherever – then so always . . . "; a law of probabilistic form asserts that "whenever – then so, in this percentage of cases, will . . . ". As a result of this distinction it follows that whereas the deductive-nomological explanation always implies "deductive certainty", the probabilistic explanation does not.

To return to our repelling balloons – it may well be objected that the explanation given is all right so far as it goes, but it goes neither far enough nor deep enough. Why is a charge developed in the balloon? Why do like charges repel? The brief answer is that empirical laws as well as being the basis for explanation are themselves susceptible to explanation by theoretical statement referring to structures and processes underlying the uniformities in question. If in some area of enquiry a degree of understanding has been reached by establishing empirical laws then a good theory will both broaden and deepen that understanding; for example, the relationship between the volume and pressure of a gas is covered by Boyle's law and this law may be explained in terms of a Kinetic Theory of gases. There are five characteristics of scientific theories which deserve brief description and comment here.

(1) A scientific theory necessarily involves two types of principles, principles being, as earlier, any relationship of concepts. One type of principle deals with basic entities and processes and the laws governing them; these may be called 'internal' principles. Assertions about the random motion of molecules and the probabilistic laws governing them are internal to the Kinetic Theory of Gases just mentioned. The second type,

the so-called bridging principles, indicate the relationship between underlying processes and empirical phenomena that are already familiar or, if
you like, between microphenomena and macroscopic features. The
pressure of a gas in a vessel comes from the collisions of the constituent
molecules with the containing walls; the pressure is equal to the average
value of the momentum that the molecules deliver to unit area of the walls
per second —these are bridging principles within the Kinetic Theory.
Because they link theoretically assumed entities with observable or
measureable aspects it is the bridging principles which give a theory its
testability.

(2)   The Kinetic Theory of Gases shows that a wide range of empirical
uniformities can be traced back to the same underlying processes; this is a
regular characteristic of scientific theories — they provide a unifying
account of a diversity of phenomena.

(3)   Theories do not necessarily account for unfamiliar occurences by
a *familiar* explanation; a theory may well be less satisfying psychologically
than the situation it is invoked to explain. It is necessary only that the
theory achieve some systematising unification in a way that allows of
specific, testable principles; if this can be done in terms of analogies that
make it readily accessible and provide a feeling of comfortable "at-
homeness" this is an added bonus.

(4)   Theories frequently cause a re-appraisal of the laws they are to
explain, in other words there is a reciprocal movement between laws and
theories directly related to the dynamic notion of chemical structure
already outlined. The theory may show that the empirical laws already
formulated hold only approximately and within certain defined
conditions, rather than strictly and unexceptionally; they may also explain
why this should be so.

(5)   A scientific theory should also be able to predict the occurrence
of phenomena not taken into account in its formulation; this predictive
success increases the corroborative support for the theory and commonly
provides the link between the theory and its practical applications (i.e.
between "pure" science and technology).

(6)   All scientific theories are, as it were, on probation, they may be
scrapped for something better.

The concepts of science are related by principles; these principles are
conveniently called laws and theories and give science its structure. What

then of the "tests of validity"? The notion of testability has occupied a crucial position at several places in the foregoing discussion and it will regularly recur, suffice it to say here that scientific testing rests on observation by the unaided senses, or with the help of tools which extend their range and improve their accuracy, of objects and events under specified and controlled conditions and takes place in such a way that some other competent person can repeat the procedure with the same result.

We have thus asserted that science has concepts, structure and tests and indicated something of the nature of these. Are they, however, distinct from those in other domains of human enquiry?

DISTINCTION BETWEEN SCIENCE AND OTHER FORMS OF ENQUIRY

Even if we accept that Hirst's concepts, structures and tests are features sufficient to characterise separate disciplines, the attempt to demonstrate that science is an autonomous discipline in the Hirst sense must remain outside the scope of this chapter; it requires a rigorous inspection of all the accepted concepts, of the relationships between them and of the procedures for testing in all those areas of enquiry which might lay claim to the status of forms of knowledge. But more than this it requires the development of defensible rules for deciding how much similarity and transfer can be allowed before a dividing line becomes meaningless.

Science is concerned with the physical world and with living organisms; it is empirical in that its base is in observation and experimentation. In science the tests of observation in experiment are often decisive; it necessarily involves deduction, but not from an axiomatic base, a feature which distinguishes it from mathematics. Its aim is a theoretical formulation which explains observable 'facts' and the concepts of obligation and goodness, for example, are no part of the explanation as they would be in ethics and morals.

If the status of science as a discipline is allowed, this is not, of course, to assert the manifest nonsense that it is isolated from the others. All science regularly uses mathematical knowledge but the validity of that knowledge is established by mathematical and not by scientific procedures; an historical treatment of the reign of George III uses the scientific (biochemical/physiological) knowledge of acute porphyria, but the characterisation and explanation of that condition is not an historical concern.

Having given an important place to the empirical base of science we should however, examine it a little more critically. Many thinkers have been exercised over the problem of the demarcation of science from religion, metaphysics, pseudo-science and so on; three components of empiricism have on various occasions been favoured as appropriate criteria of demarcation.

(1) *Observation*. This is almost too naïve to require criticism; the view implied is that science is firmly grounded in the sense-data of observation whereas 'non-science' is not. If one adopted this view astrology with its great mass of observations would be admitted as scientific, as would phrenology, psycho-analytic theory and the rest; the criterion lies elsewhere.

(2) *The logical treatment of the results of observation*. The crucial significance of induction in scientific method has had illustrious supporters (John Stuart Mill and Karl Pearson, for example) and despite the injurious blows of Popper, Medawar and others induction stubbornly refuses to die quietly. Crudely stated the inductionist school believes that science accumulates a large number of specifics or 'facts' by observation, then operates on these logically to produce generalisations, laws and theories; whether or not the generalisation or law is acceptable depends only on the objectivity and accuracy of the observations and the validity of the inductive logic which follows. When Max Born says that he "cannot compel them [i.e. anti-vaccinationists and astrologers] to accept the same criteria of valid induction in which I believe: the code of scientific rules" he identifies himself with this school. Unfortunately no valid induction procedure is available, nor can it ever be expected.[1]

(3) *Experimentation*. The detachment, objectivity and logical rigor of the stereotype scientist are not to be found in his production of laws and theories but in his testing of them. The serious role of experimentation is always to test the validly deduced implications of science's generalisations. It is of interest and importance how the testing is done — and both

1 For a full treatment of induction in science see Hempel (1966), Medawar (1967) and Popper (1963).

procedures and technical devices may be forbiddingly complex — but it is necessary also to ask what the testing is for, what it aims to do. If one possesses a theory, and particularly if one possesses some kind of pride of ownership, it is tempting to look for confirmations of that theory and easy to find them; it is just as easy to neglect unfavourable evidence. In addition any number of confirmatory pieces of evidence cannot prove a theory "true", but a single refutation demands either rejection or rescue by modification. This provides the clue; the criterion of demarcation of a scientific theory from a non-scientific one is that it must be "falsifiable", that is, capable of being refuted: no theory is scientific if it is non-testable or irrefutable. Similarly a criterion of scientific procedure is that testing is carried out not "to prove the theory right" but in an attempt to prove it wrong. It is not necessary to conclude from this that a theory can never receive experimental support — corroboration comes from an unsuccessful (but serious) endeavour at refutation.

Distinguishing requirements of science are that its theories be testable by experiment and that its practitioners attempt refutation rather than verification.[2]

THE DIVISION OF SCIENCE INTO COMPONENT DISCIPLINES

Perhaps science can be accepted as a *distinct* form of knowledge. Is it defensible to think of science as only *one* discipline, not to be divided?

Science is conventionally separated into 'natural' and 'social'; the former may be further divided into 'physical' and 'biological'. For Philip Phenix (1964) all the divisons form one realm — the empirics; for Paul Hirst there is some doubt. In 1965 he listed "the physical sciences, the human sciences" as distinct disciplines, distinguished "(perhaps) . . . by the nature of their empirical concepts." (For physical one should read natural as, presumably, Hirst would put biology with the physical sciences rather than with he social sciences — but the point is not clear.) In 1966 science is one discipline, although "maybe there are good grounds for thinking that the human sciences are logically distinguishable from the physical sciences." Hirst then continues to argue that science can be conveniently

2 But see Kuhn for criticism of this view.

subdivided according to its content (i.e. according to the selection of empirical phenomena which it chooses to be concerned with), but these divisions "do not result in domains which are logically distinguishable, for in logical respects the *sciences* are *all* strictly similar" [my italics]. There is clearly a gross inconsistency here unless Hirst intended to write "in logical respects all sciences *that are not human sciences* are strictly similar". With this confusion it is dangerous to summarise Hirst's view, but it would seem to be: social science may perhaps be distinguished from the other sciences either on logical grounds or by the nature of its empirical concepts, but there are no logical distinctions within the physical and biological sciences. We cannot leave the issue there.

The essential question is whether the different content of the branches of science necessarily results in differences in the method by which the knowledge is obtained; content differences need not make several disciplines of science, but epistemological and methodological differences may.

One way of claiming the one-ness of science is through theoretical reduction. For example, the thesis of the reducibility of biology to chemistry and physics implies that living organisms are nothing other than very complex physico-chemical systems, but what does this mean? Two claims are made: (a) that the characteristics of living things can be fully described in terms of the concepts of physics and chemistry and (b) that the behaviour of living things which is explicable at all can be explained by laws and theories that are physical or chemical. It is not possible to assign physico-chemical meanings to the terms of biology by arbitrary stipulative definitions (this is to have the same meaning as that); it may be possible to provide loosely descriptive definitions, which are sometimes called "extensional" definitions. Such definitions will express necessary and sufficient physico-chemical conditions for the applicability of biological terms; for example, being a compound of such and such a chemical structure is both a necessary and sufficient condition for being a hormone. A connection of this type is not established by analysis of meaning, by philosophy or by any other non-empirical procedure, but by chemical analysis – it is a biochemical discovery. The question of the 'definability' of biological terms is one that cannot be answered independently of empirical evidence. A somewhat similar discussion of the second claim of mechanistic reductionism would lead to the similar conclusion that whether or not biological laws can be explained by physico-chemical ones depends on the establishment of suitable connecting laws — here again the answer is in experimentation. The present state of knowledge is not sufficient to allow acceptance of the reductionist claims; this is not to deny that they provide stimulating and fertile research maxims for biophysical and biochemical investigation.

It should be noted that the idea of *reducing* biology to physics and chemistry could well become meaningless; the previous paragraph assumed that a clear distinction could be drawn between the terms of the physical and biological branches of science. In many cases this can be confidently done today — as once it could be done with chemistry and physics — but precise criteria which would hold for distinguishing future terms are difficult to imagine. If new terms in comprehensive unifying theories can account for phenomena both of the kind now considered biological and of the kind now called chemical, the distinction between biology and chemistry becomes no longer significant or helpful.

The question of reducibility is also of considerable interest in psychology where the reductionist view holds that all psychological phenomena are essentially biological or physico-chemical in character and can ultimately be explained in terms of those subjects. It recurs in the social sciences where one version of the doctrine of methodological individualism insists that all social phenomena are to be described, analysed and explained in terms of the individual agents involved and by the laws and theories of individual behaviour; the social sciences are then reducible to individual psychology and then to biology, physics and chemistry.

The behaviourist school of psychology is reductionist in the sense we have described in that it attempts to reduce all psychological states and properties to overt, publicly observable, behavioural ones. But whereas 'behaviourists, agree in their insistence an 'objective' behavioural criteria for psychological phenomena they disagree on (or ignore) whether or not the psychological phenomena are *distinct* from the behavioural ones (i.e. the latter are only the public appearances of the former) or are, in some clear sense, identical with them. Let us not plunge here into the eternally turbulent waters of the mind–body question but observe, perhaps naïvely, that although no-one has proved that the reduction of psychology to behaviourism is impossible neither has it been established that it is possible. Theoretical reduction may be able to demonstrate the 'one-ness' of science — it has not done so yet.

There are some familiar notions which have at times been suggested as demarcation criteria for constituent disciplines of science. Four of these are of particular interest.

UNIQUENESS AND VARIABILITY

Not one of the billion toads at the bottom of Lake Titicaca is identical with any other; a sample of sodium chloride can usually be taken as identical with all other samples. No toad is the same today as it was yesterday; today's sample of salt will, for most practical purposes, be the same tomorrow. These simple distinctions are reflected in the different types of statement we can make about toads as against salt and in experimental methods used to test them — biological laws are regularly probabilistic, biological experimentation requires the use of controls, sampling procedures and statistics. The difference is, however, more apparent than real. Chemical theory has to cope with change both at the macro level (this substance takes in water from the air, that substance is undergoing a photo-chemical reaction) and at the micro level (these atoms are decaying radio-actively); it also has to ask whether apparently identical samples are in fact so. (Is the isotopic composition the same?) Many physical laws are probabilistic and statistical procedures can be highly sophisticated in statistical mechanics and thermodynamics. It is roughly the case that, variability and probability enter biology at an early stage and at an observable level, whereas they tend to be necessary in physics and chemistry at a later stage and at the level of theoretical explanation. This is far from asserting that these concepts divide the physical from the biological.

COMPLEXITY

A simple living organism is inestimably more complex than any chemical compound; to characterise it fully, to describe all its properties and processes is an incomparably more daunting task. If one holds that the difference is only in complexity — a reductionist view — it is thereby one of degree and not of kind. Nevertheless, the repercussions on experimental procedures are considerable. With an experiment in the physical sciences the *relevant* variables are usually identifiable; they are also isolable and can be independently varied. In the biological, and even more in the social sciences the *number* of variables is enormously increased, the identification of the *relevant* ones is more difficult and so too is the experimental control of them. Relevant variables may go unsuspected as may their *interaction* with those variables that are being considered. It is little wonder that research in the behavioural sciences is so difficult to do and so easy to criticise.

The large number of variables which may have to be considered when dealing with living things is not entirely due to the complexity of the organism itself; it comes also from the vastly increased number of environmental factors which can be influential. The behaviour of gases is the same in Russia as in America; the behaviour of animals and people is not – because of a host of environmental/cultural variables. A fully developed science of animal behaviour would be able to explain the differences but for the moment many findings are notoriously non-exportable.

The social/biological sciences have developed more slowly than the physical sciences and their findings are more open to dispute; the reasons lie largely in the complexity of the phenomena they try to describe and explain. Although the complexity can give rise to almost insoluble methodological difficulties, it does not demand a distinct methodology.

INTERFERENCE AND OBJECTIVITY

The biological/social research worker interferes with his subjects – the observer unavoidably alters what is to be observed. The Hawthorn effect, for example, is a familiar feature of sociological and psychological investigations. Unhappily its mode of operation, the effects it has and ways of dealing with it are very incompletely understood. Some knowledge of how observer intrusion may be assessed and minimised is available but a scrutiny of any guide to social science research will show how rudimentary that knowledge is.

Within the physical sciences the Uncertainty Principle is in a way similar – crudely its message is the same; there is a limit to the precision with which one can characterise the location and speed of particles because the attempt to observe them will alter them — but quite distinct in that the type of interference and the nature of the result are specified and the sphere within which the principle must be taken into account is clearly prescribed. The chemist, for example, need not consider the effect of his observation when measuring the melting point of naphthalene.

It may well be that this intractable problem is a genuine distinguishing feature between the social sciences and the macro aspects of physical sciences; it is, however, extremely difficult to say where the dividing line would occur — in some aspects of biology observer intrusion is a major consideration (say, the study of the behaviour of higher mammals), in others it is of no importance.

The issue of observer-interference is not identical with that of observer-objectivity. To anticipate a later conclusion — all observation is a selective process, winnowing out from the blooming, buzzing confusion those observations which are relevant to the answering to a particular question or which are appropriate in the light of some hypothesis. *All* observation has a subjective component determined by both experience and expectations. However, in the social sciences more exists which is "potentially observable", the hypotheses are more ambiguous and the selection of what is relevant is more unreliable — for these reasons, and others, subjectivity in observation is more significant. The expectations, attitudes and values of the social scientist can exert a profound and subtle influence in the collection of his data — as they do also in the inter-pretation of his conclusions. Science would appear to be unified in its insistence on attempting objectivity, even if the possibility of success varies widely from area to area.

MORALITY IN EXPERIMENTATION

Experimentation frequently requires the manipulation of one variable in order to assess the effect on some other dependent variable. Varying the temperature of a chemical reaction so that reaction rates may be measured involves no moral considerations; it is conceivable but unlikely that objections might be raised to depriving plants of light in order to study tropisms; it is certain that moral indignation would be aroused if, in order to test a theory concerning the psychological effects of maternal deprivation, one denied some children the care of their mothers. Within both biological and social sciences there is a moral prohibition on certain experimental techniques and disagreement on whether many others are morally justifiable. The place where moral concerns conventionally enter would seem to be within biology – perhaps they are a distinguishing feature of zoology as opposed to botany, or perhaps they distinguish vertebrate from invertebrate zoology.

All the sciences are alike in that the application of their knowledge may raise moral issues.

These four headings can encompass most of the features held to separate the branches of science one from another. The reader may think of more: accuracy of measurement (directly related to the precision with which operational definitions can be made), ease of replication and so on. But the further this line is pursued the greater the conviction that the exercise is unfruitful; of course there are distinguishing features, but dividing lines can be drawn in a multitude of places and the reasons for asserting that any one place is consistently better than another are very far from clear.

Although later and deeper analysis may prove the conclusion wrong there are at present no strong contra-indications to accepting the sciences as one form of knowledge. Sub-division of science takes place on the basis of selected content and on the grounds of practical, administrative convenience and historical accident rather than on clear-cut logical or methodological distinctions. The phenomena investigated by science form a kind of continuum or spectrum and as one moves across this some methods gain in usefulness and applicability, whilst others recede; this kind of analogy has more to offer than one in which science appears in separate compartments.

What is Scientific Method?

As always, a question so deceptively simple has no easy answer. The scientist, in seeking to know, has to collect, characterise and classify; he has to explore and detect, to dream and to think, to engage in large amounts of technical, literary and numerical hack-work. Because the phenomena he investigates may be of the physical world, of plants and of animals (including man) alone or in social groupings, he has to do all these things at different stages of his investigations, to different extents and with different tools. With this multiplicity of activities we can provide "no system of rules for the pursuit of truth which shall be universally and peremptorily applicable". There is no precise procedural imperative which can prescribe for the individual scientist what he must do in order to get where he wants to be.

The prescription for what scientists ought to do is elusive, but so too is the description of what they have done and are doing. The history of science has only recently gained the respect it deserves as a serious and important study; it is still, in the early stages of its development. What scientists do has rarely been the subject of serious empirical enquiry. The attempt to infer what scientists do from published accounts of scientific work is fraught with pitfalls; Medawar has written "It is no use looking to scientific 'Papers' for they not merely conceal but actively misrepresent the reasoning that goes into the work they describe. If scientific papers are to be accepted for publications, they must be written in the inductive style. The spirit of John Stuart Mill glares out of the eyes of every editor of a Learned Journal" (Medawar, 1967).

Scientific Method is convenient shorthand for an incomplete and incoherent collection of guide-lines, some suggested by philosophical/epistemological, considerations some being insights of pragmatic value. Much still remains unverbalized and indeed unconscious, a circumstance which leads to the view that all scientists need to serve a lengthy apprenticeship. (During this period the day to day experience of working in a laboratory and with the masters results in scientific method being acquired by some osmotic process.) The notions of scientific method *may* determine the procedures adopted by any individual scientist; they are rather more successful in helping one scientist to assess and criticise the work of others, to determine its scientific respectability and acceptability. Criteria for assessing validity are available but it would be foolish to imagine they are complete and unambiguous.

About ten years ago a science department in one of our universities taught a brief course in history and methodology in which the essential progression in scientific method was stated to be from Collection to Cogitation to Justification. The scientist starts by collecting data through his senses (alone or with the help of instruments); secondly his brain operates logically on the specifics to produce a generalisation or theory; thirdly he does experiments to prove his theory true. One hopes it is unnecessary to criticise this view and that, in Medawar's cruel phrase, merely to expound it is to expose it. Very briefly:

1. One cannot start by *observing*: the idea of naive or innocent observation is mere flummery, the simple injunction "observe" — fatuous. All observation has to have some direction and purpose and one has to *learn* to perceive using the 'intelligent eye'.

2. Induction as a logical process is mythical.

3. The belief that an experiment can prove a theory true is childish; all it can do with certainty is repudiate that which is false. The intention of the experimenter should be refutation and the design of the experiment such as "to give the facts a chance of disproving the hypotheses."[3]

Bradbury (1969) sees beneath all the varied activities of science the simple theme Observe, Think, Experiment. This three-fold process is superficially similar to the one we have just dismissed, but Bradbury is strong in his insistence that the three activities are not hierarchically ordered but are cyclical; in addition although they are first mentioned in the order given above Bradbury starts his analysis by dealing with thinking. The thinking stage may be either imaginative (in the formulation of hypotheses) or critical (in the testing of hypotheses); the inductive process for building theories is rejected — the use of deductive logic in testing is accepted. Observation is selective in that the scientist observes in relation to what he seeks to establish, but objective in that "he observes dispassionately and does not let his prior views distort what he sees and reads". (There is a difficulty here that Bradbury does not satisfactorily deal with: observation requires prior knowledge and that knowledge can influence expectations (what one hopes to find) and selection criteria (how one decides what is relevant to one's purpose.) Our man of science must aim to be dispassionate and objective but he cannot be wholly successful nor can he easily know how far he has failed. Observations can be qualitative or quantitative. In both types reliability and reproducibility are matters of concern; so in the latter case is accuracy. Experimentation is a special form of observation in which conditions are contrived to remove disturbances so that observations crucial to the testing function can be made.

3 All these points are dealt with at length by Popper and Medawar.

The kernel of this description is that science is a hypothetico-deductive system. Although Karl Popper must be given credit for the first convincingly argued exposition of this, it is difficult to find a more elegantly economical account than that of Medawar.

"First, there is a clear distinction between the acts of mind involved in discovery and in proof. The generative or elementary act in discovery is 'having an idea' or proposing a hypothesis. Although one can put oneself in the right frame of mind for having ideas and can abet the process, the process itself is outside logic and cannot be made the subject of logical rules. Hypotheses must be tested, that is criticized. These tests take the form of finding out whether or not the deductive consequences correspond to reality. As the very least we expect of a hypothesis is that it should account for the phenomena already before us, its 'extra-mural' implications, its predictions about what is not yet known to be the case, are of special and perhaps crucial importance. If the predictions are false, the hypothesis is wrong or in need of modification; if they are true, we gain confidence in it, and can, so to speak, enter it for a higher examination; but if it is of such a kind that it cannot be falsified even in principle, then the hypothesis belongs to some realm of discourse other than Science. Certainty can be aspired to, but a 'rightness' that lies beyond the possibility of future criticism cannot be achieved by any scientific theory."

The first paradigm can be represented iconically as:

COLLECT ———►COGITATE ———►JUSTIFY

The second as:

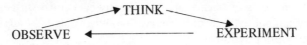

It is tempting to suggest a third:

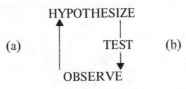

Process (a) is imaginative, speculative, a leap in the dark; process (b) involves logical rigour and careful, informed planning and design. The whole is better considered as cybernetic rather than logical: "The adjustment and reformulation of hypotheses through an examination of their deductive consequences is simply another setting for the ubiquitous phenomenon of negative feed-back." And if anybody asks which comes first, the hypotheses or the observations the only answer is a simpler kind of hypothesis.

If the activity to be called science begins with a conjecture at explanation some interesting questions follow.

A great deal of 'scientific' endeavour has been and is not immediately concerned with explanation. Is this endeavour scientific or not? Thomas Huxley's famous division of the development of science into three states is a useful context in which to consider this. All science, he believed, started from minimally organised, experiential common-sense knowledge, moved into the natural history phase where characterisation and classification were central activities, and might progress into the third stage of full explanation, the unravelling of all cause and effect relationships. The first phase would now normally be described as pre-scientific, but what of the second? Biology has been principally in that phase until comparatively recently, much of social and human science is still there; it is not surprising then that physical scientists argue that only when a subject becomes genuinely explanatory does it merit the name of science whereas social scientists contend that the descriptive, characterising process is not just the prerequisite of science but an essential part of it.

We have already said that before any observation there is some, perhaps lowly, type of hypothesis; hypothesis is often taken to mean a guess at explanation; parts of science are not directly concerned with explanation, but they undoubtedly involve observation. What then has happened to the supposedly prior hypotheses?

A simple example: a scientist is presented with a lump of solid material and asked if it is a metal. He makes certain observations; it is shiny, it clangs when struck, it conducts electricity. As a result of his observations he pronounces it a metal. Where in this process are the hypotheses? What seems to have happened is that the scientist had a (crude) operational definition of metals which implied testing procedures and as a result of applying the tests a decision was reached. It is, however, perfectly possible to reconstruct this episode in hypothesis-observation style. (Metals are shiny, *if* something is shiny *then* it could be a metal, I see this is shiny, thus this could be a metal.) Such a reconstruction seems strange and unnecessarily involved to the educated scientist, it nevertheless corresponds to the thinking-testing procedures characteristic of that period when people first started to call things metal and non-metals. In other words the hypothesis-observation theme is clear in the early stages of scientific enquiry but with the development of the science all the hypothesis-observation strands become simplified and transformed into a set of testing situations or a set of rules to decide the applicability of terms.

This is more important than it seems. Much writing on scientific methodology is concerned only with the scientist's questions, "What is going on here and why?" But all practising scientists spend much, perhaps most, of their time in dealing with the questions "What is it? How am I going to talk about it?" These are questions of identification, classification and full characterisation; the answers may, at one time, have been found by a method clearly showing the hypothesis-observation alternation, that rapid reciprocation of guesswork and check-work, but the substance of the subject has grown since then. Can these terms be used to describe this phenomenon? How is this specific to be related to the established concepts of science? The operational definitions of concepts provide us with testing situations to decide and the techniques and instruments of our laboratories provide us with the means of testing.

The answer to the question "What is it?" often has practical importance. The boy scout who identifies a tree as an elder then knows the wood will be slow-burning and smoky; the chemist who discovers uranium in a rock sample has unearthed information of commercial interest. This question and the related one of "How am I going to talk about it?" have significance beyond the practical, however, as the explanatory phase of science cannot deal with any phenomenon unless it can be adequately described with the vocabulary of the developed science; the new instance has to be handled within the existing structure.

If we return then to Huxley's theory of scientific development, we see his second phase as a necessary part of science in that it describes the properties of objects and processes in the vocabulary which is necessary for any subsequent explanatory phase. The physical scientist may not see the characteristic methodology of discovery operating in the natural history phase because *his* subject has progressed beyond that phase to acquire a fairly well-developed theoretical framework.

Hypothesis formulation is central to the scientific discovery. Can anything more be usefully said about it? Variously described as inspiration, happy guess-work and the felicitous strokes of inventive talent it is not clearly distinguishable from the operation of imagination in the arts. As in the arts the production of hypotheses in the sciences comes suddenly as a result of mental events outside the conscious mind. Although the value of a hypothesis cannot in any way be judged except by the testing of its deductive consequences it is as well to clarify that it is not *merely* a leap out of ignorance into the dark.

Arthur Koestler's grand theory (Koestler, 1964) that all acts of creation involve the bisociation of previously unrelated matrices may be translated into the more mundane language of this article as, all hypotheses result from the union of previously unconnected sections of the substantive structure of science. To bring about such a union one has to withdraw from total immersion in one section of the field and, perhaps dreamily, explore possible relationships with other sections. Archimedes withdrew from the accepted procedures of volume measurement to have a bath; the happy bisociation of volume measurement with water displacement was the result. It may be productive *reculer pour mieux sauter*, but one has to retreat *from* something, one has to possess matrices before they can be bisociated, one has to have some of the concepts of science before they can be related. Some instructions from science teachers to their pupils, and perhaps even more from college lecturers to teachers to their pupils, and perhaps even more from college lecturers to teachers in training, come periously close to "Go, ye ignorant, and discover."

On the other hand any suggestion that only Archimedes, Einstein, Darwin, Kekulé and the rest could be genuinely creative is nonsense. It rests on the misconception that hypothesis formulation is only creative if it leaps from the boundaries of existing knowledge into the unknown; however, creativity depends not on knowing everything there is to know but on the *relationship* between the learner's state and discoverable knowledge. If some youngster who knows what is meant by oxides of non-metals and what is meant by acids comes up with the idea that nonmetallic oxides are acidic his hypothesis formulation is a creative act for him.

Process (b) in the paradigm on page 47 was said to involve logical rigour and careful informed planning and design. What are the features of the experimental, or refutation, stage of scientific enquiry? This cannot be covered thoroughly and comprehensively here, the reader will be aware of the enormous literature available on experimental procedures, instruments and techniques. Some short comments on recurring themes must suffice; much of what will be said has already been implied.

The hypotheses of science have test implications of a conditional kind; they suggest that under certain specified test conditions a certain kind of outcome will occur. In any experimental test one brings about the conditions and observes whether the implied outcome *does* occur. If the conditions have been acceptably arranged and if the outcome is *not* observed then the hypothesis may be rejected; if the expected outcome *is* observed the hypothesis is not to be regarded as true but as having acquired some corroborative evidence. Details of the experimental procedures (the manipulation of conditions and the observations) should be publicly available and repeatable — that is, a competent, but unbiased, second person should on scrutiny of the test agree that it was properly conducted and should also be able to repeat the experiment and come to the same conclusion.

Although this is the normal usage of 'experiment' today it must be recognised that it has not always been this and that echoes of a previous usage can still be heard. The scout who rubs two sticks together to see what happens is conducting an experiment in the older, Baconian, sense of "contriving experience"; if, on the other hand, he is finding out whether there is enough heat generated by friction to produce a spark then his actions, to test a hypothesis, are an experiment in the sense we have described. The distinction is not unimportant to educators as much of children's activity is doing experiments "to see what happens". Such exploratory play is certainly not to be despised, but it must be defended, not on the grounds that it is scientific, but on the grounds that it is necessary as pre-science — or on some other educational grounds.

Many hypotheses are quantitatively expressed and yield indefinite numbers of test implications. Boyle's Law — and it is somewhat arbitrarily called a law rather than a well-corroborated hypothesis — can be tested by varying the value of the pressure of a mass of gas, keeping the temperature constant, and checking whether the volume assumes the values predicted from the mathematical expression of the law. It is regularly asserted that in a test of this kind only one quantity must vary at a time while all the other variables are held constant; this cannot be done — one cannot keep the lighting intensity of the room, the humidity of the atmosphere and the distance of the apparatus from the moon all constant. Fortunately it does not matter; the hypothesis contends that for a given mass at a fixed temperature the volume is fully determined by the pressure, the variables we have not controlled are automatically irrelevant. If, however, one has a hypothesis, say, that the resistance of a wire depends on the length of the wire, its cross-sectional area and the metal it is made of, then on testing any one relationship the other two variables *must* be kept constant — they are relevant to the hypothesis. The most that can be done in cases like these is to keep constant all but one of those factors that we believe to affect the phenomenon being studied; it is always possible that other important factors may not have been identified.

It is the great methodological advantage of the natural sciences that many of its hypotheses admit of fairly easily contrived experimental test, and the scope of such testing increases steadily with advancing technology. However, not *all* hypotheses can be submitted to immediate experimental test (they must all be testable in-principle); on occasions the conditions of the test implications cannot be brought about by any available means. Then one must seek out, or wait for, cases where the necessary conditions occur naturally and then check whether the implied outcome is observable. This will be seen to apply most obviously in astronomy but it is also relevant to ethological studies of animal behaviour.

In this account of scientific method we have made no mention at all of three features often said to be characteristic of it; growth, chance, and model-building.

GROWTH

This is the feature which Jevons describes with admirable clarity in *The Teaching of Science* (Jevons, 1969): "The main and crucial fact (is) . . . that in the natural sciences genuine and substantial progress is beyond reasonable doubt, whereas in typical non-sciences it is not."

Science has progressed (in the sense that the frontiers have moved further and further from the starting point of every-day, pre-scientific knowledge) and accumulated (the total volume of substantive knowledge has increased). No individual scientist has to start from the beginning but stands on the shoulders of his predecessors. The reason for this is partly in the subject matter of science (the more stable and permanent it is the further the advance), but more importantly it lies in the method of enquiry. Powerful research traditions have influenced the direction of scientific work and the way it is carried out. Sets of scientists adopt a common framework of intentions, procedures and assumptions — albeit implicity. This has profound consequences. The specialist has a lengthy apprenticeship to serve in his subject; the activities of the specialist seem to others conceptually difficult and terminologically recondite.

Some of the terms of science are linked to those of pre-science by fairly simple operational definitions; in other words *introduction* to some scientific concepts is an easy business. Familiarity with, or a full grasp of the implications of, those same concepts only comes with a knowledge of their relationships with other concepts — a much lengthier process. Certain other terms can only be meaningfully defined in terms of previously refined scientific usages; to these second order terms there is no short cut. It is considerations like these which erect a language barrier between the expert and the novitiate.

I have a suspicion, however, that science can baffle the layman for a reason other than this. The scientist observed seems regularly to be engaged on enormously complex procedures with highly sophisticated technical assistance. Clearly it is impossible for him to describe precisely what he is doing without assuming in his audience some knowledge of the subject involved; on the other hand scientists have been slow to develop any facility in describing the procedures of their work. If men of science were convinced of the desirability of making clear the *process* of enquiry as well as its results, and if they acquired an adequate vocabulary for the task, there would be real hope that the "rules of research" might become explicit, rather than remain, as now, unverbalised mysteries to be absorbed through the skin during apprenticeship. This, as much as Medawar's request for an ethological enquiry into what is actually *done* by scientists, could help remove barriers between science and other disciplines; the substance would be less remote if the syntax were understood.

The impressive growth of science raises questions for the education of scientists, but it must not be assumed that progress piles up pedagogic problems in proportion. As science advances particulars become comprehended within general statements of increased systematising and explanatory power; the more highly developed the conceptual framework, the less crippling the factual load. "In all sciences we are being progressively relieved of the burden of singular instances, the tyranny of the particular" (Medawar). We shall return to the implications of this for science education.

CHANCE

It is a recurring theme in writing on the history of science that many of the most significant advances are made when the individual scientist grasps the implications of some chance occurrence. The faculty for doing this has been called serendipity after the three princes of Serendip who "were always making discoveries, by accident and sagacity, of things they were not in quest of". Perhaps the most often recounted example is that of Fleming's role in the discovery of the therapeutic power of penicillin; he worked in an old, dusty building and on observing that some of his cultures of staphylococci had died, followed up the cause of contamination.[4]

Unless one brings in some metaphysical notion of a benign deity taking pity and casting down lucky clues the 'accident' in serendipity is less interesting than the 'sagacity'. The time and place of a chance occurrence need, by definition, no explanation; what is of great interest is that the *relevance* of a chance observation to some problem or another should be seen. Such an observation is unexpected in that at the time it is made the observer is not expecting anything of practical importance or theoretical significance; it is not naïve or innocent (to an ignorant eye nothing would be unexpected) as the person who makes it has expectations determined by his conception of the problem he faces. This particular problem may well be in the forefront of his mind, but it is not the only problem the scientist is aware of and, however it is to be explained psychologically,

4 Beveridge (1950) gives detailed accounts of about 30 chance discoveries in *The Art of Scientific Investigation.*

issues do advance and retire on the stage of attention, minds retreat from problems and people day-dream. An observation, unexpected because of our pre-occupation with problem A, may well be relevant to the solution of problem B which has also concerned us. This is a beginning, but it is still an inadequate explanation of those "who discover what they were not in quest of".

Until a proper explanation arrives what can be said of practical interest?

1. Chance discoveries are not given; chance occurrences may be taken advantage of.
2. The scientist who is confident that the solution to a problem lies within a well-defined 'box' runs the risk of missing the solution elsewhere.
3. All unexplained or unexpected observations need both scrutiny and contemplation.

There are echoes in the last few paragraphs of what has already been said about hypothesis formulation. To connect the previously unrelated requires temporary withdrawal and then an imaginative leap forward from knowledge already possessed; to see the relevance of the unexpected requires a contemplative rotation of interest round existing problems. These are not logical procedures and their creative, intuitive character provides science with much of its romance. They do not occur in cold, calculating or closed minds; nor can they occur in empty minds.

MODEL-BUILDING

In our description of science as a form of knowledge and our exploration of the features of scientific method frequent mention has been made of 'terms' and 'statements'. It is possible to make science too verbal or linguistic; there is perhaps even a danger of making science into a nature story telling us the truth about the empirical world. Balance may be restored by looking at science as the painting of pictures and the building of models.

At the level of theoretical explanation when dealing with inferred or hypothetical entities science does not make positive pronouncements about the certain existence of such entities; the statements, as we have said before, are much more tentative, humble and perhaps temporary. Strictly, instead of asserting that matter is composed of atoms, one can only say that our experience is the same "as if" matter were composed of atoms or that matter may be "seen as" atomic. The atomic theory is then an analogy or picture which is a representation of reality and which has a useful, but limited, correspondence with it. Corroborative evidence for the atomic theory is not evidence for its ultimate truth but evidence for the applicability of the picture we have.[5]

This approach adds vividness, but just as the analogy between theory and "reality" cannot be confidently extended, neither can the analogy between picture painting and science.

The function of models is to simplify, but not over-simplify: they collect, summarise and store information making it more readily grasped and handled. Theories are themselves models – they are representations (or pictures) of the world which simplify aspects of that world in a useful way, useful in that they suggest applications which may be tested. The expanding literature on types of models (iconic, analogue and symbolic) has provided a new vocabulary for characterising theories, for making their nature and utility more explicit.[6]

Science Education and the "Forms of Knowledge" Approach

Science may be accepted as a form of knowledge with its own central concepts, its structure and its tests of validity; some broad outlines of scientific method can be sketched in although many details are unknown. The reader may still legitimately ask, "Why bother?" "What is the relevance of all this to the content and method of science education?" I believe it is too early to attempt a complete, definitive answer to these questions: too little thought has taken place, too little research has been done. What follows is intended to show that the "forms of knowledge" approach to some important issues in Science Education has already demonstrated its worth and that further development of this approach is desirable. Most of the examples are taken from the natural sciences (i.e. physics, chemistry and biology).

5 The argument is given at greater length in *The Contribution of Science to Education* (Tricker, 1967).

6 This brief paragraph opens up many issues. For the use of models in science see Bradbury (1969). For description of types of models see Clarke (1968).

THE FORMS OF KNOWLEDGE APPROACH TO
SCIENCE EDUCATION USEFUL IN CLARIFYING OR
QUESTIONING OTHER THEORETICAL CONTRIBUTIONS

(a)   In the second half of the 1960s it seemed as if no writing on the school curriculum was acceptable without a reference to B. S. Bloom (1965). (See, for example, *Science for General Education*, H.M.S.O., 1969.) To say his *Taxonomy of Educational Objectives* is fashionable is not to dismiss it as mere fashion; far from it. Those educators who were convinced of the value of breaking down broad general statements of intent into more specific objectives in behavioural terms needed some system of classification and nomenclature which would help them deal with and talk about objectives of different types and levels. This system Bloom effectively supplied.

It is, however, important to ask how the taxonomy was obtained. Briefly, and thus perhaps crudely, Bloom and his colleagues collected objectives suggested by teachers, i.e. the objectives to be 'taxonomised' were those derived from existing practice. Objectives such as "to describe metallic transformations in the light of alchemical theory", "to produce a horoscope from astrological considerations" do not appear; it may be that they were never suggested. But if they were, the grounds for excluding them would have to be made explicit – this could only be done from consideration of what is, and is not, scientific. "Bloom tacitly assumes that cognitive objectives in education are tied to standards of truth and procedures for arriving at truth" (Gribble, 1970). To put this differently, if a taxonomy is to cover acceptable objectives for science education as opposed to all objectives that could be produced by science educators, selection criteria must operate; such criteria can only be introduced from the consideration of science as a form of knowledge.

Bloom distinguishes between knowledge and skills and abilities; one might think that analysis, say, was a kind of general ability that could be exercised without regard to specific knowledge content and that any knowledge could be justified on the grounds that it developed general analytic ability. Bloom only makes it clear by his sets of examples that this is not his view; his illustrations for analysis confirm that he means "analysis according to accepted canons of science, or history or whatever". Whenever one asks that a pupil acquire the ability to analyse such and such a communication in an acceptably scientific way, one has necessarily to inquire further as to what is acceptable science.

A clarification of the nature of the disciplines is required in order to decide what objectives are educationally satisfactory. If a classified list of the educational objectives of, say, natural science is produced it still gives no guidance as to the relative importance to be attached to any objective; it can usefully describe but not prescribe. The attention to be paid to objectives of a given type is decided by considerations quite independent of any taxonomic exercise and important amongst those considerations is the form of knowledge involved. If science is considered as principally a collection of facts concerning the natural world (which God forbid) then the science educator's main concern is with Bloom Category I − knowledge; if it is maintained that the prime characteristic of science is the ability to devise ways of testing hypotheses then Bloom Category V − Synthesis − is given top priority and the other categories are only important in so far as they are prerequisite for synthesis. (Although the latter contention is greatly to be preferred, it is still, of course, inadequate.)

(b)   In his important, influential and pellucid book *The Conditions of Learning* Robert Gagné develops learning structures based on types of learning behaviour given fairly precise meaning by learning theorists (Gagné, 1965). In these hierarchical structures problem-solving appears as the highest human intellectual capacity; it is dependent on the prior acquisition of relevant principles which in turn require the possession of constituent concepts. Concepts depend on multiple discriminations, verbal associations and so on. The acquisition of any particular competence in the hierarchy always depends on the possession of subordinate, pre-requisite capabilities.

Given a problem in science and knowing the method by which it can be solved the science educator can devise a learning structure with the problem-solving behaviour at the apex of a pyramid. (This analysis may be a very demanding task.) The structure obtained is then a guide to the design of effective instruction in that the learner has to be led, pushed or otherwise encouraged to ascend the hierarchy.

This approach provides many helpful insights and deserves much more than brief mention. However, let us consider just one issue in the context of the 'forms of knowledge' approach. It should be made clear that what follows is not a criticism of what Gagné has said but a warning against over-simplified interpretation of it.

A learning structure for a scientific topic expresses in a static two-dimensional diagram a guide to teaching methods. It is naïve to assume that by integrating all possible learning structures one would arrive at that intangible, complex thing we have called the structure of science. This is to fall into the trap of describing the structure of a discipline in terms of an architectural rather than a biological analogy. This point has practical relevance: the Gagné-type hierarchical structure emphasises that if a learner has, say, the concepts pre-requisite for a certain principle it is easy for him to "step-up" — it is tempting to continue that once the principle is acquired there is no further need to "step down" to the concepts. What the learner has acquired is an ability to use the concepts in the context of one principle, relevant, presumably, to the solution of one problem; this is not the same as having a grasp of the concepts as determined by their systematic import. We have previously described how, in the development of scientific knowledge, it is sufficient at an early stage for a concept to be defined in simple operational terms, but as the concept becomes a constitutent of proliferating principles its inter-relationships with other concepts refine and modify the original meaning.

One example will demonstrate the simplicity of this point. A pupil shows by his solution of a problem in elementary chemistry that he knows what acidity is — he has acquired the concept acidity in the learning structure for that problem. It is absurd to suggest from this that the acidity concept then needs no further attention. Perhaps this is straining at gnats and making mountains of molehills — no practising science teacher needs to be reminded of something so elementary. There is, however, a real need for designers of instructional programmes based on Gagné-type analyses to be so reminded.

(c)   Two influential views held by Jerome S. Bruner should also be scrutinised from the forms of knowledge standpoint.

Bruner's arguments for a "spiral curriculum" are well known. In such a curriculum "instruction should begin as intellectually honestly and as early as possible in a manner consistent with the child's forms of thought. Let the topics be developed and redeveloped in later grades" (Bruner, 1960). How acceptable is this in the light of what has been said of the nature of scientific knowledge?

Earlier we made a distinction between first-order and second-order scientific terms; the former were initially to be defined in terms of an antecedently available, pre-scientific vocabulary, the latter were dependent on the development of the former. Fortunately many important scientific terms can be reached directly with a very limited vocabulary and as a result the concepts denoted by these terms can be acquired at an early age in a way that is 'intellectually honest'. The inadequacies of this introduction clearly need to be put right at a later stage — to this extent the Brunerian spiral curriculum is happily compatible with our view of the concepts and principles of science. One must regard with suspicion any notion that *all* scientific concepts can be quickly grasped by the young learner even given strenuous attempts by the teacher to present them in a way appropriate to the learner's developmental stage; there are problems of sequence which prevent this. Concept B may only be meaningfully grasped if concept A on which it depends is part of the child's mental equipment; in this situation, however important B is, it is foolish to attempt to introduce it before concept A.

This caveat must not obscure the validity and importance of the central claim, however. Many of the crucial concepts of science can be approached simply and directly by young pupils. In British physics syllabuses the treatment of energy used to be delayed until students could be provided with a formidable list of formal definitions (Energy is the capacity to do work. Work is done when a force . . . . Force is that which . . . . etc.) In *The New Scottish Physics Syllabus* (S.E.D., 1962, 1964) energy, its conservation and propagation, is one "of the basic themes which continually present themselves". This syllabus laid stress on introducing and later revisiting basic unifying concepts to such an extent that even in 1962 it was described as a cyclical (spiral?) syllabus. In *The Scottish Integrated Science Course* (H.M.S.O., 1969) energy is introduced in the first term of the first year; the simplest of operational definitions suffices at this stage — this hardly even needs to be verbalised, but is of the form "If it's got energy it can do something, if it hasn't, it can't."

Bruner also describes the structure of a domain of knowledge as characterisable in three ways, one of which is the mode of representation. Any domain, or any problem within the domain can be represented by a set of actions (enactive mode), by a set of summary images (iconic mode) and by a set of symbolic or logical propositions (symbolic mode). The example Bruner gives for science is convincing; the very young child can act on the basis of the principle of movement when playing on a see-saw, when somewhat older he can represent the see-saw for himself as a model, eventually he can describe the principle in linguistic or even better in mathematical terms. The relationship of this to Piagetian psychology and its implications for pedagogic practice merit extended treatment and will no doubt receive it elsewhere. We shall allow ourselves a single comment.

Bruner's see-saw example is a good one, but it is difficult to find others equally satisfying and highly doubtful if the search can always be successful. Explanations at a theoretical level and involving inferred entities are a large part of the domain of science; they can frequently be translated into an iconic mode, indeed they regularly exist only in that mode but it is not at all easy to specify what the *enactive* mode of a theory could be — yet Bruner asserts that *all* domains and *all* problems within a domain can be so represented.

My son aged five is allowed, when a parent is present, to heat water on a gas cooker to make himself cocoa. One day recently he filled the kettle, put it on the gas, took it off again and emptied out three-quarters of the water saying "It won't take so long to boil now." A young child has demonstrated the possession of experiential, intuitive, enactive knowledge of concrete materials; it may be that experiences of this kind will facilitate the acquisition of scientific concepts; it is certainly the case that teachers should capitalise on them to encourage cognitive growth; it is good if such experiences can be engineered in nursery and primary schools. This is all part of an enlightened and humane strategy of education which arranges the environmental conditions to help optimise intellectual development. My son's activities with the kettle may help a later under-standing of calorimetry; they (or something like them) may be *necessary* for that understanding, but does he in any meaningful sense possess a principle relating heating rate to volume?

A principle is a generalised, verbalised statement with some explanatory import; specific personal experiences may later come to be comprehended *within* that principle, but is it helpful to say that they *are* that principle represented in an enactive mode? One can say to educators, search out an enactive mode of representation for that principle of science; alternatively one can say look for specific concrete experiences which may help in later generalisation of a scientific kind. My preference is for the latter.

THE FORMS OF KNOWLEDGE APPROACH
HELPFUL IN CRITICISING THE OLDER SCIENTIFIC
SYLLABUSES

The defects of conventional curricula in science are well known and many of them have been, or are being, put right in revised curricula. Changes that have taken place have not necessarily been initiated because of philosophical considerations; the reasons have been practical, educational, empirical and "common-sensical". My point is simply that the pressure to change could have been greater if it had been grounded in an appreciation of science as a form of knowledge.

Consider three oft-repeated criticisms of old science syllabuses:

(a)   School science consisted of a load of facts, usually unrelated and consequently very difficult to learn.

Many people asked today what they remember of school chemistry recall most vividly their abortive attempts to learn the preparations and properties of a large number of noxious gases. Such criticism was common to all the science subjects and often valid.

One cannot, of course, operate without facts, specifics and singular instances but it is a feature of the development of scientific knowledge that its conceptual framework gains ever more systematising and unifying power. The learner who is "guided into the structure of science" progressively grasps those concepts, principles or "underlying themes" which subsume particulars, give them relevance and make them memorable. Any practising scientist learns a good deal of factual material but it comes as a by-product of being concerned with the solution of problems; if he needs the factual material he knows where to look for it. He never learns it in the hope that it will be relevant for some future enquiry.

(b)   School science was taught in a formal, didactic authoritarian way.

"My teacher always gave me the impression that he had the knowledge and I didn't, therefore his job was to give me what I lacked, to hand it to me on tablets of stone" — a criticism levelled at teachers of all subjects and perhaps meant more as a comment on an authoritarian role-concept than as a condemnation of a teaching method.

There always exists a danger that the statements of a person in authority will be considered authoritative in themselves; certainly the science teacher who repeatedly said "There it is, write it down" tended to confirm in his pupils' minds that the statements of science were final statements of truth, permanent and not to be questioned. All scientific principles, laws and theories, however, are on probation – to be approached with scepticism, to be used as long as they are adequate, and to be scrapped whenever something better offers. Whether or not they are authoritative is a matter of experimental corroboration and systematic import only.

There is a perennial problem for all teachers of science as, on the one hand, they have to teach their pupils that all scientific propositions must be met with scepticism and a demand for evidence and yet, on the other hand, they have regularly to say "This you must take on trust, on my authority." The latter course has to be adopted on grounds of expense, safety and, most obviously, time (science is cumulative, scientists have to stand on each other's shoulders, no person can retrace the whole history of science).

Hearing a teacher say "It is true, take it from me, metals expand when heated", one can immediately suggest an alternative approach which is preferable on theoretical grounds. ("O.K. Bill, you've got this idea that metals expand when heated, how would you set about testing it? Right, go ahead and see.") But if a teacher happens to state that there are over 100 elements in the world and Bill interjects, "Prove it, show me them, how do you know they are all elements?" must the teacher then set about amassing all the evidence? Sometimes the teacher must tell and the pupil must accept. The science teacher has to inculcate a questioning attitude – but he has also to decide that some statements are not going to be questioned. The statements he does select for thorough scrutiny and testing are those which are likely to lead to some important insight into central scientific concepts and which are feasible on the practical grounds of time, apparatus, safety and so on – and his only qualifications for the selection are his own scientific training and his pedagogical wisdom i.e. he acts as an authority.

Many of the old syllabuses expected pupil experimentation and critical reasoning; that so many teachers did not provide them was for very mundane reasons – it is always quicker, cheaper and less tiring for a teacher to tell than to test. It is a commonplace that the new syllabuses, which require much less telling and much more testing, demand more time and more money. They also require much more patience, energy and imagination from the teacher — a point which is recognised but not always allowed for. Ten years ago there were relaxed, even lazy, science teachers claiming happily that they could teach science in any old classroom as long as they had a voice, a blackboard and a piece of chalk; today they are likely to be found in a sea of equipment, in a bigger, lighter laboratory, themselves, grey and exhausted. If teachers are not to relapse once again into the telling of science, if they are to succeed in the much more difficult job of helping their pupils to become scientists and to acquire scientific "know-how", they need informed support from headmasters and local authorities and practical help from technical auxiliaries.

(c)   School science involved too few experiments. Those there were often seemed pointless.

Some teachers of science have put less emphasis on experimental work, on pupil activity, than they themselves liked — for the practical reasons indicated. Many others did not believe that more experimental work was desirable. This latter stand is only supportable if it is held that the function of science education is to pass on some distillation of scientific content: if one holds that pupils should learn what science is, what kind of knowledge is scientific, the procedures by which science extends its knowledge and what is involved in acting scientifically then experimentation, and essential constituent of science, is an equally essential part of science education.

Science teachers! Next time your class is doing practical work go round asking each pupil what he is doing and why. When you have got over your dismay at the vagueness of the answers, then ask *yourself* precisely what the point of the work is — and be further dismayed.[7]

---

7 The purpose of much practical work was, and still is, unclear; occasionally it was indefensible. This may seem harsh but consider an example. Generations of science students were told, without any preamble, there is a thing called The Law of Constant Composition and that they would do an experiment which would prove it true. This methodological horror was then compounded by the Examination Board which required that in any description of the experiment the candidate should include the equation for the reduction reaction. (The writing of the formula for copper oxide *presupposes* that the Law holds.) It is, of course, possible to include the Law in a syllabus and approach it in a methodologically respectable way; the reader will be able to devise the procedure and to indicate the appropriate language of hypothesis — test — observations — probationary acceptance.

I am firmly convinced that we should have a much clearer view of the function of experimental work, that we should develop a more precise vocabulary to describe such work. That clearer view can only be obtained by taking into account psychological knowledge of the role of concrete experience and self-activity in learning and philosophical knowledge of the function of experiment within the discipline of science.

As a tentative start to the development of helpfully descriptive terms I offer the following classification of types of practical activity in the science laboratory.

1. *Exploration.* This ranges from creative play to experimentation in the Baconian sense. Some of it is necessary in science as enjoyable activity likely to trigger off spontaneous questions which may then be followed up. Too much exploration, insufficiently guided by the teacher, becomes aimless and time-wasting.

2. *Technical familiarization.* The purpose of this is simply to introduce pupils to pieces of apparatus and useful techniques. It is doubtful if it should often be undertaken *in vacuo* or with hopes of future utility; if the knowledge and expertise are seen to be necessary for some accepted purpose they will more readily be acquired.

3. *Demonstration.* This term is to cover demonstration by teacher to pupils and by pupil to himself. Its purpose is illustrative, to make some property or process vivid or memorable. When it finds a place in a science curriculum it does so for wholly educational reasons – it is no part of science as such.

4. *Characterization.* This describes the practical activities undertaken to answer the questions, "What is it? What (numerical) value can be attached? How am I going to talk about it?" As has been described earlier such activities regularly follow a procedural recipe as, for example, in the identification of an unknown substance by qualitative analysis or in the determination of some physical constant. They can, however, often be transformed into experimental procedures following the hypothesis – test – observation theme.

5. *Experimentation.* It would be helpful if this term were reserved only for practical work designed to test the implications of a hypothesis – if it were used only in the strict sense in which it was earlier

defined. There are good grounds for demanding more genuinely experimental work in school science and this does not simply mean more pupil activity.

THE FORMS OF KNOWLEDGE APPROACH VALUABLE FOR CLARIFYING THE INTENTIONS OF THE NEWER SCIENCE SYLLABUSES.

An Example from Nuffield Chemistry (Nuffield, 1966)

Topic A 1.1 in the Nuffield Sample Scheme – the first investigation in the first year of a secondary school course – is entitled, "How can we get pure salt from rock salt?" Can this investigation be described with the language usages we have developed in this account?

The principle purposes of the lesson can be inferred to be:
1. The introduction of the concepts of chemical purity, solution, evaporation etc., by linking them to a simple pre-scientific vocabulary.
2. "Technical familiarisation" – with beakers, filter funnels and hand-lenses and with filtration, evaporation and crystallisation techniques (Practical Activity – Type 2).

With a minimum of alteration this lesson could be changed into a practical exercise involving characterisation and experimentation (Activity – Types 4 and 5). "Here's some stuff – I wonder what it is? Any ideas? Suck it and see. It could have salt in it. How could we be more definite? Get rid of the dirt. How? . . . Try it . . . Looks like salt, tastes like salt, behaves like salt . . . The stuff we began with can be called rock salt." With this approach one avoids telling the pupils at the beginning what the substance is, one provides some (though incomplete) evidence that the substance is what it claimed to be, one introduces the notion of "hypothesize and test" and all the technical familiarization and definition of terms can be treated incidentally.

Examples from the Scottish Physics Syllabus (S.C.E.E.B. 1969)

Syllabus Section A.1 "Laboratory techniques – to catch the pupil's interest and to teach techniques of using apparatus and reading scales."

This is clearly practical work Type 2. There is an implied admission here that pupils have to acquire skill in observation; even the reading of a volume on a measuring cylinder requires an educated eye. One can question whether it is wise to do this teaching initially; it could well be postponed until the skill is necessary for some genuinely scientific purpose.

Syllabus Section A.2 "Experiments with observations and some conclusions."

More guidance should be given on the nature and purpose of the "experiments" to be included. As usually laid out in 'stations' the pupil activities are of all the five types we described. Too many experiments of type 1 (Exploration) are time-wasting unless the teacher can be on hand to deal with spontaneous questions. In too many experiments of type 2 the learners are assumed to be able to observe without knowing what counts as observation and without being guided in the acquisition of the necessary skills.

The well-known black box "experiment" is an exercise in characterization with no prescribed procedural rules. Instead of being asked to "observe and conclude" learners should be asked to "guess and test".

Syllabus Section D 4 "Resistance. Effect of change of length and gauge of wire. This introduces a situation where two variables exist and each must be suppressed, in turn, to investigate the effect of the other – an important principle of scientific method."

With experiments of this type the science teacher has great opportunities to teach some essential features of scientific methodology in an unobtrusive, but telling way. It is highly desirable that the learner should "discover" the principles relating the concept of resistance to length, cross-sectional area and so on; that having arrived at hypotheses with clear test implications he should be able to design and perform properly designed trials in which he can check the implications against his own observations. Having done these experiments the student ought to be able to answer such questions as, "If you had taken two separate wires of 34 s.w.g. one 1 m long and the other half as long, and made of different materials, what could you have concluded?" If the learner has not grasped the concept of relevant variables and their control, the teacher has failed to make the most of the situation. The syllabus guide should make it clearer to the teacher the precise points of scientific method which can emerge.

THE FORMS OF KNOWLEDGE APPROACH AND SOME SPECIAL CLASSES OF LEARNER

The primary-school child

The idea of science as a body of information to be handed on has too often produced gross educational malpractice in secondary schools; fortunately this has rarely happened in primary schools. However, at a time when there is increasing emphasis on developing primary school science it is important to clarify what kind of science this should be.

A great deal of the activity in a modern primary school is genuinely scientific already. If you ask a young pupil engaged in a project on "Our Weather" what temperature is, you may well get the answer, "This thing is a thermometer and the mercury has stopped at the 20 mark so the temperature of the room is 20". Through simple practical activity, i.e. operations, the young child is being introduced to concepts important in both mathematics and science such as temperature, length, weight, solution and so on; the operational definition of concepts has begun and the child is developing the vocabulary which later science will need. He is also gaining some technical familiarization with the instruments and apparatus of science.

In much creative play with water, sand, constructional toys and the like the very young child acquires direct experience of the concrete which will help him in later generalization and explanation. Whether or not in this activity the principles of science are acquired in their 'enactive mode' the teacher can, by unobtrusive comments and questions help the young child along the fascinating path that leads to the full symbolic verbal or numerical expression of scientific principles. To take Bruner's example – two boys A and B are on a see-saw in the school playroom when the teacher passes and asks A why he is sitting nearer the centre than B is. Later when A is drawing, the teacher comments on the fact that A has put the thin figure in his drawing right at the end of the plank and asks why. This kind of guidance is not only encouraging linguistic development but also providing a gentle introduction to the structure of science.

The questions which children ask about their immediate environment are the same questions that concern and motivate science – What is it? What is happening? Why? Children do not need to be taught to ask these questions but teachers *do* have to be helped to answer them; wrong or misleading responses from the teacher can decrease the frequency with which such questions are asked, they may not impede intellectual growth but they certainly fail to encourage it. If in our weather project a child asks "Why is it raining?" it is desirable that the teacher recognises this as a question which does have a scientific explanation; this recognition is much more important than knowing precisely what the explanation is. Hence the answer "Perhaps because the clouds are cold," is, at least in embryo, scientific however inadequate and temporary it may be; the answers "Because God sends the rain" or "To help the flowers grow" are theological and teleological – they answer a question from one form of knowledge with the concepts of a different form.

There are many spontaneous 'scientific' questions – "Why is it raining?" is one – which teachers do not immediately follow up by a series of observations and experiments, partly because they do not possess enough knowledge themselves and partly because it would take too long to teach all the knowledge pre-requisite for a detailed answer. In these cases the honest answer is the best one: "Part of the answer is ... Science has a better answer but it would take the rest of the year to tell you about it." Nevertheless, there are many questions which can most profitably to taken up: for the ensuing pupil activity and teaching it is a great advantage if the teacher has a clear insight into the language and procedures of scientific method. The following dialogue is from a primary school classroom:

Pupil   : Why are the windows steamed up?
Teacher   : Let's think, have you any idea what makes them look "steamed up"?
Pupil   : Perhaps it's water.
Teacher   : Could be, how can we be sure?
Pupils   : Collect it. Taste it. See if it makes the mustard grow.
(*Activities to test suggestions, i.e. experimentation and characterizations.*)
Teacher   : We've got some evidence for thinking it's water. Where did it come from? Any ideas?
Pupil   : It came out of the glass.
(*Teacher now has to decide whether to test this hypothesis and thus refute it or close this avenue for practical reasons of time etc.*)
Pupil   : The water came from the air.
Teacher   : Did it? How do you know there is water *in* the air?

It is possible to multiply examples like this where the primary teacher can provide guidance and activities which are entirely appropriate to the developmental level of the learners but which are also defensible as genuine science.

Much of the material suggested for primary schools involves activities of types 1, 2, and 3, i.e. exploration, technical familiarisation and demonstration. There need be nothing wrong in this as long as the activities do not become aimless, routine or merely vivid; these unfortunate outcomes can be avoided by the teacher who, although not a professional scientist, is still sufficiently aware of the nature of science to raise the activity to the levels of characterisation and genuine experimentation. There is a real need, in addition, for all teachers to be supported by kits and learning programmes which incorporate insights both from learning theory and from considerations of science as a discipline.

Approaching science in the primary school through stories of the great scientists of the past has fallen into some disrepute — there is nothing to be said in favour of dull little tales of forgotten men facing problems now of only academic interest. But we must be careful not to condemn the general method because of the incompetence of some who use it. I have had the privilege of witnessing a teacher of ten-year-olds transform the worn old anecdote about Archimedes into a vivid, arresting account of an important problem solved in a scientific way. The pupils took from this a little substantive knowledge and an insight into the place of imaginative hypothesis-formulation in science. Provided that (a) the elements of the problem are accessible to the pupil, (b) the principles used in its solution are still part of the structure of science and (c) some of the features of scientific method can emerge, the re-telling of episodes from the history of science can be a valuable tool in the armoury of the science teacher.

The less-able pupil, the early school-leaver

The days when it was considered that an ability to recite the properties of carbon monoxide and to state Ohm's Law were likely to help the early leaver cope with his post-school environment have now receded far into the past. There are, however, many people now actively concerned with how to provide for a less-able pupils a scientific education worthy of the name

(Nuffield, Schools Council, Association for Science Education, Scottish Consultative Committee on the Curriculum, etc.) Their successes and problems remaining deserve a book of their own; but three points:

(1)   Some specific factual knowledge and some practical skills are clearly indicated on the grounds of relevance to daily life. There is an obvious case for including human physiology and basic practical electricity in any science syllabus but there is remarkably little content which can be justified on such grounds.

(2)   Every pupil should gain some understanding of the conceptual framework of science. For the less able this means grasping a few basic concepts, e.g. growth, energy, chemical change, through a great deal of carefully planned practical activity and being led to discover for himself some of the linking principles. We do these pupils, and eventually society, a great disservice by suggesting they are incapable of this initiation into the structure of science.

(3)   All pupils, including the less able, should appreciate something of the way science extends its knowledge and of the way it tests its propositions. Only with this know-how are people equipped to criticise the pseudo-science with which they are inevitably bombarded in this age. One simple illustration: a current television advertisement "proves" that a biological (What does that mean?) washing-powder is better than a conventional one by soaking a dirty cloth in the biological powder and boiling another cloth in the conventional powder. Science education has failed any person who does not immediately say "Stop! the experimental conditions have not been properly arranged — the conclusion is worthless."

There is a lack of good texts for the teacher concerned with the process rather than the content of science. A teacher who wishes to introduce the average pupil to operational definitions of concepts, subjectivity and selectivity in observation, the arrangement of controlled experimental conditions, hypothesis testing and characterization will find the Consumer Association's magazine *Which* a far better source than any presently available text-book.

The non-science specialist

Courses in science for those who have decided, however early, that their main activities are to be in the arts have been relatively neglected. Jevons

(1969) outlines four possible types: the introductory or foundation course, the general survey course, the course in scientific method and the case histories approach. He points out the criticisms that can be levelled at all of these and decides in favour of the case histories course – which gives the 'feel' of the 'tactics and strategy' of science from a detailed study of episodes from the early development of science subjects.

The criticisms of the first two types of course are valid and powerful, but those of the third seem rather less so. "The trouble is that there is no agreement on how the method by which science progresses is to be described and in what terms it should be analysed." There is, as we have been at pains to point out, no *complete* agreement as to the method of science; there is, however, and increasing measure of agreement and there is no good reason why this increase should not continue – it awaits the more strenuous efforts of philosophers and scientists and of observational research.

A better solution than any of the four in isolation is to devise a course which integrates the method course with the case-studies course. Indeed, this is inevitable unless the 'tactics and strategy' of the case histories are to remain vaporous and unverbalised. The approach through case-histories can only be given point as *science* (as apart from history) if it pays attention to the nature of scientific knowledge and to the procedures of scientific method. Conversely a course in scientific method can best be given substance by an examination of examples in which the method is presumed to operate.

To anyone who clings to a Gradgrind view that learning some of the facts is the same as studying science, the 'forms of knowledge' approach remains irrelevant. As soon as it is suggested that the questions "What is science?" and "How does science proceed?" are appropriate to science education, then a consideration of science as a form of knowledge is necessary.

REFERENCES

BEVERIDGE, W.I.B. (1950) *The Art of Scientific Investigation.* London: Hutchinson.
BLOOM, B.S. *et al.* (1965) *Taxonomy of Educational Objectives,* Volume 1. London: Longmans Green.
BRADBURY, F.R. (ed.) (1969) *Words and Numbers. A Students' Guide to Intellectual Methods.* Edinburgh: The University Press.
BRIDGMAN, P.W. (1927) *The Logic of Modern Physics.* New York: Macmillan Co.
BRUNER, J.S. (1960) *The Process of Education.* New York: Random House.
BRUNER, J.S. (1966) *Toward a Theory of Instruction.* Cambridge, Mass.: The Belknap Press.
GAGNE, R.M. (1965) *The Conditions of Learning.* New York: Holt, Rinehart and Winston.
GRIBBLE, J.H. (1970) Pandora's box; the affective domain of educational objectives. *Journal of Curriculum Studies,* vol. 2, No. 1.
H.M.S.O. (1969) *Science for General Education.* Curriculum Paper 7. Edinburgh: H.M.S.O.
HEMPEL, C.G. (1966) *Philosophy of Natural Science.* New Jersey: Prentice-Hall Inc.
HIRST, P.H. (1965) Liberal education and the nature of knowledge. In *Philosophical Analysis and Education* (ed. R.D. Archambault) London: Routledge and Kegan Paul.
HIRST, P.H. (1966) Educational theory. In *The Study of Education* (ed. J.W. Tibble). London: Routledge and Kegan Paul.
HOLROYD, C. (1969) The concept of structure. *Scottish Educational Studies,* vol. 1, No. 3.
JEVONS, F.R. (1969) *The Teaching of Science.* London: Unwin.
KOESTLER, A. (1964) *The Act of Creation.* London: Hutchinson.
KUHN, T.S. (1962, 1970) *The Structure of Scientific Revolutions.* Chicago: Chicago U.P.
MEDAWAR, P.B. (1967) *The Art of the Soluble.* London: Methuen.
NUFFIELD, (1966) *Chemistry, The Sample Scheme. Stages I and II.* London: Longmans and Penguin Books.
PHENIX, P.H. (1964) *Realms of Meaning.* New York: McGraw-Hill.
POPPER, K.R. (1959) *The Logic of Scientific Discovery.* London: Hutchinson.
POPPER, K.R. (1963) *Conjectures and Refutations.* London: Routledge and Kegan Paul.
S.C.E.E.B. (1969) *Physics; Syllabus and Notes.* Edinburgh: H.M.S.O.
S.E.D. (1962) Circular 490. *Alternative Physics Syllabuses.* Edinburgh: H.M.S.O.
S.E.D. (1964) Circular 490 (revised). *Alternative Physics Syllabuses.* Edinburgh: H.M.S.O.
TRICKER, R.A.R. (1967) *The Contribution of Science to Education.* London: Mills and Boon.

HISTORY

P. J. ROGERS

THIS chapter is concerned with three related problems. Firstly it examines the nature of history and seeks to determine in what way, and to what extent, it may be regarded as an independent discipline or form of knowledge. Secondly, in the light of this, it attempts to establish what contribution history has to make to general education. Thirdly it explores the implications (if any) which answers to these questions may have for the practice of teaching.

I

In a well-known article[1] Professor Paul Hirst defines a form of knowledge as "a distinct way in which our experience becomes structured round the use of accepted public symbols" (p. 128), and goes on to list four related distinguishing features which characterise all forms of knowledge.

"(1) They each involve certain essential concepts that are peculiar in character to the form, for example, those of gravity, acceleration, hydrogen and photo-synthesis, characteristic of the sciences: number integral, matrix in mathematics: God, sin and predestination in religion. Ought, good and wrong in moral knowledge.

"(2) In a given form of knowledge these and other concepts that denote, perhaps in a very complex way, certain aspects of experience, form a network of possible relationships in which experience can be understood. As a result the form has a distinctive logical structure. For example, the terms and statements of mechanics can be meaningfully related in certain restricted and limited ways only and the same is true of historical explanation.

1 P. Hirst, *Liberal Education and the Nature of Knowledge.*

"(3) The form, by virtue of its particular terms and logic, has expressions or statements that in some way or other, however indirect it may be, are testable against experience. This is the case in scientific knowledge, moral knowledge, and in the Arts, although in the Arts no questions are explicit and the criteria for the tests are only partially expressible in words. Each form, then, has distinctive expressions that are testable against experience in accordance with particular criteria that are peculiar to the form.

"(4) The forms have developed particular techniques and skills for exploring experience and testing their distinctive expressions, for instance, the techniques of the sciences and those of various literary arts. The result has been the amassing of all the symbolically expressed knowledge that we now have in the Arts and the Sciences."[2]

The last two of these seem uncontroversial. "Distinctive expressions" means that historical expressions or propositions are clearly different from aesthetic ones. Each, that is, has a distinct character which makes it what it is and not something else. Similarly, "techniques and skills for exploring experience and testable against experience in accordance with particular criteria peculiar to the form" obviously point to the distinctive *modus operandi* and tests for truth which each form has developed. The nature of the techniques and tests is determined by the interplay of basic rational criteria such as consistency and appropriateness with the nature of the subject matter, historical, scientific, aesthetic or whatever, with which one is concerned. Each will represent a particular twist or adaptation given to fundamental rational postulates, such as appropriateness and relevance, by the nature of what is to be studied.

However, Professor Hirst's first two points seem to call for further discussion. The "distinctive logical structure" allegedly peculiar to each form in virtue of the limited network of possible relationships created by its peculiar concepts could hardly be defining characteristic of a *discipline*, for the same is true of any form of intelligible discourse whatever. Within branches of knowledge which Professor Hirst specfically excludes from the realm of disciplines, such as geography or engineering, which he characterises as fields,[3] this same rule clearly holds – for example, the

2 Hirst, pp. 128–9.
3 Hirst, p.131.

concepts of "contour" or of "profile" in geography. These terms have limited and specific uses whose limits cannot be exceeded if intelligibility is to be maintained. They can be meaningfully related in certain strictly limited ways only.

As regards the first point — sets of basic concepts peculiar to each of the forms — a more extended discussion is needed. Some of the examples which Professor Hirst uses in fact only dubiously exemplify the principle he wishes to establish. The nature of such terms as "good" or "wrong" or "ought" in moral knowledge appears to be ambiguous and debatable, and in what sense could they be held to be peculiar to the form? The physical sciences and mathematics certainly fit his model very much better. The scientific application of "wave" or "particle" is separate from, and far more precise than, the uses made of these words in common speech — indeed some such terms do not seem to enter common speech at all. But, in contrast, this is not true of certain other forms which Hirst recognises as disciplines.

In history, for example, the concepts do not possess anything like this degree of autonomy because they lack esoteric or technical meaning. Whereas the central concepts which he lists from the physical sciences such as gravity or acceleration really are central in that while they will not be met with elsewhere, they must characterise, sooner or later, any course of study which is to count as science at all. This is not true of history. In contrast with the physical sciences, history is continuous with, not distinct from, general human experiences. Conventionally, it is true, history is largely restricted to "politics": but this restriction (which Professor Hirst seems tacitly to accept) seems quite indefensible for every significant activity has a history. We should not be surprised then to find continuity between the concepts met in historical study and those met in general experience. There are not in history, as there are in science, networks of concepts which are peculiar to the discipline and which must characterise any study of it. Which concepts one meets depends upon what one chooses to study.

If, for example, the subject is international relations in the 19th century, then the "balance of power", the "national interest", "imperialism", etc., will be met with. If one is concerned with the history of Art, then beauty, "form", "gothic", "baroque", will be the sort of terms one will encounter. If one studies Ancient Greece, one will meet with, and need to understand, some concepts which one does not meet with or need to understand if one studies the history of modern Europe. On the other hand, if one studies the politics and foreign policy of both periods, one will need, and meet, many of the same concepts. Historical concepts are thus really the concepts of politics of art or science or economics, according to what one is studying the history of.[4] It must be stressed, however, that these activities are not fully independent one of another. They interlock and interact continually, and the historical explanation will be concerned to bring out those inter-relations as a part of the accurate record of change which it is concerned to give.

However, this does not of itself establish that the study of history contributes significantly to education. Indeed it may seem to rob history of all autonomy and to make it parasitic upon other subjects, to whose study it adds, at best, superfluous detail. The position now to be defended is that history contributes to other subjects by its accurate record of change through time, a particular dimension of understanding without which their study is impoverished. In general then it is claimed that there is in understanding and explanation a genetic component which makes the relevant historical perspective an element in any comprehensive, perhaps, any adequate, understanding. Two examples from the history of Art and Science will be developed in support of this claim.

Developments in Art are, of course, neither haphazard nor autonomous, but rest upon experience. This remains true no matter how innovating an artist may seek to be, for he is building upon, modifying and reacting against a tradition (or traditions). As E. H. Gombrich says: "Art itself becomes the innovator's instrument for probing reality. He cannot simply battle down that mental set which makes him see the motif in terms of known pictures; he must actively try that interpretation, but try it

---

4 If, then, the concepts employed are not distinctively historical then what is distinctive to history? The answer is really a summary of Professor Hirst's third and fourth points, which will be put together under the heading of "procedures" — for exploring, and procedures for testing the truth of the fruits of exploration! — and hence, for establishing the true developments which characterise whatever is being studied — the conduct of foreign policy, the development of scientific methods, or the concept of beauty.

critically, varying here and there to see whether a better match could not be achieved . . . ."[5]

The same is true of the viewer. For him, too, there is no such thing as neutral vision. We see in terms of our expectations and these are shaped by our experience. If then, we are to appreciate a work of art our experience must include the tradition — the grammar and syntax of style and the presumptions, social and aesthetic — of the artist. We must understand what he is seeking to do and be able to read his symbols, and in this relevant historical knowledge has an essential part to play. In the case of contemporary Art it is in terms of an understanding of how its "grammar, syntax and symbols" grow out of, or react against, the tradition with which he is familiar, that an informed, and hence comprehending, appraisal (as opposed to mere outraged rejection) is made more readily. In general, knowledge of the history of Art clearly demonstrates that no set of standards or conventions are always valid regardless of time or place or change. When this point is grasped the dominance of a particular set is loosened to the degree that the beholder understands the provisional and even ephemeral nature of the standards, conventions and expectations embedded in it and he is thus more able and willing to countenance the deviation and modification which Gombrich points out.

And this leads to a further important point. For in the absence of a clear sense of the provisional nature of canons and conventions and the strong tendency, therefore, to trust the ones that are familar as the "correct", or even as the only possible, ones, much of the point and achievement of a work of Art may be lost. For the originality of a past innovator has, exactly because he was successful, helped to determine the nature of the subsequent orthodoxy. What was really the originality of the work becomes submerged in the general body of accepted schemata and norms of expression and, hence, taken for granted. Thus the impact and intrinsic merit of work may be muted if not actually lost. There is, therefore, no way of truly appraising a great artist's work except by replacing it (as far as possible) in its original setting — which means, of course, in its historical context by means of historically-shaped imaginative effort.

5 E. H. Gombrich, *Art and Illusion*, p. 324.

An example may make this clear. In an article marking the quincentenary of Donatello's death, John Pope Henessey writes:

"If Donatello's heads were simply life-like, that would in 1430 have been remarkable enough. But they are expressive, and expressive in a rather special way. No one who visits the Brancacci Chapel can doubt the narrative intentions of Masaccio. In head after head they are made manifest. But the emotions are not stated: they are implied through inflections in fundamentally an inexpressive style. It is a strange experience now, and must have been a far stranger experience then, to pass from this generalized language of emotion to the precise expressive syntax of Donatello."[6]

Here the work of Donatello is set in an aesthetic context within which it is seen as a significant development, and by means of this historical analysis cues are given as to how to look at it in terms of a developing tradition. As Gombrich says: "A style sets up a horizon of expectation, a mental set which registers deviations and modifications with exaggerated sensitivity."[7] Deprived of that "mental set" by ignorance of style and tradition the beholder cannot really comprehend a work. Part (though only part, of course) of the greatness of Donatello lies in those aspects where his work stands in relation to a prevailing tradition. "Originality" is a prime quality in an artist. But how is this to be assessed except in terms of his aesthetic context? Really to see it one has to see it with 15th-century eyes, and this can only be done through the fullest possible knowledge of the 15th-century setting. Obviously, then, it can be fully appreciated only in terms of historical knowledge which explains, as far as they can be known, the artist's presuppositions, the social and aesthetic contexts of his creations, and what was psychologically or technically possible at the time. For at any point in time possibilities are limited.

Gombrich has rightly attacked the notion of the "innocent eye" according to which the artist, unshackled by tradition or precedent can paint what he "really" sees.[8] "In all styles the artist has to rely on a vocabulary of forms and it is the knowledge of this vocabulary rather than a knowledge of things that distinguishes the skilled from the unskilled

6 *The Times*, December 20th, 1966.
7 Gombrich, p. 60.
8 Gombrich, p. 324.

artist."[9] The possibilities within any vocabulary and hence within any style are limited and it follows that we cannot appraise a work except in terms of an understanding of style and its possibilities.[10] Consequently it is necessary to understand the constraints and possibilities of a style and why, how and when they come to be relaxed or expanded. An instance is to be found in Andre Chastel's account of late Quattrocento painting.

Professor Chastel picks out "the years round 1475" as "one of the main joints in the articulation of modern painting"[11] He shows how Antonello de Messina "aroused on his way from Naples to Venice a new interest in colour treated as a means of bringing out light, no longer simply as a function of design. In addition he stimulated pictorial techniques by spreading Flemish procedures that were already familiar to southern artists."[12] Chastel shows how this, reinforced by some aspects of North Italian Art, and combined with a great growth of interest in Flemish art and the subsequent widespread use of oil paint, produced a revolution in painting. The "new" style grew so that "at one blow the artists who . . . had become set in the methods of 1470 . . . became old fashioned".[12]

By means of historical narrative Chastel thus explains a development in Quattrocento Art. Except in terms of such descriptions we do not really understand or appraise the works of Art themselves, for, without them, the palpable differences between works before and after the change remain obvious, but inexplicable.

But not only developments in Art itself are relevant. The whole climate of a society may be crucial to the understanding of its Art. It is possible, for example, to trace the development of Greek sculpture ignoring the social context. But if this is all we do we have not understood, but merely described, a development. Why that development occurred is likely to remain largely mysterious, as is the question which arises when the development is traced back to its origins — why were the illusionist skills

9 Gombrich, p. 293.

10 Gombrich, p. 86: "The layman may wonder whether Crotlo could have painted a view of the Fiesole in sunshine but the historian will suspect that, lacking the means he . . . could not have wanted to . . . The individual can enrich the ways and means that his culture offers him: he can hardly wish for something he has never known is possible."

11 Chastel, *Studios and Styles of the Renaissance*, p. 272.

12 Chastel, p. 278.

mastered by the Greeks not also mastered in these early civilisations such as Egypt where the root influences of Greek Art are to be found? To look at Art in isolation not only does not explain: it suggests a most misleading answer — namely that the Greek Art grew out of Egyptian in the sense that it represents an improvement. On this erroneous view the Egyptians, had they had the skill, would have carved and painted like the classical Greeks.

This very patronising attitude is clearly mistaken for it implies that naturalistic realism is the ultimate goal of all art. Moreover, it effectively destroys all possibility of understanding Egyptian Art because, viewed in this inappropriate way, it cannot but look naive and childlike. The error springs from isolating Art from its social context. Gombrich has convincingly argued that the difference between Egyptian and Greek Art springs from the radically different social functions they respectively fulfil. It was not that the Greeks were keener observers and more skilful craftsmen. Observation is always for a purpose and is carried out in terms of presumptions which are socially determined. Greek Art, on the other hand, has no such narrative intent but is pictographic. The scenes on tomb walls "do not link events or explain their development; they are typical sayings belonging to typical situations". Hence their sterotyped, unrealistic character.

This example seems to answer an objection to the main argument — namely that "understanding" in terms of historical knowledge has little to do with appreciating a work as a work of art. This view really maintains that a work is to be assessed in terms of criteria peculiar to Art itself — such criteria, presumably, as form, colour, etc. But, as the Egypt - Greece example should make clear, such criteria are far from objective. In particular, they are not independent of socially determined presumptions and purposes, which can only be known by historical study of the society concerned. And these can vary radically. The truth is that the arguments and the objection are far from compatible. It is not argued that historical understanding alone confers appreciation and certainly not that there is any substitute for gaining insight into artistic criteria by engaging in artistic activity. A combination, it is claimed, gives a more comprehensive appreciation. Nor, of course, is it suggested that appreciation is the only, or even the chief, objective of art education simply that it is *an* objective to which historical study contributes. An analogous argument seems to hold in the case of Science. J. B. Conant, for example, concerned with the problem of understanding the "Tactics and Strategy of Science", argues that of the two ways of probing into complex human activities such as Science, the historical and the logical/ philosophical, the former "will yield more real understanding . . . for nine people out of ten".[13] He is not alone in this view. Hutten[14] argues that "the natural evolution of ideas, that is their history, is more important than their ex post facto logical analysis". Conant goes on: "I doubt if the philosophical treatments of science and scientific method have been very successful when viewed as an educational enterprise",[15] and recommends a "case histories" approach, meaning "a close study of a relatively few historical examples of the development of science". These examples would be so chosen as to require little factual knowledge or mathematics, and would concentrate upon the growth of concepts and techniques, the relation between imagination, observation and experiment, and the interconnections between Science and Society.[16]

Easley,[17] in a critique of Conant's "case history" approach, argues for an "inductive sequence" approach. But as he admits, and as the example he gives[18] makes clear, this is similar to Conant's suggestion. This approach is in fact a qualification or development of case history, which he feels may be inadequate because the scientific principles do not stand out boldly enough in a full-bodied historical account. Accordingly, "once principles of scientific method have been discovered in and verified by the historical record of scientific enquiry, the data and ideas need to be rearranged, so as to reduce greatly the actual complexities of the historical development of a theory". Clearly, Easley's suggestion is rooted in the historical approach. "The historical record record is the raw material from which inductive procedures are discovered in the first place[19] . . . it can

13 J. B. Conant, *Understanding Science*, p. 27.

14 E. H. Hutten, *The Ideas of Physics*, preface, p. v.

15 Conant, p. 28.

16 Conant, pp. 30–32.

17 J. A. Easley, *Is the Teaching of Scientific Method a Significant Educational Objective?*

18 Easley, p. 175.

19 Easley, p. 176.

readily be seen that accurate historical descriptions of the development of major theories would provide valuable source materials for preparation of inductive presentation."[20]

At first sight, Conant's advocacy of case studies drawn from "the early days in the evolution of the modern disciplines" might seem unacceptable to Hutten, who attacks the use of old-type experiments on the grounds that they greatly over-simplify modern science, and that, being familiar, they are not *experiments*: There is no doubt as to the outcome and the result is a travesty where science is made to look infallible, and the grossly erroneous view of scientific knowledge as both certain and totally objective is implanted.[21]

Of course this second criticism need not hold. It is a very fair description of traditional scientific teaching, but it cuts across all modern notions which insists on pupil experimentation on situations where the options are genuinely open. Every effort is made to ensure that the pupils "realise what the experiment originally involved when it was carried out for the first time"[21] — and this is of course fully consistent with the positions of both Conant and Easley.

Hutten's first objection is, however, more substantial. It is important to realise that he is objecting, not to the study of old-type experiments *per se* but to their presentation as paradigms of all scientific procedure. This is a valid, though implied, criticism of Conant: but educationally, the interesting point is that, taken together, the objections emphasise the disadvantages of the logical-analytic approach to science. For old-type experiments are untypical, and contemporary ones are too difficult for any but scientists to understand.[22] What is left as a valid approach — and this is Hutten's programme — is the historical, not limited as in Conant's argument to a few traditional case studies, but as "a long chain of interpretation reaching from the more familiar kind of knowledge through various degrees of abstraction until we arrive at the ideas of today which themselves are always accepted only temporarily".[23] As a particularly dramatic example, Hutten quotes the Michelson-Morley experiment of

20 Easley, p. 177.
21 Hutten, p. 4.
22 Hutten, p. 4.
23 Hutten, p. 3.

1881 as the culmination of 150 years of work and shows how it gained its significance from previous connected study, and how the work of Einstein in turn rested upon this chain.[24] This "crucial experiment shows . . . that it is the integration, the consistency, of a number of different experiments that makes us accept a theory. If we divorce the crucial experiment, or any experiment, from its historical background we fail to see the criteria implicit in scientific research."[25]

Implicit in the discussion so far is the assumption that developments in Art or Science (or government, or transport or education) occur only partly in response to internal stimuli and enjoy only a limited autonomy. More important is the pressure of the complex interplay of social facts. But in either case the contribution of history to understanding is significant and, perhaps, central. In so far as developments within a field enjoy relative independence (as perhaps in Pope-Hennessey's comments on Donatello) history highlights and explains what the developments were: when they are essentially the result of wider influences then it is the re-creation of the social matrix which history contributes. It is thus less a discrete form of knowledge marked by peculiar concepts, then a dimension of knowledge which contributes to the understanding of social phenomena by re-creating, the circumstances of their development through appropriate procedures and techniques.

II

These two examples – Art and Science – should have established the initial claim that History is a component of understanding. But they bring out only one aspect of the contribution History has to make – namely that in the understanding of some complex phenomenon – such as Renaissance Art or scientific method – knowledge of its historical background and development plays a very helpful, perhaps a necessary, role. Beyond this, History is an indispensable corrective for, and check upon, the assumptions, attitudes and information which go to make up our cultural inheritance. For clearly a part of that inheritance is a version of the past and a bundle of attitudes and expectations towards the world

24 Hutten, pp. 5–7.
25 Hutten, p. 7.

which have grown from it. The appropriateness of attitudes and expectations – the degree to which they are based upon reality – depends upon the comprehensiveness and accuracy of the "version of the past" which has been inherited – that is, the degree to which it is the product of history rather than of folklore. Of course the fact is that a "cultural inheritance" often embodies a version of the past which is biased and untrue. This point is admirably discussed by Dr. Kitson Clark[26] who describes the growth of the distortions of history which shape men's behaviour in the present. Many of them "may have been derived from confusedly remembered lessons learned at school, some inculcated by the reiterated assertions of politicians. Some associations survive from misty recollections of newspaper controversies, from scraps of special information or of personal experience, or the stories of chance acquaintances... (The result is that)... intelligent and apparently highly educated adults are curiously at the mercy of very questionable generalisations and descriptions against which any normal historical education should have guarded them." Nor is it possible to escape from this predicament by simply ignoring the past "for to disregard the past is very often the surest way of becoming its slave. A man who ignores history will still make the historical assumptions which are implicit in most languages and in all political judgements, but he will not know he is making them and so will be unable to criticise them or reconsider the evidence on which they are based ... There is only one way to escape ... it is to use history more effectively."

Contemporary events in Ireland seem a perfect illustration of Dr. Kitson-Clark's case, and of the way in which cultural inheritance is by no means synonymous with what can be learned from history. On the contrary, it is just as an astringent corrective to competing mythologies which constitute that "cultural inheritance" that the historical record is required.

Moreover, by correcting myth and thus modifying the mental set, the historical record also modifies the frameworks of expectation which grow from past experience and in terms of which all fresh experience is classified and understood. Thus the record affects anticipation, and it may therefore be claimed that history enables a certain limited kinds of

26 G. Kitson Clark, *The Critical Historian,* pp. 6–9.

prediction to be made. This claim is best developed by examining objections to it.

Mr. R. Brown, for instance, criticises Professor W. Walsh for his claim that "A person who knows a good deal about the History of Germany is in some respects at least better equipped to say how Germany is likely to develop in the future than one who is utterly ignorant of that History." For, argues Mr. Brown, "In what way is he better equipped?" It can only be if "Some scientific laws about the behaviour of people in societies were available then he would be able to add his detailed information to those laws in such a way as to deduce some statements concerning the future behaviour of the relevant people. Unless the historian is in possession of laws of this kind his predictions can only be obtained by assuming that present trends will continue in the future. Since a trend is merely a progressive change in a property common to a sequence of events, there is little reason, in the absence of knowledge about its causes, to believe that it will hold beyond the present."[27]

The short answer to Mr. Brown is simply to point out that as a matter of fact we simply assume continuity between past, present and future and form sets of expectations which depend on this assumption. Moreover, we know perfectly well that upon the whole these expectations are not disappointed. If, as a regular thing, they were, then the word "rational" could have only a very restricted application to the world. There could be no coherence between intention and outcome — i.e. no purposeful and planned behaviour — because there could be no way of judging what steps would be likely to produce a particular outcome. There could be no conceivable generalisations about human nature or motivation because these generalisations rest upon what reflection about experience has taught us to anticipate.

However, this merely establishes that we do in fact make, and act upon, assumptions drawn from experience and that it would be very inconvenient if we could not do so. It does not establish them as valid. The problem is how to justify the root assumption that the future will resemble the past and to counter the argument of extreme scepticism which holds that this cannot be done. *A priori* (the sceptic holds) it is impossible since it is in principle perfectly conceivable that the future

27 R. Brown, *Explanation in Social Science*, pp. 29–33.

might be quite different from the past: and, by definition it cannot be established by evidence, for no evidence concerning the future can exist except by inference from the very past experience whose validity is questioned.

The answer to this sceptical argument is limited but sufficient for the present purpose — to establish that historical knowledge permits a form of prediction. Dr. F. L. Will[28] has suggested that the key question is "What future is being spoken of?" He suggests that the whole difficulty only arises because of a confused and double meaning given to "future". If at any point of time it were claimed that "the future will be like the past" (the context would almost certainly show in what respect(s) the similarity was predicted) and after an interval (say, a year) had passed the similarity was found to hold in the specified sense, this would be evidence in support of the assumption that the future resembles the past. This can only be contested by maintaining that the future has not yet come — that by the time evidence is available concerning a future which exists when the prediction is made, that future is no longer the future, and the evidence is thus no longer evidence. Before we had it, it counted as evidence: now we have it, it is evidence no more.

Now this, Will argues, is sleight of hand; for in this sense the future being spoken of is a future which never comes and of which, consequently, nothing can be known because it does not exist. By retreating into such a future, the sceptic makes his criticism impregnable by making it impossible to test. Reasonably, however, the original statement applies to a future which does come, in which things do happen and, hence, in which the prediction can be tested. "This kind of future is constantly being revealed[29] . . . there are beliefs about the way the future will be like the past which have been and are being confirmed constantly by the uniform experience of countless positive instances in everyday life and in vast areas of Science.[30]

In short, Will insists that "future" must have a degree of specificity so that it is taken to refer to some definite point(s) in time and the prediction

28   F. L. Will, *Will the Future be like the past?*
29   Will, p. 47.
30   Will, p. 49

is made testable. He also adopts as his criterion the frequency with which similar events, or patterns of them, are repeated.

Applied to historically-based prediction, both these points need further development. For it is not true that historically-based predictions rely only on the mere frequency with which similar events or patterns recur: historical scholarship is concerned amongst other things to expose the *reasons* for their occurrence. In explaining the conduct of Foreign Policy for example, one of the starting assumptions is not an assumption at all, but a fact – namely, that there exists no effective and impartial arbiter for international disputes. (The United Nations cannot yet be said to fulfil the role.)

Now this is at least one important consideration which has determined the conduct of foreign policy, and, since essentially it still holds, still determines it. It might be argued that we do not know that this may not change suddenly and inexplicably. But (apart from the extreme implausibility of such a suggestion – quite sufficient in itself to settle the matter for practical purposes) the fact is that this is true *now*: and since policies decided upon in the present are designed to have effects, and do so, in the future, we have excellent grounds for supposing (from the state of present observed facts) that the short-run future (made up of events shaped by those facts) will resemble the present (and recent past), made up of events which are the effects of similar facts.

It is not asserted that present facts (for example, the absence of an all-powerful world order with which to replace, or control, present sovereign States) will never change, but that, because the facts are what they are in the here and now, (no such world order exists) events of the type we have become accustomed consequentially to associate with them, for reasons we understand, must be expected to occur in the near future. There may be no way of specifying with any precision how long a span of time that "near future" may occupy, but that does not mean that there are not points in time against which the expectation can be checked (and, if falsified, corrected): on the contrary, such points are ever-present.

It is not claimed that this argument entirely obliterates the difficulty of induction. But, both in terms of the frequency with which types of event occur, and, more important, the (comprehended) reasons which account at least in part for their occurrence (initial conditions, which existed in the recent past and which still exist in the here and now, in terms of which decisions are taken which will determine much of the character of the near future) we have far better grounds for cautiously assuming a conditional continuity in the sense set out above than we have to entertain the contrary hypothesis that no such grounds can exist. As against what Mr. Brown clearly implies, we can, and do, have knowledge about the causes of trends, and, consequently, often have good reason to believe that trends will (or will not) hold beyond the present. It is in this restricted, but practically useful, sense that historical knowledge can enable us to make restricted, but practically useful, predictions.

Indeed, Brown's separation of prediction based on mere observation and that resting on knowledge about causes seems to ignore his own warning that the two "must not be too sharply separated" (p. 31). A prediction about, say, a likely move in German foreign policy is not based just upon a collection of similar moves in the past — it is less random than that. The historian has clear ideas as to why those moves were made and has in mind a whole panoply of insights and generalisations about how States conduct their foreign relations — and why. He will also appreciate what is peculiar in the German position — her long frontiers resting on no easily defensible natural features, the strategic advantages and dangers stemming from her central position, and so on. In a word he has "knowledge about causes of a trend" and that knowledge of causes grows out of observed similarities linking a sequence of events. The separation of the two — basic to Brown's objection to Walsh — seems impossible to maintain.

It is this line of reflection that also compels disagreement with Mr. Brown's treatment of C. H. Phillips' book *India* which, he says, "contains the unauthorised use of a certain type of prediction". What Mr. Phillips has done is to give an analysis of partition and the state of affairs in the Indian sub-continent. Since he was writing of contemporary affairs, this analysis, insofar as it is accurate, amounts to a knowledge of the antecedent conditions appropriate to the prediction he then makes — that India and Pakistan will "gird" at each other.

Brown insists that this prediction strips the writer of his role of historian. But this seems to erect a rather unreal barrier between observation and the expectations which this may lead one rationally to entertain. It is difficult to see how a historian could not form this expectation when carrying out this particular study; it seems rather pedantic to criticise putting it into words as unprofessional. Because of his subject matter, Phillips' expectations concerned events which had not yet occurred — this is the sole, and accidental difference between his "prediction" and that which any historian at least tacitly makes in giving an explanation. For in constructing an explanatory account of (say) Bismarck's foreign policy an historian in effect predicts. In showing how one step was followed by another he takes it for granted that this is not just a fortuitous succession, but that the first was a condition for the second — i.e. that given the first, the second could be predicted in our "likely" sense. If this is not so then he has failed to establish connection between the events, and has explained nothing.

There is, moreover, a very significant phrase in Mr. Phillips' prediction, "For some time to come each of the new Dominions is likely to gird against the other." Now this means that Phillips is not dogmatically predicting at all: nor is he (in Brown's words) saying, "Perhaps it will happen but it is equally likely that it won't." He is saying, "The position is such that unfriendly relations between the two countries are likely for some time." He is drawing a conclusion from a body of analysed and ascertained facts which constitute the antecedent conditions for the outcome he suggests as likely: and the degree of confidence with which that outcome is said to be likely is proportioned to the weight of evidence which supports it. In a word, Phillips is making a rational inference based upon the empirical generalisation that in certain sets of conditions, for comprehensible reasons, neighbouring States tend to "gird" at one another, and the judgement that the particular example falls within the scope of the generalisation by exemplifying at least some of the "certain conditions".

Whether we are to call this inferring "prediction" is not just a matter of terminological preference: if we are, then we must distinguish a strong and a weak sense. "Strong" sense prediction — such as the Marxist prognosis of inevitable class war with a predetermined and inevitable outcome — surely goes far beyond what historical study can justify: but weak sense prediction — or, better, rational inference, modest and circumspect, drawn with a degree of confidence proportionate to the strength of the supporting evidence — is of the very nature of the historian's work: for it means that we draw the conclusions (tentative, perhaps) in which study eventuates. It is, in short inherent in the nature of explanation.

But what is it that causes us to see those explanations and inferences as rational? What is it that enables Phillips to draw his conclusion and causes his readers to accept it as an appropriate outcome of his argument? It seems there are two criteria — firstly that the explanation is consistent with one's sense of what is probable; secondly that the writer exhibits appropriate professional skill in his handling of sources and in the construction of his narrative. Explanation thus involves both conceptual "evidence" and particular evidence — both a general conceptual framework of expectation and understanding, shared by writer and reader, and an adequate mastery of the specific evidence on the matter in hand.

A further example will assist. Consider, for instance, how one would set about explaining the Russian intervention in Czechoslovakia. Why did the Russians intervene? "Because", the political commentator will reply, "she feared the ideological consequences of Czech 'liberalisation' upon the other satellite countries, and, indeed, within the Soviet Union itself: because, herself with many different nationalities, she feared the disruptive force of growing nationalism among her satellites: because the extreme strategic importance of Czechoslovakia made the possibility, though disavowed, that she might drift out of the Warsaw pact militarily intolerable: because Western, and more particularly German, activity in Eastern Europe, both diplomatic and economic, was, in Russian eyes, reaching dangerous proportions . . ." and so on. But of course, all these explanations rest on unspoken assumptions about how States behave, about the nature of the national interest, and the main-springs of foreign policy. They are factors which fill out the skeleton generalisation "States protect their interests" — a generalisation of the type which historians take for granted their readers share[31] and which makes such explanations explanatory. To go beyond these premises, to ask why States in general, including Russia, act in such ways is to invite the answer "Well what do you expect, that is the way things are."

It is within this general framework, provided by the mesh of relevant conceptions, that particular facts fit together and come to life, as it were — it is the difference between a narrative and a mere list. But of course the particular facts of the case are equally important. It is the interplay between general and specific, between conceptual and empirical

31 Take for granted, that is, when writing for an adult and sophisticated audience. In education, it is the *creation* of such frames of expectation which is at stake.

evidence, that generates an explanation. In fact the two elements — conceptual and empirical which we have distinguished cannot be separated except for analysis. It is only the empirical that can call the conceptual into play, and only the conceptual which permits the empirical to be intelligibly marshalled. Consider again the intervention in Czechoslovakia. To explain the Russian invasion we have to pick out numerous specific events and factors which presuppose and activate relevant generalisation and concepts — embody them in this instance as it were. To try to give an explanation in terms of the concepts and generalisations alone would reduce one just to saying "It was in Russia's self interest to do so, or at least her rulers thought so," But that would obviously be no explanation at all because it would lack any particulars of the events which took place.

To try to explain without any conceptual frame, on the other hand, is equally impossible. If no conception or example of how States, particularly Great Powers, react to a threat to their security (and of what constitutes such a threat) exists apart from the question in hand, the reader could only say "But why should these events be associated in this way?" (He might be content to say "I see: so I am to infer that it is reasonable to expect that given A, B, and C — X, Y, and Z are likely to follow.")

But in that case the matter would not be explained. The writer would be taking an untested inference on trust. He would also be laying the foundations of exactly the type of general conception we are speaking of — and this latter process is exactly what both explanation and education involve here: the use of the relevant general conception if it exists: its creation if it does not. Its grasp grows from a multiplicity of analogous cases each of which modifies or deepens the conceptual frame by the different chain of particulars it brings within it. And such a multiplicity of cases is to be found only in history, not only because the great bulk of analogous events lies in the past, but because the historian's knowledge of the outcome of past events, his hindsight,[32] makes his account of them much more reliable than those of contemporaries, distorted by unavoidable ignorance and confused by direct involvement.

However, this argument rests on the assumption that events may be

32 The question of hindsight is developed more fully below.

classified into types in virtue of important similarities which characterise them. In reply to this the claim is made, not that the future cannot be confidently expected to be like the past, but that no event, past, present or future is sufficiently like any other to permit useful generalisation. To some extent the foregoing discussion has forestalled this objection, but by no means adequately and this is the question now to be examined.

In his imaginary discussion between an historian and a logician on the causes of Louis XIV's unpopularity W. R. Dray[33] claims to show that the historian's explanation would consist solely of particulars, and that the only generalisation the logician could give which would really include them all would be one so wide as to be identical with the sum of them. It would come to "any people like the French in the respects specified would dislike a ruler like Louis in the respect specified"; "the respects specified" being exactly the historian's list of particulars. In short our generalisation (or "Law") is one with only one case − that is of course, no law at all.

Professor Dray goes on to criticise Mr. P. Gardiner who maintains that the absolute uniqueness of events is disproved by the language the historian uses − words such as "revolution" and "conquest" which clearly indicate that events can be classified as similar in at least some important respects. Dray replies that this merely indicates that events, or some events, can (by being classified) be brought under a general law − not that they actually are so brought − that explanation of them is merely consistent with, not dependent upon, general considerations. He denies that the explicability of, say, the Norman Conquest is dependent upon there having been other invasions of one country by another.

This really amounts to denying the use of conceptual evidence, as an example may make clear. Consider Christopher Hill's claim that under Cromwell "The Protestant interest became once more an asset of English Foreign Policy."[34] This might, at first sight, seem a rather puzzling statement. However, Mr. Hill means that from time to time Cromwell used the antagonism of Catholics and Protestants in Europe at large to increase the influence and prestige of England by championing the Protestant cause. Mr. Hill suggests that "this was a purely nationalist policy". When the role of champion could be expected to benefit England it was played:

33 W. R. Dray, *Laws and Explanation in History*, p. 32.
34 C. Hill, *Puritanism and Revolution*, p. 143.

when it could not, it was abandoned. The key word is thus "asset". Ideological considerations, it is suggested, were no independent variable but were wholly subordinate to Realpolitik.

Now this must surely raise the question of how likely this is as an explanation; and while this may involve an evaluation of Cromwell's judgement, personality and temperament and a close scrutiny of the particulars peculiar to the situation, fundamentally the answer depends upon whether foreign policy is likely to be conducted, and ideological weapons used, in this way. If no other instance in which this was so could be found then belief in the explanation given would be weakened. In effect, then, tacit reference is here made to a principle of experience as to how foreign policy is conducted: the explanation of Cromwell's policy rests upon a general frame of relevant expectation in terms of which it is understood, of which it is an instance, and which, accordingly, it helps to establish and articulate.

In fact, of course, historians take it for granted that schema exist in the minds of their readers which make their explanations explanatory: and these schema can only come from experience, from knowledge that human beings in fact tend to behave in certain ways in certain circumstances. This must mean that the circumstances in question bear a paramount if partial resemblance to some which have existed on previous occasions. The whole notion of being able to explain any event at all necessitates the repudiation of its uniqueness if that term is so stringently defined as to exclude the possibility of comparisons with other events. If an event really is unique in that sense, it cannot be explained. It is not a question of replacing judgement "by deduction from empirically validated laws". [35] The point at issue is that it is only such generalisations growing from a plurality of cases which enable judgement to follow explanation at all.

Dray continues that "unique" can be a relative term, that "historical events are often unique simply in the sense of being different from others with which it would be natural to group them under a classification term". [36] This is perfectly true of course: the same thing — exactly the same thing — never happens twice, so that any two events whatever are different in some respects. But Dray concludes from this that the historian

35 Dray, p. 51.
36 Dray, p. 47.

"when he sets out to explain the French Revolution is just not interested in explaining it as a revolution – he is almost invariably concerned with it as different from other members of its class. Indeed, he might even say that his main concern will be to explain the French Revolution's taking a course unlike any other; that is to say, he will explain it as unique in the sense distinguished above."[37]

This seems altogether too facile an argument. Obviously if the historian sets out to explain the French Revolution he is concerned to bring out what distinguished it from other revolutions. This reduces to saying that it is the *French* Revolution he is explaining. But the term "Revolution" is also a part of the explanation given – we all know perfectly well in general terms what sort of events earn and justify this title. It arouses a set of general expectations of what the "ingredients" of Revolution are. It is thus only possible to use a descriptive word like "Revolution" in this connection because there are other events sufficiently like this to be grouped with it as "Revolutions". The very existence of such classifications surely indicates that here similarity is essential and disimilarity is in some sense secondary. For if things are more unalike than alike, how – in virtue of what – could they possibly be grouped together?

Moreover, it is very doubtful whether historians are "just not interested" in references to Revolution in general when setting out to explain the couse of one particular revolution. Given the model of class struggle, of which all Revolutions are seen as dramatic manifestations, it would be a fair inference that all Marxist historians are so interested; and among more Conservative historians consider Sir Lewis Namier's account and analysis of the Revolutionary year 1848.

"The French Revolution of 1789 and the Russian of 1917 were made and sustained by the converging action of the two greatest revolutionary forces: the people of the capital, effective through concentration at the very centre of government, and the peasant masses, invincible through their numbers, their dispersion, and the primitive, practical character of their demands (they never seek by revolt to establish new and higher forms of production, but to free themselves of burdens, or seize more land in order to cultivate it in their traditional, inadequate manner)."[38]

37 Dray, p. 47.
38 Sir Lewis Namier, *1848: The Revolution of the Intellectuals*, p. 5.

It could not, surely, be denied that this is analytical explanation, or that it is given in terms of generalisations — study the sentence in brackets for instance. Namier continues that "There was something incongruous about the Revolution of 1848" because "the mob had . . . no articulate aims and no-one will ever be able to supply a rational explanation of what it was they fought for".[39] In short, Namier implies that 1848 was not a Revolution in the thoroughgoing sense of 1789 and 1917. "The mob (came) out in revolt moved by passions and distress rather than by ideas."[39] And "accidents and misunderstandings epidemic in character . . . converted revolts into risings". When "the proletariat was defeated in Paris and the peasants bought off in the Habsburg Monarchy the social forces behind the Revolution of 1848, disjointed and insufficient from the very outset, were . . . practically eliminated. What remained was the middleclass led by intellectuals"[40] and these did not want Revolution but "a share in the Government of States to be remodelled in accordance with the National Principle".[41] The Monarchs thus survived. They "had merely to turn constitutional and receive liberal intellectuals into political partnership".[42]

Now this surely explains the "incongruity" which Namier has been tacitly probing. "Incongruous" implies expectations (contrasted to which an actual outcome can *be* incongruous) and because of the forces he selects for special mention in the successful, or "true", Revolutions — proletarians in the capitals and a mass of peasants in the countryside—Namier's explanation of 1848 is partly given in terms of what one would expect because the situation is revolutionary: and this, in turn is determined by what is the case in other instances of Revolution.

In short, Sir Lewis has compared two Revolutions — the French and the Russian — which are alike in the respect he regards as crucial, and has contrasted with these a quasi-revolution which, because the crucial respect does not apply, is held to be not fully a Revolution at all. Both comparison and contrast are given partly in terms of generalised considerations drawn from considering more cases than the one in hand.

39 Namier, p. 7.
40 Namier, p. 23,
41 Namier, p. 24.
42 Namier, p. 7.

Dray's contention that the historian is just not interested in a Revolution as a Revolution thus seems ill-founded. The "events are unique" school of thought will not do, for by denying meaningful comparison, it greatly reduces the possibility of anything being explained at all.

Dray's first mistake is the apparent assumption that generalisation is necessarily concerned only with establishing similarities, and for that reason the historian, being concerned with particular events and, hence, with particulars which·are unique, cannot, as he comes to grips with his task, make use of generalisation. In fact, however, dissimilarities and the unique facets of events are often revealed in terms of generalisations, non-conformity to which reveals the precise character of the event under examination — as in Namier's description of 1848 in terms of its dissimilarity with 1798 and 1917.

There is, moreover, a further point. Not even particulars are fully "unique". The "unique" events of the French Revolution — i.e. those which distinguish it from other Revolutions — are not really unique in the sense of totally dissimilar from any which have occurred before. Consider such a factor, surely important, as the personality and ability of Louis XVI or Charles I. Now it is obviously true that no situation from which Louis or Charles was absent could be exactly the same as one in which either of them was involved. But Louis and Charles exemplify traits and limitations which are observable in many human beings and whose consequences in given circumstances can be roughly assessed because of what we know of the range and productivity of human characteristics. When a historian cites the "obstinacy" of Charles, or the "stupidity" of Louis he is in fact referring to widely known and experienced human characteristics — or he would not be explaining — and is indicating that a certain outcome is made likely by the concatenation of the characteristics in question with a particular set of circumstances.

Yet these very terms (such as "obstinate" or "stupid") must themselves be descriptive in a general way, because they necessarily imply a connection between an acting agent and the nature and outcome of his actions — they reduce to such a generalisation as "men who, in such circumstances as these, act in these ways are stupid" (because such actions tend to bring about consequences which the agent could not possibly be thought to want). But this loose causal relation between type of action and type of outcome, and our expectations of what men want to achieve could have neither meaning or existence except as generalised notions of what is in fact the case — and this necessarily implies a plurality of instances from which to generalise.

"Uniqueness" is thus conditional and limited. This fact meets Dray's complaint of "pseudo explanation", where he maintains that the attempt to explain a paticular phenomenon like the French Revolution in general terms cannot be true explanation at all since the particulars unique to the French Revolution are (by definition) not susceptible to generalisation. [43] But, in a perfectly reasonable sense, they are.

Dray's mistake seems to have been that he ensured the outcome he sought — a vacuous "covering law" — by looking for *one* law which was to cover a whole explanation. For of course in one important sense events *are* unique — in that the claim of particulars picking out *this* event constitutes a unique assemblage which taken together, builds into a total explanation; but each, or at least many, of these particulars rest upon, or are instances of, and are related to the whole event by, (possibly implicit) generalisations. And the whole body of such generalisations makes up "conceptual evidence". It is only the peculiar combination of particulars that is unique — the generalisations are widely applicable. But, on the other hand, there are many of them. A historical explanation rests upon not one 'Covering Law' exemplified by an event, but several or many law-like generalisations which here coalesce.

What History offers is really a series of analogies. It is never the case that events are exactly repeated (how could it be?). It is that different events may be alike in respects which our judgement and experience suggest are particularly significant. This is how comparisons are made, and categories are formed. It is also what analogy is. Things are not analogous if they are identical.

This section has been concerned to argue for the importance of history as the source and touch-stone for valid generalisations in terms of which aspects of experience can be understood, and limited, but necessary, prediction made. In developing this argument two interlocking types of historical "evidence" were identified — the conceptual and the particular — and their nature and relationships examined.

43 Dray, p. 52.

Two related objections were encountered: that past experience is use-less as a guide to conduct because there can be no way of knowing that the future will be like the past, and that nothing in the way of useful general-isations can be learned from history since all events are unique. Both objections, it is suggested, are invalid — the first because it refuses to occupy a position where evidence could challenge it; the second through a seeming misconception of what historians do (and, indeed, are obliged to do because, without some generalisation, explanation cannot be given) and through a greatly exaggerated idea of what is claimed for generalisation in history.

The next section is concerned with the process of giving an historical account.

III

So far it seems to have been assumed that the particulars of an event, and, hence, of an historical account of it, are somehow given. In fact, of course, selection of particulars is required for, clearly, not all the facts about the past interest historians all of the time. The criterion of selection and emphasis will be relevance to what is to be explained. The events of the year 1832 in Britain which appear in an historical narrative, and the distribution of emphasis amongst them, will vary markedly according to whether the historian is primarily concerned with Franchise reform or living conditions or public health. (To many contemporaries 1832 was less the year of Reform than that of the cholera.)

Of course, there might well be some overlap between the two narratives, and in a general survey of the year both sets of particulars would be comprehensively covered: but that brings out a more radical difference which exists among past facts. Some facts would not enter into any historical narrative, not because the historian is ignorant of them but because they do not interest him. Many ships, no doubt, had been wrecked on the East coast of Greece by late summer gales blowing from the Black Sea. But only the occasion in 480 B.C., when much of the Persian invasion fleet was destroyed, concerns historians — because, by altering the balance of forces, it contributed significantly to the ultimate victory of the Greeks — i.e. it had significant consequences.

An historical fact is thus not *any* fact about the past. It is a fact (properly attested, of course) which historians actually use by a process of selection in the course of explaining something: and it can only be so used if it had consequences for or connections (casual, qualifying or illustrative) with other facts which make it important for that explanation. However, it is not true that the division between past facts and historical facts is fixed or permanent. Since the variety of things historians may wish to explain is so large, and the explanations they offer may vary, it follows that the distinction between past facts and historical facts is not fixed.

E. H. Carr has an illuminating example of this relationship. He considers a fact, hitherto unused by historians in an historical account — namely that at Stalybridge Wakes in 1850, a gingerbread seller was kicked to death by a mob. Does that make it an historical fact? Mr. Carr suggests that "its present status is that it has been proposed for membership of the select club of historical facts. It now awaits a seconder and sponsors."[44] If, as time passes, more and more narratives come to refer to it, it will in due course, qualify. And this is not an arbitrary matter. If it is taken up that will be because it is acknowledged to satisfy the criterion for use — utility in explaining something(s) with which historians are concerned: and the recognition that it satisfies the criterion is that historians in fact use it.

Constructing an historical narrative is thus a process of winnowing, of differentiation between the various members of a mass of crude facts and of showing their intrinsic relations. In a word, historical narrative is the product of colligation — of "explaining an event by tracing its intrinsic relations with other events and locating it in its historical context".[45]

Consider a phrase such as "Napoleon's foreign policy". Now literally this is a mere abstraction. It consisted of thoughts and purposes "floating in the mind" of a man long since dead — indeed, even that goes beyond what we know directly. We assume certain thoughts and purposes to have existed in the mind of Napoleon because of actions which he performed or attempted to perform and events which followed — in short we infer purpose from action. But it is of the nature of purpose that it is frequently, or even usually, wider in scope than any specific action — that its realisation requires a plurality of actions. If Napoleon's foreign policy

44 E. H. Carr, *What is History?*, p. 12.
45 W. H. Walsh, *Introduction to the Philosophy of History*, p. 59.

could be summed up as "French hegemony in Europe" we could not deduce this from any one action: we can and do deduce it from a whole panoply of actions. It follows surely that no one of those actions can be fully explained in isolation from at least some of the others. Some – the Treaty of Lunéville for instance – are more nearly self-contained than others because they have a sort of summary quality which lays bare and sums up what has been at stake in the past:[46] but none would be fully explicable alone.

Or consider the Sarajevo Crisis and the outbreak of war in 1914. It would clearly be quite wrong to say that the one caused the other in any but a superficial sense. In order really to understand what was involved one would need to know the course of events in European History generally for decades before – probably since 1871 – and to understand the aims and ambitions and fears of the various Powers. Then – with a background knowledge of how foreign relations are in general conducted, and what sort of purpose statesmen in fact have, we could place Sarajevo in an intelligible context.

This last example should have removed the suspicion which the Napoleon example may have created – that what is being argued for is explanation given necessarily in terms of the plan of a master-mind. Walsh certainly seems to view colligation as tied firmly to the "deliberate attempts to carry out a previously formulated programme".[47] On this view, of course, colligation has a limited applicability – more limited indeed than he seems to claim. But having, and seeking to realise, a purpose is by no means synonymous with "a previously formulated programme"[47] or "deliberately planned happenings" and there is moreover a crucial ambiguity in the word "plan".

Consider for instance Hitler's conduct of German foreign policy. Looking back after the event this may assume the appearance of a neatly time-tabled blueprint, a plan duly implemented in all its pre-conceived detail. Mr. A. J. P. Taylor,[48] in a recent book, has subjected this interpretation to sharp attack, and having demolished it, has concluded that it is nonsense to talk of Hitler having had a plan at all. But the conclusion by

46 See H. C. Deutch, *The Genesis of Napoleonic Imperialism.*
47 Walsh, p. 61.
48 A. J. P. Taylor, *Origins of the Second World War.*

no means follows from the argument. Hitler may have had no plan in the sense of a time-tabled stage-by-stage blueprint to be implemented: But he had a purpose — to tear up the Versailles Treaty and perhaps secure German predominance in Europe. To secure this end he had to review and take note of circumstances, some of which were favourable and others less so, and formulate plans using the one and coping with the other. As action develops, unexpected, or at least unforeseen, opportunities and snags develop and these have to be responded to.

In this way "opportunism" is built into any political enterprise whatever and is in no sense imcompatible with planning — it is simply a synonym for necessary flexibility in pursuing some purpose — which purpose ties together and explains all the various actions which spring from its pursuit. Partly Hitler took advantage of facts. (That is, he conceived, and sought to implement, plans based on an appraisal of what the situation allowed or dictated.) Partly, by means of deliberate planning, he created new facts — a mighty German army and air force, and an excellent communications system for instance, which altered the nature of what was possible for him.

The fact that events do not conform to a neatly regimented programme, therefore, does not mean "no planning" in the sense of "no purpose or objective and no attempt to realise it by intelligent action"; it simply means that a "plan" is not something dreamed up in vacuo by wise men divorced from reality: it means that an attempt is made to recognise, utilise, or neutralise the facts of a situation — and, of course, to seize any unforeseen opportunity which presents itself for furthering an overall aim.

This responding to the facts of a situation in the attempt to ward off dangers, or turn them to advantage is central to the point under discussion. Consider, for instance, the rise of monopoly capitalism which Professor Walsh rightly allows to be in no sense "a deliberate attempt to give expression to coherent policy". Clearly, no one planned it. But it by no means follows that it will not fit the "colligation" model. For the nature and features of the capitalist system were such that capitalists were faced with the need to rationalise production, to reduce ruinous competition in some industries and reap the benefits of very large-scale production in others. The changes grew out of the bleak facts of the situation.

Professor Walsh's division between the planned and the unplanned — at least in the examples he gives — seems thus to break down. He makes undue concessions. There seems to be no need to "hanker" after "some substitute" for "teleological explanation";[49] nor is anything gained by categorising some sequences as only "semi-teleological" simply because they were manifestly not planned in detail in advance in precisely the way they occurred.[50] Colligation does not require "deliberate attempts to give expression to coherent policy" in the sense of fully articulated premeditation by a master agent. It is not disproved of even damaged, by the agreed fact that no-one "planned" monopoly capitalism. The case is simply that given a knowledge of men and of the facts of the case, we can make sense out of what they do because we can entertain accurate conceptions of their purposes, and of the sort of steps they are likely to take in seeking to implement them.[51] An event in the career of J. P. Morgan fits into the colligation model just as well as Hitler's occupation of the Rhineland. In both an event is explained "by tracing its intrinsic relations with other events and locating it in its historical context".

But how exactly is this done? What is it that reveals "intrinsic relations" and identifies "historical context"? The answer, implicit in what has already been said, lies in the sort of account an historian gives. It is not the case, as is so often assumed, that the ideal for an historian (though one which paucity of sources prevents him from ever reaching) is to describe the past "just as it was" − to write, in short, the sort of account an omniscient and unprejudiced contemporary witness, were there such a person, might have produced. For the historian has a priceless asset, his hindsight.[52] The real significance of events is often not available to a

49 Walsh, ibid.

50 Indeed such a view − that they were − would surely end by making the "colligation" model very rarely applicable: for almost any case would probably prove upon examination to be over-simplified. As we saw in the Hitler example, events were the outcome of an amalgam of deliberate purpose and what circumstances permitted, inhibited or encouraged − though the two (purpose and circumstance) merge and interlock ceaselessly. Purpose is shaped and determined by circumstance − Hitler never would have entertained his purpose had the facts been radically different − and some facts can be altered by purpose − German rearmament meant that the situation was no longer the same. Nor would rearmament have been possible if initial circumstances had not been what they were. Versailles forbade it: and resolution on the part of the other powers could have frustrated it. And this same interplay between purpose and circumstance seems ubiquitous in human affairs.

51 This is, of course, an instance of the operation and importance of conceptual evidence.

52 On this point see A. C. Danto, *Analytical Philosophy of History*, chapter VIII.

contemporary because their significance consists in consequences which often do not appear until after, perhaps long after, the events themselves. These consequences, and, hence, the significance, of events, are available to the historian, and his narrative will consist of a selection of events chosen as we have seen on precisely the criterion that they had consequences of significance and are, for that reason, deemed to be important. The narrative will embrace those (chosen) events and will relate their significance in terms of consequences.

However, historians compose narratives of different kinds, and one type of difference is especially relevant here. For genuine history can be written on many different levels of generality,[53] from the most detailed account of the shortest time-range to the wide, sweeping "studies" or "surveys" of the entire history of countries or civilisations. Within wide limits the historian may choose at what level he wishes to operate and, obviously, what evidence is directly relevant to him will depend in part upon his choice of level.

However, limits exist. Even the most detailed narrative of the most limited period represents a selection of facts from the sum total which exists, and their intelligible arrangement: even the most highly generalised survey must respect the facts. While it will actually use only a fraction of the evidence which appears in more detailed narratives, and, even so, in a very abbreviated form, the "use" must amount to a faithful précis, and its argument and conclusions must be consistent with those facts which it does not incorporate. Each successive level of higher generalisation rests upon, or presupposes full mastery of, the evidence uncovered and employed at the more detailed levels of enquiry.

It should be clear that the "colligation" account of historical explanation well fits the different levels upon which that explanation is given. The different levels alter the shape (so to speak) of the colligation, the less general thickening it with detail, the less detailed elongating it with generalisations which assume, summarise and represent the body of detail. And this admirably suits the structure of historical events. For events are not discrete entities side by side like beads on a string. The "Second World War" is an event: so is "The War at Sea", "The Battle of the Atlantic" and "the sinking of the Bismark". Each of the last three events is contained

---

53 On this point see A. M. MacIver, *Historical Explanation*.

within the preceding ones, and even the last named is, of course, made up of a great number of other events. Each of the four events can thus be the subject of a colligatory chain, or can be an element, more or less emphasised, within a chain devoted to the more general events which include it.

Obviously, the evidence drawn upon will vary in identity and emphasis according to which level of generalisation (and hence which colligation) is chosen. Just as narratives proceed at different levels of generality, the most general incorporating, and often presupposing the less, so an event lies within other events and includes yet others within itself. Indeed it is this which determines the variable nature of historical narrative. Colligation matches the level of generality chosen to the "level" of event appropriate to it. The sinking of the Bismark will occupy a more, or less, central place according to which of the first three narratives is given.

However, it might be argued that there are dangers in the "colligation" account of history which need to be guarded against. The colligation model is clearly reinforced by what has already been said about historical events. Events are chosen (or rejected) by the historian because they are, or are not, relevant to what it is he is trying to narrate – the chosen events are those that enable the narrative to proceed by making the process of change intelligible. But this principle of selection, by concentrating on the relations of an event, may cause the historian to overlook its unique character.

The Reform Bills of the 19th century, for instance, might all get run together as "franchise reform" or "the growth of parliamentary democracy" to the neglect of the study of the unique circumstantial context of each and half the value of the study would be lost: for in that event little idea could be gained of the kind of circumstances and pressures which preceded and accompanied the Bills of 1832, 1867 and 1884 respectively. We would fail to obtain a comprehensive explanation, and such explanation as we had would not be useful since we should be able neither to gain nor to check any well-founded ideas as to how the franchise was reformed or how parliamentary democracy "grew". We should be unable to check any of the superficial generalisations to which the chain of events so summarised might give birth – as, for example, the common claim that all reform has to be wrested, more or less forcefully, from reluctant rulers.

A second, related, danger (it might be claimed) is that by locating an event within a particular colligation, only some of its connections, and hence only some of its features, are exposed, and by the emphasis thus given to these, other connections and features are overlooked. Colligation, by the very process of revealing some relations, might thus effect an artificial dissection of reality by separating events which are in fact related. (The commonest example is perhaps the conventional division between Home and Foreign affairs when the two are in fact intimately related.)

The cause of both these difficulties, in so far as they are real, is that colligation tends to stress conceptual evidence. For, by seeking to make explicable a course of change, it embodies appeals, probably tacit, to a special complex of generalisations. The answer is to complement this process by close attention to each particular event in a colligatory chain. This will take two forms. Firstly, the narrative should include analysis designed to isolate the aspects of the event which are relevant, as causes and effects, to the chain being built up. Secondly, as many chains should be constructed as are necessary to exhaust the sum of relationships with other events which the event possesses, each such chain respecting the analytical requirement just set out. Chartism, for example, might "belong" to colligations dealing with "franchise reform" and with "working class movements".

Clearly these principles are connected. In exposing the features of an event by analysis in the course of constructing one chain, it is almost inevitable that its relations to other chains will be opened up. These can be fully articulated by building up those chains as the second principle requires.[54] And the whole process is in no way a modification of the

54 How far one narrative can embody all that needs to be said about an event, and how far (and how many) separate chains are needed obviously depends upon the particular case. The Suez crisis, for example, belongs mainly to foreign policy, but opinion within the Conservative Party obviously had a bearing upon Sir Anthony Eden's conduct of affairs. Reciprocally, it is clearly the case that Suez affords an illustration of that opinion and it may have had an important bearing upon the development or modification of it. Whether this (and the several other aspects of Suez which are not central to foreign policy) require another chain or chains, or whether they can all be fully accommodated by sub-ordinate mentions in the course of the one chain is a matter for the historian's judgement. The important point is that (ideally) all the significant aspects of the Suez event should be exposed and treated. (On this question see G. R. Elton, *The Practice of History*, chapter III, section 7, especially pp. 138–140.)

colligation model. The objections point to dangers which need to be guarded against, but, properly carried out, colligation will avoid them both. For history is the record of change occurring through time, and such a record can only be made intelligible if the relations between the events, which make up change, are exposed. But the complexity of those relations, and of change, is such that only close scrutiny of individual events is capable of showing what the relations were, though this is carried out in terms of general considerations.

However, there is an extension of the first objection (that colligation, because it works through hindsight, may impose upon the past a pattern so precise and tidy as to make it a mere caricature of the past that happened) which needs separate mention. The possibility is that an historian, starting from his present, may attempt to use a study of the past for some practical purpose in the present. This intention, it is argued, must warp the historian's choice of subject, and of the facts and evidence he recognises. The clearest statement of this position is that of Professor Oakeshott[55] who distinguishes between "practical" and "objective" history. The practical attitude towards the past is marked by the desire to have clarified specific problems which occur in the now-existing world, to assimilate the past with the present.

A practising lawyer exemplifies this attitude towards the past. "He considers the past event solely in relation to its present consequences . . . and . . . is interested only in past events which have present practical consequences."[56] This attitude is perfectly valid within its own universe of discourse, but statements in this idiom are "non-historical" statements about the past. For the historical attitude – that of the true historian – is concerned with "an interest in past events for their own sake, or in respect of their independence of subsequent or present events".[57]

To the "practical" attitude Oakeshott claims "the past consists of happenings recognised to be contributory or non-contributory to a subsequent condition of things or to be friendly or hostile to a desired condition of things".[58] (These two are clearly not the same, and should

55 M. Oakeshott, *On the Activity of being an Historian.*

56 Oakeshott, p. 147.

57 Oakeshott, p. 155.

58 Oakeshott, p. 153.

not have been grouped together.) In contrast, for the "specifically historical attitude . . . everything that the evidence reveals or points to is recognised to have its place: nothing is excluded, nothing is regarded as non-contributory. The place of an event is not determined by its relation to subsequent events."[59]

It is the "hindsight" aspect of historical writing and its necessarily organising and explanatory nature that casts doubt on the clear cut distinction that Oakeshott has set up. For "its relation to subsequent events" is what gives an event narrative vivacity because those subsequent events are its consequences or outcome or point. Of course, these may be rather trivial or indirect: but if there were none at all — if the "event" were totally unconnected with any subsequent happening or if it failed to illustrate or enlighten any aspect of the story being unrolled it is hard to see what place it could have. In short, any historian is concerned with "happenings recognised to be contributory or non-contributory to a subsequent condition of things": and if they are non-contributory they are unlikely to figure in his narrative.[60]

However, allowing that the principle of selectivity is relevance to the purpose in hand, it might still be argued that a fundamental distinction exists between the historian's quest for relevance and the "practical" man's in that, for the historian, relevance is not determined by anything extrinsic to the historical account itself. But, for once the subject for study is chosen, the same is true of the "practical" approach. For, if the background to a state of affairs is to be helpful in understanding it, then it must be the *true* background which is given. Regardless of motivation, then, history must be studied *as if* "for its own sake". If the "relevant" history to be studied is that which, it is hoped, may throw light upon, say, the present troubles in Ireland, then exactly where the enquiry leads is determined by the evidence available and the criteria and standards of historical work — just as would be the case with an "objectively" motivated study.

Oakeshott's claim that in the genuine historical enquiry "everything that the evidence reveals or points to is recognised to have its place" is perfectly well founded. But this is not a description of an enquiry

59 Oakeshott, p. 154.
60 For a lucid and amusing example of this essential point see Danto, p. 131.

springing from a particular motivation, but of any enquiry which is to count as history at all. It might be that enquiries stemming from the interest in present problems failed to measure up to these requirements: but that is an empirical matter, not a necessary connection, as Oakeshott seems to suggest. It would have to be shown, and it has not been shown. There seems no prima facie reason for believing that a genuine historical enquiry may not have as its starting point the desire for explanation of some present problem.

The fact is that "everything the evidence reveals or points to is recognised to have its place" is a general principle of procedure which always operates, and can only operate, within the particular context of the original choice of subject and level. It is only within a general frame of relevance which those choices provide that evidence could "reveal" or "point to" anything – or indeed that there could be "evidence".

Oakeshott is quite right in asserting that an unhistorial attitude to the past, motivated by practical considerations, does exist. What is wrong is the illegitimate extension of this point to cover all enquiries which have as their starting point a concern with some present problem and a desire to elucidate it. In fact, unless the evidence or procedures are violated, the distinction is not between studying history and doing something else, but between different motives for conducting an historical enquiry. An enquiry springing from a practical interest does not "impose on the past an arbitrary teleological structure" unless it fails to do justice to the evidence or the procedures appropriate to its selection and use. And the test here is not motivational but criterial.

More will be said about procedures below. For the moment it is important to note that Oakeshott has identified a real danger, although he seems to have wrongly identified its cause and remedy. For it is true that colligation, and the hindsight through which it works, brings with it the danger that an over tidy and precise pattern will be imposed upon a reality which was in fact shot through with doubt and uncertainty – that statesmen, for example, may appear to be almost entirely rational in their calculations. The remedy is (as far as possible) occasionally to set hindsight aside and seek to place oneself in the position of the agent one is studying, trying to reconstruct the situation as it bore in upon him. In a word, reconstruction is a vital part of historical work in that it imposes a powerful check upon the various forms of distortion discussed.

The most emphatic argument for reconstruction is that of Collingwood,[61] who held that historical explanation involves "getting inside" the subject of historical inquiry — Julius Caesar or Cromwell — in making their thoughts our thoughts and hence apprehending the full significance of what they did; and this feat is performed by sympathetic intuition — not by reference to, and inference from, general considerations. In this way, "When the historian has ascertained the facts there is no further process of enquiring into the causes. When he knows what happened, he already knows why it happened."

Now it is true that historians do try to do something which can be described as trying to "get inside" their subject although the psychological possibility of recreating thought by intuition in the absence of the appropriate and accompanying emotions (and Collingwood insists that only thought is recreated — "all history is the history of thought") is highly dubious. The intuitionist explanation works very well in some cases, and this means that carefully selected examples, such as Collingwood's own, can give it an apparent authority. But really this is due to the fact that the explanation of some events or actions are rather obvious. Why Nelson did what he did at Trafalgar is explicable in general terms to anyone who knows enough of naval tactics at that period to see how his actions contributed, or were expected to contribute, to victory: but this is because no-one doubts that victory was what Nelson was trying to achieve.

By contrast if one attempt to intuit the explanation of Cromwell's actions between, say, Naseby and the King's execution, that would be a most hazardous undertaking because whereas Nelson's objective is clear, it is simply not true that it is obvious what Cromwell was up to. On the contrary, this is a point which is still hotly disputed. Intuition seems to work well in proportion as the explanation required is more and more obvious. For while the intuitionist does very well until doubts or disagreements are expressed, in the face of these (supposing they do not concern ascertainable matters of fact — such as points of chronology which are, of course, specific to the case in question) he can only persist in his assertions: for to do otherwise would be to invoke general considerations, to support his case by reference to what it would be reasonable to expect. In fact, no historian who wished to be taken seriously would ignore the challenge to defend a proferred explanation.

61 R. G. Collingwood, *The Idea of History*.

This means that there must be some testing and evaluating of an intuitively based explanation other than the intuition itself – for it is exactly the inherently esoteric nature of the latter which causes the challenge to be made at all. The historian is in fact asked "What grounds have you for these statements?" and the answer cannot be that he has intuited their truth, that for private reasons he knows them to be true, for it is precisely this which is in need of justification.

The solution is clear. Reconstruction can only be undertaken on the basis of evidence, not just of particulars, but of that interplay between conceptual and particular evidence already described.

But what is the nature of this evidence? E. H. Carr,[62] in a penetrating illustration of this point, shows how printed collections of papers "gratefully accepted by historians in default of the originals" are frequently grossly unrepresentative of those originals. Moreover, the originals themselves need very careful scrutiny. Apart from obvious dangers such as fraud, the contents even of genuine documents cannot be taken at face value. Thus, Carr argues, the original papers left behind by Stresemann (German Foreign Minister under the Weimar Republic) far from being an objective record of diplomatic conversations, are constructed (whether consciously or not) so as to over-represent the successful aspects of his policy, and to make his arguments seem clearly more effective than those of his opponents. "The documents do not tell us what happened, but what he wanted others to think, or perhaps what he wanted himself to think, had happened."

The difficulty, given that this is known, is to know what allowance to make for it. Indeed, the outcome might well seem to be total scepticism as to the possibility of historical knowledge. No historian can completely free himself from the presuppositions of his age, or of his own personal preferences, and if evidence, instead of being a check upon these, becomes almost the creature of his judgement because of its uncertainty, the result would be innumerable conflicting accounts all equally valid as explanations – which amounts, of course to no explanation at all.

Collingwood seems to have reached the lip of this abyss when he said "St Augustine looked at History from the point of view of the the early Christians... Gibbon from that of an 18th century Englishman:

62 Carr, pp. 16–19.

Mommson from that of a 19th century German. There is no point in asking which was the right point of view. Each was the only one possible for the man who adopted it."[63] This would restore the intuitionist claims in their fullest and strongest form. An "explanation" of, say, Cromwell's motives and actions leading to the execution of the King could be no more than a mere reflex of predetermined religious or social prejudice. But the position is by no means so desperate as this. In the first place, the existence of difficulties in the evidence does not mean that they cannot be overcome, or at least detected, and the evidence thus used with proper caution. Elton gives as an example Sir John Ramsey's mistake in imagining that the receipt issue rolls of the Exchequer for the 15th century can be taken at their face value[64] — a mistake that will not be made again precisely because it is seen to have been one.

Secondly, by no means all evidence is as uncertain as Carr's example might suggest. There is an enormous bulk of evidence which places events — the meetings of Parliaments, the passing of laws, the outbreaks of plagues and so forth — beyond any reasonable doubt.[65] The strength of much of this evidence is cumulative — that is more than one source testifies to the same event or events — and some of it is complementary — that is, two independent facts strengthen one another because one of them supports expectations which the first causes us to entertain. This clearly strengthens confidence in each of the pieces of evidence (and, hence, confidence in any narrative they may be used to support).

Moreover evidence in itself is not history. History is the result of the use of evidence, and this is characterised by minimum standards of procedure, accepted by all historians, which, together with the "framework of fact" place a stringent check upon arbitrary interpretation. Suppose two historians disagree over an account given by one of them, and consider what sort of statements the critic would make. They will invariably be found to be one of two types — that his opponent offends the general sense of credibility — that his conceptual frame seems mistaken, or that his handling of evidence is in some way faulty. Setting aside the first point,[66] the whole notion of evidence ineluctably

63 Collingwood, p. 12.
64 Elton, p. 60.
65 See Kitson-Clark, p. 42.
66 This is, of course, the question of conceptual evidence already discussed.

presupposes agreed criteria and procedures. For without this notion of evidence, and the acknowledgement that it must be respected, i.e. treated in certain ways, how would any account be said to be wrong? What could be wrong about it?

No rational dispute is possible except in terms of agreed criteria, for without these "right" and "wrong" are meaningless concepts. No evidence can be adduced and no argument advanced in support of a contention until it is agreed what shall count as evidence and argument. Consider, for example, G. R. Elton's review of Christopher Hill's *Society and Puritanism in Pre-Revolutionary England*.[67] The first point to be noticed is Professor Elton's opening: "In the last few years Mr. Hill has come to the fore as our leading authority on the earlier Stuarts and the pre-history of the Civil War. The mantle he wears may not be quite that of Tawney, but no-one looks so likely to fill that vacant place. And let it be whispered that in many respects he is the better historian." High praise, surely. And yet Professor Elton goes on to write a somewhat critical review of the book. But this apparent incongruity is not incongruous to anyone acquainted with what history is. Professor Elton does not question for a moment that Mr. Hill is writing history: he simply gives a qualified disagreement to the interpretation Mr. Hill offers. Obviously, then, the disagreement takes place within a broad framework of agreement, and what can the framework possibly be but a set of procedures and criteria as to what qualifies as history at all which is accepted not merely by Elton and Hill, but by any historian whatever: for if this were not so, then how could Elton's criticisms be cogent or even intelligible? How could he take it for granted, as he clearly does, that his criticisms really are such? And what sort of faults does Elton specify?

"The learning is prodigious and varied . . . but it is also oddly restricted. Not a single unprinted manuscript is quoted . . . the account of the Puritan lectureships suffers from the failure to enquire how many parishes may possibly have harboured these prophets of the new order. The great bulk of the evidence consists of contemporary comment, complaint and propaganda.

---

67 See also Hill's own critique of Recent Interpretations of the Civil War, in *Puritanism and Revolution.*

"Such material though entirely legitimate (*N.B.*) is also very difficult. It needs criticism and here it receives none ... I have noticed only three instances in which the reader is warned of a possible bias in the author cited, in each case an opponent of Puritanism. On occasion a writer says something manifestly wrong (for instance, that Protestant colonists made the American Indians work while the Spaniards let them remain idle), but Mr. Hill refrains from comment.

"In the result the historian's interpretation of the facts of the day too often embodies only the views held by one section of contemporary opinion. Contemporaries were not, of course, always wrong; it is less certain that one part of them were always right. Mr. Hill's method enables him to demonstrate beyond doubt the existence of an identifiable social philosophy. But it can do little to elucidate the rightness or effect of this philosophy, and it positively bars one from understanding its opponents or the truth about the situation under attack from radical reformers.

"A preoccupation with public archives is not only the creator of unconscious bias in the historian. Admirable as Mr. Hill's range and verve are, it must remain uncertain whether the clarity and coherence of his picture does not owe a good deal to a preference for contemporary statements rather that the critical analysis of contemporary facts."

Some of the criticisms of Hill's work — i.e. the criteria of historical scholarship which are taken for granted — may now be listed:

(a) The evidence is alleged to be selective — it "too often embodies only the views held by one section of contemporary opinion", i.e. the conclusions drawn fit only part of the evidence available.

(b) That Mr. Hill is wrong in assuming that the public utterances of those living through events can be taken at their face value — that what a man says is necessarily concerned with truth rather than to stir others to act in a particular way, i.e. the evidence is inappropriate to the conclusion drawn because it is treated as given truth not something to be scrutinised. And in addition Elton suggests that private unpublished sources, not being open to the same objection, should have been used, and were not.

(c) That the actual influence of the Puritan lectureships is assumed to have been great merely because it plainly was potentially so: whereas this claim could only be advanced with assurance if it

could be shown that many such lectureships existed, i.e.
inadequacy of evidence for a conclusion.

(d)   The allegedly unjustifiable assumption is made that contemporary
statements can be taken at their face value — that men's motives
and opinions are necessarily the same as those they consciously
express and that those who live through events necessarily clearly
understand what is happening.

Now it is surely obvious that no objection could rationally be made to
the principles of Elton's criticisms. No one could possibly maintain that
evidence need not be representative or appropriate and sufficient to the
conclusions drawn from it. But this is because it could not rationally be
denied. It is qualities like "appropriateness", "sufficiency" and "relevance"
which give a conclusion its validation and truth. Intrinsic in the very
notion of rational discourse is the notion of justification — that one can
and will give grounds for one's contentions. But this entails, not merely
that grounds of *some* sort be given, but that there is agreement on what is a
"ground". And it is qualities such as relevance etc. which are the
"ingredients" of justification and which constitute grounds. In the case in
hand, Professor Elton's critique can only be answerable, arguable, or even
meaningful (and it is clearly all three) because there exists an agreed
notion of coherence between evidence and conclusion, and of what that
coherence consists in a particular case.

So far it has been argued (a) that sensible disagreement between
historians is only possible at all because of agreement as to the criteria and
procedures which must be followed and satisfied if a narrative is to be
classed as history, and (b) that what does satisfy them in particular cases is
bound by considerations of rational coherence and this must limit the
occurrence of disagreement.

But it does not remove it. Historians do differ: and does this not weaken
the second contention, and indeed the first too? For if the existence of
agreed criteria and procedures does not preclude disagreement as to what
does, or does not satisfy them in practice, how useful are they? It could not
be denied that there is force in this criticism, but how much force clearly
depends on how often, and to what degree, incorrigible disagreement as to
what is evidence occurs. But relevance is not always hard to demonstrate
and it seems clear that there is indeed a very considerable measure of
agreement. For whether or not particular considerations are relevant to

whatever business is in hand is largely a rational matter. An historian is not and cannot be a wilful and perverse individualist free to accept or reject anything without acknowledging or being under any obligation rationally to defend his opinion if called upon to do so.

However, it is true that apparently incorrigible disagreements do exist. And they appear to spring mainly from two sources — the presumptions and value systems a historian brings to his work, and the tendency to develop paternal affection towards one's own theories, so that one becomes unwilling to recognise as relevant evidence those sources and arguments which seem to place them (the presumption and theories) in jeopardy.

But how far does this make history viciously subjective? It is true, of course, that there is no autonomous and independent "umpire" and no infallible way of settling exactly whether agreed procedures have been faithfully observed — if historian (a) maintains that historian (b) has mishandled his evidence and historian (b) insists that he has not then there is no means of incontrovertably determining the matter because it is judgement which must decide. Whose? The alleged unreliability of the two contestants is exactly what is in question. But this does not leave us helpless. History is an open enquiry.

Any man of appropriate training may write and publish free from any censure but that of his peers. Certainly this is most unlikely ever to result in one universally accepted version — in Lord Acton's "scientific history":[68] but it does strictly limit the type of disagreement which significantly exists. It is safe to say for example that no trained historian alive today, or at any future time, would or will take seriously the frantic vituperation of Motley's *Dutch Republic.*[69] At a less extreme level consider the famous contemporary controversy over the "rise of the gentry". While most certainly there is no emerging consensus on this, disagreement falls within bounds, and it would be generally agreed that traditional views need to be sharply modified.[70]

In principle the explanation of Cromwell's conduct or of the decline of Athens must remain partly matters of opinion: but the only opinions

68 Lord Acton, *The Cambridge Modern History*, pp. 10–12.

69 Take seriously, that is, as a history of the Dutch Republic. It has considerable significance as a document about values and assumptions of Motley's own time.

70 See, for example, J. H. Hexter, *Reappraisals in History*, pp. 117–62.

worth noticing are those of men who are trained to observe and actually do observe the principles of enquiry intrinsic in the notion of rational investigation. Historical knowledge (like scientific) is thus always provisional: but this does not mean that nothing at all is agreed or that anyone can hold any opinion he likes and still be taken seriously. We are, in fact, half way between Acton's *Ultimate History* and the thoroughgoing subjectivity of Collingwood in his remarks quoted earlier. For these two extremes merely mark limits: they do not exhaust the possibilities. There may indeed be no point in asking which point of view was "right" because that kind of "truth" does not exist in history. But there *is* certainly point in enquiring whether any of them was wrong: the only point of view 'possible for the men who adopted it' may prove on examination to be no kind of history at all because it may flout those requirements which an activity must satisfy if it is to rank as history. It may be vitiated by lack of imaginative sympathy for the assumptions and normal practices of a past age: it may be ruined by an overwhelming intellectual presumption so that "evidence" becomes what confirms a preconceived (or "party") line: it may, through dishonesty, carelessness or incompetence, mishandle sources in the ways discussed earlier, or in others: and so on. And these are not matters where criticism is palsied or rational objection dumb. The fact that no historian can be guaranteed to be entirely free from these faults does not preclude him from detecting them, or thinking he detects them, in the work of other men. And while it would be futile to expect argument always to produce agreement, to assume the ubiquity of dissent is to fly in the face of what is palpably true.

Not only is there "a very large body of agreed historical knowledge on which no dispute is possible", but this is constantly being augmented, regardless of the fact that disagreement persists. For it is quite mistaken to suppose that the continuance of disagreement and the growth of knowledge are incompatible. G. R. Elton shows how Sir Lewis Namier's radical revision of 18th century political history, although by no means commanding general assent in itself, nevertheless destroyed the older interpretation so completely that while many "object to the Namierite explanation . . . No one now would dream of interpreting the England of the unreformed Parliament in the way universal before Namier wrote." And as Elton points out, "what makes his revision so solid that it has now become, even to opponents, the new conventional framework was his firm foundation of scholarship" — that respect for evidence and rational procedural criteria discussed above.

This section has been concerned with the construction of an historical account. Such an account necessarily involves selection of facts on the criterion of relevance to what is being explained, and takes the form of setting the selected events in a context which brings out their intrinsic relationships. This process of "colligation" works through the historian's hindsight, his knowledge of the consequences and significance of events which can only be grasped after — perhaps long after — their occurrence. However, colligation, because it involves hindsight, involves certain dangers. The "chaining" of events may result in their range of connections being grossly under-exposed and, in particular, the desire to elucidate some present problem may cause them to be forced into an arbitrary teleological pattern. The danger ought really to be illusory since, if explanation is to be given (whether this is sought just for its own sake or for some more utilitarian motive), its value depends upon its truth, which involves, of course, a just and comprehensive survey of each event. However, to ensure that this happens, as many chains as are needed to exhaust the connections between events should be constructed.

This really means the reconstruction of events by the interplay of imagination and evidence. Evidence, although not unambiguous, is not wholly subjective either. A great deal of agreed and incontrovertible fact exists and further there are reputable procedures which confine disagreements of interpretation within the limits of rational dispute. The criteria underlying the procedures are in part logical and in part concerned with the knowledge and meaning of sources.

The final section attempts to relate what has been said to the problems of teaching.

IV

In so far as this account is acceptable certain considerations seem to arise for the teaching of history in schools. The first general point to be made is that schools are not attempting to train professional historians. It is obvious from what has been said that great erudition and professional skill are required to write satisfactory history — it is a lifetime's work to master one chosen period. It follows that there will be very significant differences between the professional historian's practice and what the teacher attempts to do with his pupils. What the latter should be doing, it is suggested, is to give them some competence in the use of the skills of historical enquiry, some information established and authenticated by use of those skills and some more generally applicable frames of expectation built up from that information which may enable them to understand, better than would otherwise be the case, certain aspects of experience. It follows that although fully professional competence cannot realistically be aimed at nothing should be done which is inconsistent with, or false to, professional practice.[71]

It should be obvious from what has been said that the skills of historical enquiry cannot be learned apart from engaging in its study – which alone calls for their exercise. There is, for example, no way of criticising (and hence – perhaps – correcting) an erroneous version of some part of the past embodied in public myth except to demonstrate its lack of firm foundation and, if possible, to confront it with a properly authenticated alternative version. And nothing counts as demonstration of error, or as "properly authenticated" except an argument based upon, and checked against, a careful review of the evidence. If, therefore, pupils are to learn to make such criticism, or to recognise them as valid when made, they must master the procedural criteria such arguments must satisfy, and come to know upon what evidence they rest. As both these requirements concern, at bottom, the quality of sources and the ways in which they are used there is no alternative to the pupils having experience – and, by implication, extended experience – in the case of sources.

This is true of course, not only of "public myths" but of widely accepted academic doctrines. The Weber thesis, Namier's correction of the "Whig" version of 18th century political history, or Lenin's

71 There are situations in teaching when this requirement must be somewhat relaxed. In general this is due to psychological and sociological factors. Obviously the age of the pupils must in part determine what is studied and how. The psychological evidence (in so far as it is reliable and unambiguous) concerning the mental operations which children of a given level of maturity can be expected to possess, and sociological evidence concerning the effects of home background upon (for example) motivation and language skill are obviously important considerations. An enforced modification of full-bodied historical enquiry which seems especially important – the emphasis upon reconstruction rather than hindsight – is dealt with below. But while professional practice cannot be attained in full, its attainment remains the only proper ambition and guide.

"Imperialism", for example can only be effectively examined and assessed in the light of relevant evidence.[72] If, for example, the last named work is criticised on the ground that its argument does not fit the chronology of capital export, then the only way of evaluating the criticism is to ascertain the facts concerning the export of capital — that is, to consult the relevant sources. It is not enough (although, of course, if is helpful) to read critical accounts of these works, for, in absence of familiarity with the evidence, no rational choice among the various conflicting accounts can be made. Since it is not possible to judge the merit of an argument from a standpoint of ignorance concerning its basis and content, the tendency will be either to evade the issue altogether by the flabby assumption that truth lies somewhere between the various conflicting accounts, or to adopt the account that seems most plausible — which may well mean no more than "most in tune with personal prejudice". This point is all the more pressing in education because of the growing tendency to lead pupils into the study of a historical problem by means of selections from the writings of historians who disagree about the matter. There is no harm in this — quite the reverse — provided the student is, in at least some measure, equipped to make a critical review of the alternative argument through knowledge of the sources.

Analogous arguments hold for all the other important aspects of history. The importance of reconstruction has already been emphasised. It was shown that this is quite impossible except on the basis of evidence and this needs to be emphasised in the context of teaching. For in recent years it has become much more common to modify formal instruction with "creative" or "imaginative" activity. Often, however, this activity is not practised upon, or disciplined by, genuine evidence, and, consequently, is not shaped by its proper use. All too often little genuine evidence is presented (in which case the reconstruction becomes mere imaginative composition or art, or hardwork, without any basis in fact) or it is presented uncritically, not as something out of which a narrative or picture or model can be constructed by inference, cross referencing and so on, but

---

72 At a still higher level of abstraction the "laws" of sociology, in so far as they claim support from, or make reference to, the past need the discipline and corrective of an independent check against the evidence they allegedly rest upon and mobilise.

as a subsitute for any such operations.[73] Frequently the pupil is simply told "Find out all you can about . . ." without being given any idea of what sources of genuine information are available or even that some of the things he may find out are better founded than others. Unless his work is then criticised in terms of evidence, this is clearly inimical to that training in relevant selection of facts which (as was shown above) is fundamental to colligation and, hence, to the whole historical enterprise: quite apart from the tacit but pernicious suggestion that what the book says is true because the book says it.

The remedy lies in the proper use of sources both for composing the work and for criticising it. Certainly the open ended, or "free thinking" approaches rightly insisted upon by modern educationists are necessary in history: but "the price of effective free thinking . . . is submission to the disciplines imposed by the principles of historical method".[74] In history (as so often in life) inferences have to be drawn, and decisions taken on the basis of evidence which is incomplete, by means of imaginative reconstruction limited and disciplined by that evidence and criticised in terms of it.[75] True, not everything can be directly based upon evidence — that is the consequence of its incompleteness and the reason

73 This does not differ in principle from another common practice — that of decorating the pages of "text" books with passages of original material. Frequently this degrades the sources into mere (dispensable) illustrations of points already made by the text to which, since they are uncriticised, they can lend only illusory support. Often they lie inert upon the page merely encumbering what they lack the power to fertilise.

74 David Thomson, *The Arms of History*, p. 35.

75 This fact is of much interest in connection with the stress laid by educationists in recent years upon "creativity", the fostering of which is urged as an educational aim as valid as the development of conventional intelligence, from which it is, allegedly, clearly distinct. A more realistic claim would seem to be the "threshold" theory, according to which "creativity" only separates off from conventional intelligence at a threshold of about 120 I.Q. Its exercise consists not in making random stabs or guesses at a problem using mere whimsical personal predilection, but of the application to it of sensible and controlled insights growing out of a firm foundation of relevant knowledge. Certainly, this theory admirably fits the practice of history. The exercise of creativity is guided by, and checked against, clear mastery of the evidence, which alone can raise it above the level of unsubstantiated speculation.
For a discussion of creativity and the "threshold" theory, with full references, see A. J. Cropley, *Creativity*.

why imagination is required at all. But imaginative reconstruction must be consistent with the evidence and this necessarily requires that the pupils be introduced to sources.[76]

The sources are the only proper basis for knowledge for, strictly, there are no such things as historical facts but only "traces" — evidence from which facts may, more or less confidently, be inferred. While it might seem pedantic to insist upon this in the face of the mass of "facts" securely established and known, it is a principle which should never be forgotten. If it is, the sorcery of the printed page will extinguish, for immature minds, the possibility of a critical attitude. It is better to cause the pupil to doubt what he need not doubt than to allow him to accept what he should strongly question. For sources are, in fact, always incomplete, often ambiguous and sometimes contradictory. They cannot just be used, but must be criticised. To present the pupil with nothing but an account which has "solved" or removed all these difficulties (supposing that to have been accomplished) is not only to plant an entirely false sense of the certainty of knowledge in his mind: it is to rob him of most of the point of the exercise by a confusion between a process and its outcome. The professional historian's narrative is an outcome of the skills of enquiry of which he is a master: but those skills are precisely what the pupil has in some measure to learn. He has to build, from the study of particular evidence, the structures of conceptual evidence and to acquire, along with those expanding conceptual frameworks, a steadily growing sense of relevance which sharpens and makes more appropriate his handling of particulars.

The interplay of conceptual and particular (upon which such stress was laid above) can be only tenuously and intermittently experienced or grasped apart from working with sources: and even that degree of insight which might be otherwise acquired is of limited value, for, without the sources, the pupil cannot adequately criticise what he tacitly infers. It follows that a historical education which consists solely of reading other

76 It should be obvious that the same is true of the use of hindsight, if anything of the reality of problems and decision taken is to be presented, and a disastrously over-simplified caricature is to be avoided. The exercise of hindsight must, as already stressed, be conditioned by close and constant reference to evidence so that justice is done to the identity of each event drawn into the colligatory chain.

men's work — even work of genuine scholarship, which, outside the sixth form, is very rarely the case — and makes no provision for the pupil to learn, by extended practice, the way in which such narratives are to be constructed and criticised is quite inadequate.

The pupil needs practice in learning how facts are established (with varying degrees of confidence) by cumulative evidence, by complementary relationships, and by inference, all involving an estimate of the reliability of sources. It is not suggested, of course, that the learning of skills is all that is at stake, and that knowledge of content is unimportant. On the contrary, it is not really possible to separate the two. The skills of historical enquiry can only be practised and, hence, acquired, on material appropriate to their exercise. Reconstruction, for example, can only be carried out on the basis of evidence and relevant background knowledge — that is, of historical material.

The point to be emphasised is not that knowledge is unimportant but that it can be confidently acquired only through the informed exercise of the relevant skills. This does not mean that the pupils must never read, or be told, anything, but that this must be combined with training in the skills of enquiry which enable them to assess as well as to assimilate.

Indeed, it is not the stress upon procedural skills which splits these off from knowledge of material, but conventional teaching which does so by setting up the learning of material as an almost exclusive objective. Moreover, this unbalanced concentration impoverishes the nature and effect of historical education. For, if skills are to be ignored, then whatever benefit is to be found in a programme of studies must be found within the material itself. But, with the younger and less able pupils this condition is difficult to fulfil. Either they study material which is beyond their grasp — as has commonly been the case with the conventional courses of political history (a state of affairs not fundamentally altered by the inclusion, or substitution, of social and economic history) or, if material is found suitable to their capabilities, it is likely to be of a trivial or ephemeral nature, and difficult to justify on educational grounds.

If, on the other hand, mastery of procedures is included as an important objective, the case is altered, for now material which is, perhaps, trivial in itself, is made worth doing because it confronts the child with genuine procedural learning at a level, and within a context, which he can handle. A beginning might be made with an historical investigation of the local football team. Solely as information this would not be educationally very significant, but as a properly conducted inquiry using records, cross-referencing and checking sources of information against one another it could be the entry point to a valid course of study.

Past living conditions in the district might also serve. In the 1860's, for example, the City Improvement Trust in Glasgow employed the photo-grapher Annan to make a survey of some of the worst slum areas which it was proposed to demolish. His pictures showed hideous conditions, but the filth, animal and vegetable, referred to in official printed records (and which would, indeed, have been expected) is not to be seen in the pictures. This gives an opportunity for a critical comparison of sources of evidence. Various possible explanations arise — the written testimony is wrong, the streets were specially cleaned up, the pictures are somehow in-accurate — and so on.

Official reports can be compared with newspaper accounts of the same events. Reports of committees can be set against the minutes of evidence upon which they are based. Here the matter is not simple, for the general report will not merely summarise the evidence of witnesses. Report and evidence will bear subtle testimony to the reliability of a witness — his occupation and interests revealed by cross-examination may be more revealing than what he says, just as the questions he is asked can tell a great deal about the interests involved, and thus lead into the purpose of the investigating Committee, its membership, and how it came to be set up.

"What the evidence is" is clearly not a simple question. But this shows how evidence may exist on different levels of generality, and these different "layers" make it possible to find a level of enquiry appropriate to the maturity of a range of pupils, the more sophisticated type of query being fitted in as the pupil grows in confidence and skill. [77] It is not argued, however, that narrow and detailed enquiries of this kind should be the only type of historical education. On the contrary, it has already been stated that relevant background knowledge is needed as a frame and base for reconstruction, and a combination of general and detailed study is needed. Thus older pupils studying the later 17th century might work

[77] The "spiral" model of the curriculum, presently to be discussed, fits this admirably.

through (for example) Macauley's account of Dame Alice Lisle's trial before Judge Jeffries – having first studied the context of that event and, perhaps, been given (deliberately) the conventional view of Jeffries as a bloody butcher. This would involve the double question of Macauley's use of his sources (disgraceful) and the quality of those sources themselves (dubious). In the course of the reconstruction other evidence should be drawn upon to illuminate the whole question of 17th century attitudes towards high treason and fair process at law and to gain a sense of the constitutional importance and political urgency of the matter.[78]

This study in depth of particulars is not only valuable in itself. Simultaneously the illuminating generalisations discussed earlier may be developed. In drawing an inference or hazarding a guess one is, of course, using a tacit generalisation in terms of what it would be reasonable to expect. This is both used to make the inference, or guess and is modified, extended, or confirmed according to whether the inference or guess is in fact well founded. For there may be an important and valuable difference in this respect between teacher and learner. Because the latter may be unaware of the outcome of an event he may sometimes escape from the limitations which hindsight imposes (along, of course, with the great advantages which it bestows) upon the professional historian. Given that he is firmly placed in a context structured by the evidence the questions "What would you do?" "What would you expect?" can become genuine hypotheses which, growing out of evidence, can be checked against evidence and confirmed, or modifed. In the latter case the question may then arise of why the hypothesis was incorrect and reasons, in terms of evidence, can be used to account for this. In this way expectations can be corrected in terms of the evidence, and generalisations accordingly modified and refined. In this way reconstruction rather than hindsight is perhaps to be stressed in teaching, particularly in the earlier stages.[79]

Clearly, this will only be feasible if the questions chosen for investigation are such that the pupils possess some relevant background knowledge and at least some dawning sense of appropriate expectations. So far from being a grave obstacle, however, this can be turned to good

78 For this example see Kitson-Clark, pp. 92–115.

79 This is the example referred to at the beginning of this section, of how teaching history may differ from the practice of the professional historian.

account. As was shown in section III colligation is consistent with accounts written on very different levels of generality – (and much the same is true of evidence.[80]) The higher its level of generality, the further an account is from particular evidence. Similarly, events may be more or less complex. The evidence which has to be sifted and covered to construct a colligation for the Second World War is enormous compared to that required for the sinking of the *Bismarck*. Almost inevitably, then, accounts of the more complex events will be more general and, hence, further removed from particular evidence, apart from the difficulties of sheer size.

All these considerations combine to suggest a criterion for choosing the level of generality suitable for a given group of children. It should be one where they can handle (in terms of relevant background knowledge and half-formed expectations) the evidence which the enquiry involves. The more generalised level uses as evidence the outcome of evidence used at the lower levels of generality which it should incorporate – that is, it presupposes knowledge of the conceptual and particular evidence used at those lower levels. It seems to follow that the younger the child (and thus the less he knows) the more limited in scope and the more concrete in nature the chosen enquiry should be. And since his background knowledge is likely to be heavily concentrated upon his own personal environment, if indeed it is not confined to it, there would seem to be a strong case for commencing with local studies and working through these towards matters of more general significance. The important point is that the problem is using sources is greatly eased by this approach. Local affairs obviously do not involve questions of high politics remote from the child's understanding, and a genuine study of them may be made whereas the attempt to present (say) problems of foreign policy to young pupils cannot but do violence to the complexity of the questions involved.[81] The fact that much (though not all) of the content of local studies will not be taken on to more and more sophisticated levels is not the essential point. The children are learning genuine skills of enquiry by their introduction to the use of original evidence.[82]

80 See pp. 80–81 above.

81 There is empirical evidence that children are often prematurely confronted with too high a level of generalisation in history teaching. See G. Jahoda, *Educational Review*, 1962/3.

82 An example of what is meant is briefly outlined in a short appendix.

In this way it might be possible to make use of the fertile hypothesis of Bruner when he advocated the construction of a "spiral"[83] curriculum. Arguing that each discipline has a peculiar form characterised by a set of underlying principles and key ideas, he suggests that courses should be so designed that the pupil, as he matures, constantly re-encounters these at ever growing levels of complexity. Bruner attempts an application of this model to history as follows: "If a student could grasp in its most human sense the weariness of Europe at the end of the Hundred Years' War[84] and how it created the conditions for a workable but not ideologically absolute Treaty of Westphalia, he might be better able to think about the ideological struggle of East and West — although the parallel is anything but exact."

Now this example seems faulty in that it does not represent a spirated progression at all. Allowing the rightly limited analogy to be sound, for the sake of argument, the Thirty Years' War in no way affords a simpler, less complex representation of the principle involved — namely that protracted but indecisive ideologically motivated conflicts tend towards pragmatic, "politique" solutions. On the contrary the study of what war is, is an immensely complicated task,[85] and could not be significantly undertaken at an earlier level of maturity and knowledge than that which would be appropriate to study of contemporary international relations. In fact this attempted application to history is an example, not of the spiral, but of the process discussed earlier — the helpful analogies which may be drawn between different events which are in some crucial way similar, from which sorts of comparison and helpful generalisations may be developed. Both events mentioned belong to the same level of the spiral.

Bruner's mistake is tacitly to accept the conventional view that historical education consists of the pupils coming to possess a definite and extended body of information. Because of this, chronological accident, rather than intrinsic difficulty, determines what is studied when, and any match which is achieved between the latter and the pupils' level of

---

83   J. S. Bruner, *The Process of Education*, pp. 13, 52–54.

84   Bruner, p. 25. He clearly means the Thirty Years' War.

85   This cannot be developed at length here. One point however would be to decide on the interplay between the ideological and other factors involved in the war. See G. Pagès, *La Guerre de trente ans*.

maturity is as fortuitous as it is rare. The consequence is, of course, that the earlier periods of history have to be arbitrarily simplified, often to the point of falsification, in order to be made intelligible to the younger pupils generally by a gross caricature of those aspects (for example, politics) which are too hard for them to study properly.

By accepting this linear approach to historical education Bruner adopts one which is really incompatible with his spiral model. But in doing so he nevertheless performs a valuable service by revealing what is wrong. As long as concentration was fixed on a body of information, say, English history from Alfred, the chronological approach was plausible — indeed, it looked so much the most logical that deviation from it seemed perverse. But once attention shifted to principles and key ideas as with Bruner's spiral, this plausibility vanishes. When the attempt is made to find simple manifestations of key ideas in the earlier periods, and more complex ones in the later, this usually cannot be done — as the example of the Thirty Years' War, just discussed, shows. For, of course, the later is not usually more difficult than the earlier. Medieval politics are arguably *harder* to understand than modern — quite apart from the peculiar difficulties, both linguistic and technical, that medieval sources present.

For this reason it is often held that history, unlike, say, Physics, has no structure and it might thus seem that the spiral model is inapplicable to it. But this is solely due to viewing history merely as an extended body of knowledge to be mastered. As long as this view persists it will indeed be impossible simultaneously to do justice to the material, and to respect the immaturity of (at any rate) the younger pupils. However, once attention is shifted to procedures of enquiry the matter is quite different. Throughout this section heavy stress has been laid on the necessity to use sources if history teaching is faithfully to represent the subject. This epistemological insistence is now matched to psychological imperatives by the spiral model. For, given that it is the procedures of enquiry which the pupil is to encounter at ever growing levels of complexity, it is possible to find historical material affording exercise in those principles suitable to many different levels of maturity, as in the examples already given.

On the argument so far there seem to be no criteria for choice of period since it is the skills of enquiry which have been emphasised. However, two points in the earlier discussion might suggest that the choice should favour modern history. It was argued that recent past, present and near future are not really separable and that, apart from generating conceptual frames of expectation (whose development is relatively independent of period), history offers enlightening perspectives to present problems by the particular background which study of the recent past provides. The context which gives current events much of their meaning is the perception of them as outcomes of earlier events to which they are related.

However, if this suggestion is adopted, the dangers to which Professor Oakeshott draws attention become particularly acute because of the temptation to seize upon whatever question chances to be topical and trace its background in isolation from the broad social context.

The danger can be avoided if it is remembered that developments in a field — Art, or Science, of transport — are determined partly by pressures and opportunities internal to the field itself, and partly by the elements of the general social context. Cubism is partly to be understood in terms of devleopments, technical and otherwise, within late 19th century painting, and partly in terms of social developments external to Art itself — for example, our altered conception of the mind brought about by new psychological theories: the atom bomb was the result both of the growth of scientific knowledge and of the needs of war — the latter being an especially striking example of social need determining the direction of scientific effort: development in modern transport cannot be attributed merely to the technical development of the internal combustion engine — on the contrary, that development took place within a favourable social context and would not have taken place had the context been unfavourable.[86]

In a word, no comprehensive explanation can be given in terms of crude teleogical "tunnels" which Oakeshott rightly deplored. Explanation is to be given in terms of a whole social matrix within which the full historical "contribution" to understanding is to be found in all its complex inter-relations.

But explanation need not be comprehensive in order to be useful. It was argued in section I that all significant human activities have a history and their significance cannot be fully grasped except through that history.

86 This is the objection to the "lines of development" approach — that some theme (say, transport) is selected, and its development charted as if it was a perfectly autonomous matter. "Costume (or Houses) through the ages" are popular examples of the same error.

It is now suggested, as a corollary to this, that the teaching of every subject should have an historical dimension. (The discussion of Art and Science in section I should have made this clear.) But, of course, the various subject specialists will not entertain this as their main objective and they will not, therefore, find it appropriate or practical to explore the whole, or even nearly the whole, range of connections between their subjects, other subjects, and the general social context. It is thus suggested that the role of history should be that of knitting together and fully developing the various strands of explanation which other subject courses have partially (and for their own immediate purpose, adequately) developed, showing the whole wealth and range of interconnections which exist between them, and placing the whole within the central theme of political, social and economic development — the theme of fundamental importance which will only be touched upon by the other subject courses. In this way the current objective of an integrated curriculum might be achieved while preserving the integrity of its component elements.

And this educational suggestion, of course, perfectly fits the form of narrative which characterises history, for the fitting together of related events in chains which explain them by showing their interconnections is, as has been shown, what colligation does.

Appendix. An Example of Source-based Local Studies

An attempt at a genuine historical reconstruction of life in their medium sized industrial town during some specified period in the past was made by senior primary school children. One aspect of the work may be given in illustration of the principle involved. A scale ground plan of a two-roomed house of the period was combined with information from the Census returns showing (amongst other things) the proportion of the population living in houses of various sizes. This was taken together with wages, unemployment figures, unemployment payments, supplementary grants — e.g. of clothing, information concerning diet and prices — all from official sources.[87] This was supplemented by more highly coloured material from, for example, speeches made at the time and reported in the local press. (An interesting development at a later stage might be to set

87 Obtained from Report of the Medical Officer of Health.

these accounts against others to be found in more detached (and perhaps more reliable) journals, or to test them against (for example) official figures when this was possible and appropriate.)

The reconstruction was made not only in terms of information directly obtained from the sources, but of inferences drawn from them. For example, the pupils were asked to draw up shopping lists in terms of a (rudimentary) cost of living and probable family income and in terms of the size of their families and information in the Census returns to work out in what sizes of house they would probably have lived. Then, by reference to the scale ground plan (simplified) and illustrative material concerning sanitary appointments and general state of repair, a picture could be inferred of the discomforts of living conditions.[88] Attempts could be made estimating the reliability of contemporary witnesses by reference to their professional or other interest in matters under discussion.[89]

Similar and related enquiries were mounted concerning (for example) transport, water supply, sanitation and scavenging. But enough has perhaps been said to illustrate the point.[90] The development of "spirals" from this beginning can obviously be made. For example, the period chosen was one of very heavy unemployment and this would naturally lead into a subsequent discussion of the reasons for this. This in turn would lead into more and more sophisticated explanations in terms of national, and even world, economic problems. These in turn must involve political history – and so on. In the course of the pupils' school life a comprehensive and interlocking study of the history (say) the last two hundred years can be undertaken.

88 This lends itself to modelling work; scale models of the house could be constructed and "populated" with scale people.

89 For example, one witness built up a plausible argument against more corporation housing being built on the ground that there was already a surplus of dwellings (at a time when 20,000 people were living three or more per room). It was interesting to set this argument and fact against the revelation that he was a private builder worried by the low level of corporation rents, and the number of his houses which, presumably because of their much higher rents were unlet.

90 There is a further important consideration. Most of the sources used made heavy demands upon the pupils' literacy. The question whether it might not be possible to "translate" some sources into pictorial or diagrammatic form: and if this proved feasible it would be interesting to note the improvement (if any) in the pupils' performance. An illustration of this is given below.

There is plainly no one route which must be followed, provided that
the principle of basing the work upon original sources which are multiplied
and become more complex as the pupils grow in maturity and judgement
is respected.[91] For similar reasons the approach is equally consistent with
colligation.[92] For the connections just sketched are in fact those that
reveal the logical relations of events. Building the *Queen Mary*, itself an
event made up of sub-events (such as the stoppage of work for 28 months
from December 1931), finds its place in the context of the inter-war
depression which it illustrates and of which it formed a part: and that in
turn is located within the wider framework of national and international
politics. Simultaneously, this theme connects at numerous points with
others[93] which are related, though not central, to it (just as was the case
with party opinion and foreign policy in the Suez example discussed
earlier). Each of these may be developed into a fresh colligation the whole
gradually moving towards a complete network of explanation at any
selected level.

References

ACTON, LORD. *The Cambridge Modern History – Its Origin, Authorship and Production*. C.V.P., 1907.
BROWN, R. *Explanation in Social Science*. R.K.P., 1963.
BRUNER, J. S. *The Process of Education*. Harvard, 1960; Vintage Books, 1965.
CARR, E. H. *What is History*? Macmillan, 1961; Pelican Books, 1964.
CHASTEL, A. *Studios and Styles of the Renaissance*. Thames & Hudson, 1966.
COLLINGWOOD, R. G. *The Idea of History*. O.U.P., 1945.
CONANT, J. B. *Understanding Science*. Mentor Books, 1951.
CROPLEY, A. J. *Creativity*. Longmans, 1966.

91 It will be necessary, of course, as it was in the example given for the sources
to be selected and, for the younger pupils, edited and simplified. But except perhaps
in medieval studies, selection is forced upon the professional scholar because of the
mass of material which exists. No difficulty is caused by this – provided the selection
is done in such a way that it fairly represents all the evidence available which bears
upon the investigation, whether this be living conditions in the pupils' own locality
in grandfather's day, or European capital exports in the 19th century.

92 On the role of colligation in teaching see D. Thompson, *Colligation and History Teaching*.

93 An obvious example at an elementary level would be found in the
consequences of the stoppage of work – when it has been suggested about half the
total wages of Clydebank were cut off. This in turn could be "spiralled" to more and
more general levels.

DANTO, A. C. *Analytical Philosophy of History*. C.U.P., 1965.
DEUTCH, H. C. *The Genesis of Napoleonic Imperialism*. Harvard, 1938.
DRAY, W. R. *Laws and Explanation in History*. O.U.P., 1957.
EASLEY, J. A. *Is the Teaching of Scientific Method a Significant Educational Objective?* In Scheffler, I. (ed.) *Philosophy of Education*, pp. 154–179. Boston, Allyn & Bacon, 1958.
ELTON, G. R. *The Practice of History*. Sydney University Press, 1968.
GOMBRICH, E. H. *Art and Illusion*. Phaidon, 1960.
HEXTER, J. H. *Reappraisals in History*. Longmans, 1967.
HILL, C. *Puritanism and Revolution*. Mercury Books, 1958.
HIRST, P. *Liberal Education and the Nature of Knowledge*. In Archambault, R. (ed.) *Philosophical Analysis and Education*. R.K.P., 1965.
HUTTEN, E. H. *The Ideas of Physics*. Oliver & Boyd, 1967.
JAHODA, G. *Children's Concepts of Time and History*. Educational Review, 1962/3.
KITSON-CLARK, G. *The Critical Historian*. Heinemann, 1967.
MCIVER, A. M. *Historical Explanation*. In Flew, A. G. N. (ed). *Logic and Language* second series, pp 187 – 203. Blackwell, 1961.
NAMIER, Sir L. B. *1848 – The Revolution of the Intellectuals*. O.U.P., 1946.
OAKESHOTT, M. *The Activity of Being an Historian*. In *Rationalism in Politics*. Methuen, 1962.
PAGES, G. *La Guerre de trente ans*. Paris, 1949.
TAYLOR, A. J. P. *The Origins of the Second World War*. Hamish Hamilton, 1961.
THOMPSON, D. *Colligation and History Teaching*. In Burston, W. H. and Thompson, D (eds). *Studies in the Nature and Teaching of History*. R. K. P., 1967.
THOMPSON, David. *The Arms of History*. Thames & Hudson, 1969.
WALSH, W. H. *An Introduction to the Philosophy of History*. 4th edition, Hutchinson's University Library, 1967.
WILL, F. L. *Will the Future be Like the Past?* In Flew, A. G. N. (ed). *Logic and Language*, second series. Blackwell, 1961.

MORAL PHILOSOPHY
AND MORAL EDUCATION

KEITH DIXON

> ". . . until some method of teaching virtue has been discovered, progress will have to be sought by improvement of intelligence rather than morals"
>
> (Bertrand Russell)

Part I. Can there be a philosophical basis for moral education?

1. THE TRADITIONALIST VIEW

Complaints about the insufficiency of our current moral standards make up a considerable part of the volume of lay and professional writing on the subject of moral education. Standards are alleged to be in decline; personal values are "adrift upon a sea of scepticism": a supposedly desirable communal quality of living has been superseded by mere contractual relationships and the value of persons, it is alleged, is being undermined by the depersonalising impact of a mass society. Conflict, division and uncertainty, it is felt, are characteristic of our present state. Such general allegations are often incapsulated in the slogan "the contemporary malaise" – a subject upon which it is not unknown for sociologists and social philosophers to be invited to speak. The central issue for our society is seen by critics of this persuasion as being the problem of order – not its explanation but its *defence*. And order, so the argument runs, can only be established upon the basis of normative consensus which takes into account those "tried and trusted' values which are implicit in the Western, broadly Christian, tradition.

One of the primary tasks of an educator according to this view is the transmission of traditional, intellectual and moral culture suitably interpreted, and even critically modified, in the face of continuing social change. Advocates of this "traditionalist" view press for the straightforward inculcation of a body of more or less flexible moral rules or attitudes. Emphasis is laid upon the clear-cut guidance, even the direction, of the young. When "flexibility" in moral teaching occurs it can, on this view, only be premissed upon the determinate set of moral ideals which the sceptical adolescent will come eventually to understand and to make his own. Attitudes towards youthful moral scepticism are either paternalistic or condemnatory depending upon the liberality or otherwise of the particular tradition.

Moral education is seen by the traditionalist as an *urgent* matter. Worried by what he sees as the sceptical and "morally permissive" temper of the times, the traditionalist does not believe that further critical questioning should be encouraged without limit. What is important for social and moral reasons is the *containment* of scepticism within a framework of rational or revealed moral truths.

1.1. Now clearly in labelling such general attitudes "traditionalist" I do not wish to imply that there are not marked differences in emphasis between educators who share the same general concerns. The assumptions of the "traditionalist" are complex and vary considerably according to his particular beliefs. Nevertheless, I think it useful to categorise the assumptions of an ideal-typical traditionalist since I believe that large numbers of practising teachers and educators share these assumptions either explicitly or implicitly.

Firstly, it is assumed that morality is a form of *knowledge* and that we have access to moral truths. It is held that there is an objective, often transcendent, set of moral standards for all times and all places. Such standards may not be "rigid" but they are held to be basic in the sense that they may be applied to all possible moral situations.

These moral rules or attitudes are usually Christian, frequently puritan and are often highly conventional and class-biased. The underlying assumption, rarely questioned, is that education ought to be directed towards the maintenance of a relatively morally homogeneous society. Such an assumption enables the traditionalist to use the words "moral" and "social" almost interchangeably, except in those circumstances in which social values sanctioned by law or custom clash with "transcendent" or "genuine" values. The total effect is to disguise or temper the moral authoritarianism of this view and to suggest that there already exists a widespread acceptance of "basic social norms". This latter assumption is, of course, merely persuasive; there exists no clear-cut empirical evidence to enable one to judge the degree of "basic" moral consensus.

Secondly, the analysis of society is pessimistic. Pessimism ranges from M. V. C. Jeffreys' remark: "We are witnessing the disintegration of a civilization" (Jeffreys, 1950) to less startling assertions deploring the lack of a common culture, the lack of respect for authority in general; the alleged decline in the stability and influence of the family; and the all-pervasiveness and moral degeneracy of mass culture. Such assertions are seldom supported by the relevant sociological evidence. They are more often than not regarded as self-evident.

Thirdly, advocates of traditional moral education are strongly inclined to take a tough-minded view about the indoctrination and conditioning of the young. F. W. Garforth, for example, writes: "In any society indoctrination is inevitable, necessary and desirable; the choice is not between accepting and rejecting it but between an indoctrination that is allowed to happen — a random conditioning by environment and one which is directed towards social purposes" (Garforth, 1964).

Garforth, and others like him, fail to make fully coherent the concept of "social purpose"; nor do they seem aware of the full implications of their assimilating the process of education to that of indoctrination based upon agreed social purposes.

Fourthly, there is a tendency to embrace a paradoxical view of freedom as "service" (Stenhouse, 1967). Freedom at least in one "sense" of the word is identified with "glorious liberty" (i.e. moral emancipation). There is an attempt to incorporate Christian, Humanist or conventional moral judgements into the concept of freedom. This misleading procedure often tempts advocates of a more or less morally homogeneous society to solve difficult intellectual and moral disputes by a linguistic sleight of hand.

In criticising these assumptions, I do not mean to argue that a rational case cannot be made out for the traditionalist view. What I am objecting to is the failure to elucidate and defend the philosophical and sociological bases which are held to be relevant to the educational recommendations proposed by many traditionalists. Professor R. F. Atkinson seemed to me to be right when he pointed to the existence of a conspiracy of silence amongst influential educators over the question of conceptual or empirical moral relativism (Archambault, 1965). It is to a consideration of the case for moral scepticism and moral relativism that I now wish to turn.

2. SCEPTICISM

Set against the traditionalist account of the matter are the arguments of
the moral sceptic. Beginning from the well-established fact that social
customs and moral codes are peculiar to a given culture, the sceptic is
moved to consider whether or not all moral judgements are *merely*
reflections of socially-induced and psychologically necessary subjective
dispositions or feelings. The notion of moral *knowledge*, he suggests,
disappears in the face of even the most peripheral acquaintance with
sociological and anthropological data.

But of course a careless rebuttal of moral cognitivism based upon these
simple-minded grounds will not do. The existence of "ultimate" moral
truths is clearly compatible with wide differences between actual
moralities. The sceptical thesis needs, not empirical support (although this
is always suggestive) but epistemological security. That is, the sceptic
needs to show that the possession of moral knowledge is *a priori*
impossible. In this undertaking he needs, of course, to say what is to count
as knowledge for him. A consistent sceptic, as distinct from a relativist, has
to claim, I think, that nothing whatsoever short of final and absolute
certainty, is to count as knowledge, and since absolute security of
judgement, in the sense he defines it, is simply not possible, either in the
spheres of morality, history or science, we are forced into the position of
denying that we *know* anything or can ever know anything.

Sceptical challenges to the foundations of our knowledge in general
have always been present in the history of philosophy. Indeed, it would
not be wholly untrue to say that philosophy has largely consisted of the
elaboration of sceptical challenges and the attempts to resist them.
Certainly a sceptical challenge to our commonsense or scientific
descriptions and explanations of the world leads to an increased understanding of the "presuppositions" of commonsense or science but we do
not thereby abandon attempts to understand the world or give up simple
claims to know merely because of the possibility of insecurity in our
judgements. Some of us may rely on the comforting doctrine that the false
coin of scepticism can only circulate where there is a genuine currency
(Ryle, 1954), that is, scepticism is only conceivable where there is a real
possibility of knowledge with which it can be contrasted. And however
seriously one takes the sceptical challenge one is generally content to go

about one's work unharassed by nagging assaults at the carefully constructed edifice of our knowledge.

If, however, we are only *intellectually* worried in our most abstract hours by the general problem of scepticism, why should we have to take its challenge more seriously in the field of morals?

2.1 Whatever the philosophical difficulties or mistakes implicit in the attempts to provide guarantees for our knowledge of the external world, we have at least *some* notion of what might qualify as candidates for the position of guarantor — namely, our "immediate perceptions", our memories or our introspections of our own mental processes. Further, we all do, in fact, generally agree as to the nature and existence of physical objects. We believe, unless we are mad, that the physical world exists independently of our wills, that other people see the same things that we do and that agreement about statements in the physical sciences are somehow forced upon us. Thus, as plain men we take the physical world for granted as external to us and believe that objects directly cause most of the sensations we experience. As philosophers we may argue that the sceptical question cannot be intelligently put; that the search for the foundations of our knowledge in terms of anchoring it to that which is wholly certain is misconceived or we may hold that the sceptical argument is self-refuting.

In moral matters, however, things are not so clear-cut. For here we are faced not only with empirical diversity of beliefs but by the insistent impression that values are *created* not discovered. Once we reject, or at least, question the assumption that there are absolute moral laws operating as part of the universe then the sceptical challenge presses upon us in a way we feel to be relevant to our moral practice — to our *decisions*.

For if there is an anwer in general terms to the question "What ought I (morally-speaking) to do?" which reads "It's of no consequence" or "Please yourself" then this has a more immediate impact for most people than the questions for example, "How do I know that others exist?" or "How can I be sure this desk is really here?"

We operate in the world of things, by and large, on the basis of practical certainty; in moral matters we may live with a feeling of uncertainty about the security of our judgements. And this insecurity and uncertainty is felt as *pressing* because we feel that values are made by men and that men differ in their fundamental moral evaluations.

The opponent of scepticism might well argue, however, that this "feeling of insecurity" is beside the point – even neurotic, (Holland and Harrison, 1967). We know perfectly well, it may be argued, that rape and torture are morally wrong and we regard the man who is constantly questioning his moral beliefs as being in an "ethical mess". One might not, for example, feel any more insecure in one's moral judgements than one is in accepting inductive reasoning, in spite of philosophical doubts about its status. No inductive argument can of course have the status of a deductive argument but this does not prevent us from acting in daily life upon the basis of a series of inductions, whereby one can predict the behaviour of others and oneself more or less successfully. Why should the alleged fact of values being created rather than discovered matter? Is not a claim to knowledge a matter of having rational justification and evidence for what one believes? And where the philosophical sceptic is trying to set up a paradigm of knowledge which excludes us from claiming to know, is not the moral relativist trying to reserve the concept of knowledge for application only to the physical sciences? His insecurity it can be claimed is only felt because he holds dogmatically to his own positivist metaphysic.

3. CAN THERE BE MORAL KNOWLEDGE?

There is a sense in which one can quite appropriately remark "You know what you are doing is wrong" but one needs to analyse the use of the word "know" in the context in which it is uttered.

I suppose that it is just possible for someone to understand such a remark as implying a joint "recognition" on the part of both parties to a moral discussion that there exists a body of moral law laid up, as it were, in a Platonic heaven to which both participants have special access but in such a case a claim to know these absolute moral truths would have to be rationally defended. A more plausible interpretation might credit the person to whom the remark is addressed with the belief in some generally held prima facie moral principle as "one ought to consider the interests of others" which he had neglected to apply to a relevant situation. Thus "to know" in this context could be taken to imply not that the individuals concerned had *cognised* the truth of some moral propositions but that one of them had in fact knowledge of his own beliefs which he had, for reasons of self-interest, refused, whether consciously or unconsciously to regard as relevant to his circumstances. What is implicit in the remark "You know you've done wrong" is not a statement about knowledge of right or wrong but *charge* of inconsistency. The response to such a charge might be varied, for example, as follows:

(a)   Yes, I *realise* I've done wrong, I feel great remorse.
(b)   It may *look* that way but there were circumstances you don't know about.
(c)   Nonsense, I *know* nothing of the sort.
(d)   I know I wronged him but I couldn't help it at the time.
(e)   I just couldn't have done otherwise.
(f)   Certainly I've done wrong! So what!

Each of these responses takes the utterance as a challenge and either accepts the criticism, repudiates it, or provides justifications or excuses.

If the comment "You know you've done wrong" is interpreted as "You (*and I*) know you've done wrong" then:

Response (a)   implies that both parties to the discussion acknowledge shared moral beliefs.
Response (b)   leaves open the possibility of moral consensus in the light of further discussion.
Response (c)   repudiates the suggestion of moral consensus or asks for clarification.
Response (d)   acknowledges consensus but offers an excuse.
Response (e)   acknowledges consensus but claims freedom from blame.
Response (f)   either acknowledges consensus and embraces inconsistency; questions the possible use of sanctions against his behaviour by the other; or repudiates moral terminology in a much more fundamental way.

No doubt an interpretation of "You know you've done wrong" as "*You* know you've done wrong (but I don't see it that way)" is subject to rather different interpretations of response but in each case the verb "to know" is only used to imply knowledge of *beliefs actually held* by one or both agents or refers to agreement between them as to the acceptability of certain moral principles. It is not the case that the use of the word "know" in moral contexts implies the same kind or the same degree of certainty as in statements about the colour of cornflowers or the Law of Trespass. One does not "look and see" in morals, neither does one consult authorities. One comes to a *decision* based upon more or less reasonable grounds – but there is no final court of appeal in the event of moral disagreement.

To put the point another way, it surely cannot be sufficient to argue that to know is to claim that "a particular belief we hold is a rational belief" and that the rationality of the belief can only be assessed by "those who are acquainted with the specialised procedures for establishing truth in that particular field" (Langford, 1969).

We may indeed hold for example that "X is wrong" on rational grounds yet not be prepared to assert that "we *know* X is wrong". And we may wish perhaps to withold the claim to know X is wrong precisely because we have *decided* to hold that particular moral principle or belief. Are we not justified then in feeling unhappy about dignifying our decisions with the title of knowledge?

I would want to suggest that the concepts of knowledge, truth and falsity ought not to be predicated of statements other than those which are analytic or empirical. I know that the square root of twenty-five is five, because given the axioms of arithmetic, it could not be otherwise; I know that the present Prime Minister of Britain (in August 1970) is Edward Heath because that is a fact which exists independently of my will and which I have good reasons for believing to be true. I do not know that the selling of arms to the South African government is wrong although I sincerely believe it to be so, on what are, I hope, rational grounds.

No doubt such recommendations to "restrict the concept of knowledge" will be regarded as "positivistic" − a common term of abuse in much contemporary British philosophy. Nevertheless, such a recommendation does emphasise clear distinctions between moral and other forms of discourse − distinctions which are of crucial importance in the field of moral education.

4. RESUMÉ

I have argued in rather brief compass the following:

(a)   That what I have labelled the "traditionalist" view of moral education incorporates the assumption that morality is a form of knowledge.

(b)   That the sceptic denies this and that his challenge must be taken more seriously than other possible sceptical challenges . . . since

(c)   Morality is a sphere of discourse and action which however rationally grounded rests in some sense of the word "ultimately" upon the decision of the agent rather than upon his cognition of the structure of the world . . . and hence

(d)   I wish to deny the possibility of moral *knowledge*.

5. A COMPARISON OF ATTITUDES TOWARDS MORAL EDUCATION BASED UPON A BROADLY TRADITIONALIST OR RELATIVIST VIEW

Are there, then, any necessary implications for moral education to be drawn from theories which debate the claims of morality to be a form of knowledge? Does it follow, for example, that the traditionalist is necessarily involved in a commitment to a programme of moral education whilst the relativist is not?

In my view there is no relation of strict *entailment* between the adoption of a particular philosophical stance and attitudes towards moral education although I would regard it as a very curious fact about people if there were not a contingent link between their philosophical views and their attitudes. As Renford Bambrough (1968) remarks: "Those who defend the thesis that philosophy is neutral on non-philosophical issues feel bound to conclude that philosophy is wholly irrelevant to such issues. But mutual *relevance* is not incompatible with *logical independence*" (my italics).

That is to say, it does not follow as a matter of logic that two people holding diverse philosophical positions should differ about policy recommendations. Philosophy as well as politics make strange bed-fellows when it comes to practical decision-making. Nevertheless, one could expect, other things being equal, that the holding of one belief rather than another would make a difference in most practical situations.

Let me illustrate this point further: Suppose that A holds that it is possible to know moral truths "objectively" and B denies this possibility. What are the implications for their respective attitudes towards moral education?

For the "objectivist" to be committed to moral education at least three conditions must be satisfied:

(a)   There must be objectively determinable moral propositions.

(b)   At least one person must be in possession of at least one such proposition.

(c)   Such proposition(s) ought to be taught to others.

Now clearly philosophical considerations apply only to the first of these conditions: (b) is a question of empirical fact, and (c) is a first order judgement of value.

Thus the objectivist is not *necessarily* committed to a programme of widespread moral education since he might believe either that although moral knowledge was in principle attainable, no one yet had possession of it or that, if known, moral truths should remain in the possession of an elite or cognoscenti. It is the fact that these two latter possibilities are contingently unlikely that inclines us to assume that there is a more direct link between philosophy and practice than is actually the case.

Similarly, a relativist might wish to support the teaching of a particular moral code in schools without in any way being committed to the truth of such a code. There may indeed by a tendency for objectivists to favour a movement towards moral homogeneity whilst the "open options" man may tend to favour moral pluralism but this is in no sense a logically necessary consequence of their respective beliefs.

If it is argued, however, that there are "irreducibly open options" in the field of morals at an ultimate level, then this fact has implications for the moral educator in that it commits him, if he wishes to advocate a policy of moral education, to a process of persuasion rather than instruction. R. F. Atkinson refers to the criteria for determining the validity of moral judgements as "fugitive" and he uses this assertion to distinguish between the processes of *instruction* (where the criteria for validity are public and more or less universally agreed upon) and *indoctrination* where they are not. Atkinson takes the line that the slippery nature of moral criteria is a consequence of the conceptual point that the first principles of morality are not susceptible to proof. He writes: "Morality is not unique in that its first principles are not susceptible to proof. What distinguishes morality from the formal and natural sciences is that in it different and opposed first principles are readily conceivable by morally serious people." (Archanbault, 1965).

It seems to me that Atkinson is correct in maintaining that the "open options" moral educator is committed in the last resort to a process of persuasion if he wishes to teach particular substantive beliefs. I would, however, want to resist his use of the word "indoctrination" simply on the grounds that it carries with it unsavoury associations of brain-washing and is often used in opposition to the word "rational". The fact that a

relativist may hold that moral disagreement is *in the last resort* not capable
of rational solution does not, so it seems to me, preclude the application
of such notions as consistency of judgement and the giving of reasons for
preferring one course of action to another. The word "indoctrination"
carries with it notions of lack of respect for reasons and evidence. The
word "persuasion" is perhaps more neutral since one can persuade others
by appeals to common humanity and rational considerations (in so far as
this is possible) as well as by conditioning them to respond in certain
desired ways.

6. A PROPOSED SOLUTION TO THE OBJECTIVIST-RELATIVIST DILEMMA: CAN WE TEACH VALIDATED MORAL PROCEDURES? (DIXON, 1968)

It is widely felt that moral education is at present very much an ad hoc
business and that one of the aims of education ought to be to encourage
the direction of intelligence towards the consideration of moral problems.
Liberal-minded educators, such as John Wilson and his associates, for
example, are very conscious of the fact that whilst a cognitivist
or "objectivist" stance towards moral education may tend to encourage
uncritical acceptance or, through a process of counter-suggestion,
uncritical rejection of traditional values, moral relativism may tend
towards the encouragement of irrationalism or mere emotivism Thus
cognitivism is conceived of as positive but indoctrinatory whilst relativism
is seen as liberal but negative. It is important to stress, however, the
repeated use of the words "may tend to" and "encourage" in this context
for as I have tried to insist, there is no question of the logical entailment of
practical policies from philosophical premises without the intrusion of
extra-philosophical assumptions. Nevertheless, Wilson is right in
contrasting two sets of attitudes towards moral education one of which is
conceived as "hammering home what we already know to be true", the
other which regards moral education with "the suspicion attached to
brain-washing or totalitarianism". And these attitudes do contingently
relate to the philosophical positions which are held by educators. Is there
then a resolution of this problem which would allow of a positive element
in the teaching of morality but safeguard pupils or students from the
possibility of indoctrination? It has been widely suggested that there is

such a resolution – one which recommends the teaching of validated moral procedures.

6.1. It is possible to argue that although we may differ from others in many of our actual moral judgements, there may be an area common to all possible moral judgements which may be taught without reservation. That is to say, if we could locate a number of principles which were implied by the activity of talking to others in a serious way about moral problems then we could rule out certain substantive judgements as being immoral simply because they denied the basis upon which moral discussion takes place. Not only would the location and description of such principles be useful to the moral educationist but it would at the same time refute the relativist.

At least one important version of the relativist case current in post-war analytic philosophy implied that ultimately one could choose to "say what one liked in moral terms" (Ayer, 1946; Stevenson, 1944, 1963). According to this theory, all moral judgements could be separated into two broad dimensions – questions of fact and questions of value (accompanied perhaps by a recommendation or command to act). Where moral disagreements occurred, then, there were two possibilities – either disagreement about the *facts* relevant to the judgement – (in which case the dispute was in principle resolvable) – or the disagreement about the value element. In the latter case, one could argue about the *inconsistency* of a man's evaluations but one could not refute them by reason alone. Where clashes of value occurred, one had to turn to force, persuasion, or an inescapable intellectual tolerance of the opinion of one's moral antagonists.

This view allowed the consistent fanatic a well-defined place in the moral arena. Faced with the spectacle of consistent racists there was nothing one could do but thank God there weren't too many of them (Hare, 1952, 1963). One could not deny their opinions the status of moral views although one could quite properly *feel* that they were wrong and try to persuade them to change their views by seeking to extend their sympathies and expose possible formal deficiencies in their argument. If then there was to be no question of "ultimate" justification in moral matters – and many critics were already questioning the *meaning* of such a phrase – then a coherent, philosophical rationale for moral education, it was thought, could not be given.

Nevertheless, a large and influential section of moral philosophers were not prepared to accept that the traditional questions of ethics could be resolved in such a way. They wished to preserve the "place of reason in ethics"; to deny that moral disagreements, however fundamental, were not resolvable in principle and to claim that certain substantive judgements could be ruled out of court as candidates for the status of distinctively *moral* judgements.

6.2. An ingenious answer to the relativists was suggested by Karl Popper, in a series of seminars held in London, and developed later by A. P. Griffiths and and R. S. Peters(Dixon, 1968).

Briefly, their particular theory gives sense to demands for the "ultimate justification" of moral judgements by accepting that a further rational standard *is* required but it sees this standard as operating both within and outside moral discourse. The autonomy of morals is preserved by making moral discourse, in some sense, *self-justifying*. That is, the rational standards appealed to in justifying particular judgements are implicit in the very existence of the discourse. A demand is put in the form: "Either accept certain basic presuppositions or reject the discourse itself."

I cannot here discuss the detailed arguments developed, largely by A. P. Griffiths, to support this case but perhaps an analogy used both by Griffiths and R. S. Peters will make the point clearer. In astrological discourse, for example, if one wishes to make a statement: "Gemini subjects born with the Moon in Virgo are likely to be dominant, slightly paranoid, and excitable" one needs to assent to the general proposition "The stars and planets affect human behaviour." If this latter proposition is rejected then astrology is rejected as a valid and serious activity. Or again, if one rejects the formal principle of non-contradiction one is thereby excluded from participating in logical discourse since what is rejected constitutes the necessary conditions of consistent argument.

The propositions: "The stars influence human behaviour" and "A cannot be both B and not B" are statements within separate discourses but they also appear to be external presuppositions of their respective discourses. Is it not possible then to discover such principles in moral discourse?

A hint of what these principles might be was given in Karl Popper's *Open Society*, vol. II, chapter 24. Popper (1962) writes:

"The fact that the rationalist attitude considers the argument rather than the person arguing is of far reaching importance. It leads to the view that we must recognize everybody with whom we communicate as a potential source of argument and of reasonable information; it thus establishes what may be described as the rational unity of mankind."

One should note here I think the enormous width of the gap between the claim that one ought to recognize and consider the interest of one's *immediate* moral interlocutor and the claim that one ought to make a prime facie assumption about the rational unity of mankind. Nothing is established by this argument alone.

A similar view was expressed by Benn and Peters (1959) in chapter III of *Social Principles and the Democratic State*. They write:

"If we are prepared to attend seriously to what another person has to say, whatever his personal or social attributes, we must have at least a minimal respect for him as the source of argument."

Benn and Peters go on to argue that seriously committed moral philosophers (and presumably others interested in morality) *must* demand reasons for accepting rules. They write:

"It is surely *illogical* for a man who is seriously interested in giving reasons for rules to consider any particular person's interests as being more important than anyone else's unless good reasons can be shown for making such a distinction."

The consummation of this process of argument leads to the following assertion:

"In our view the impartial consideration of the interests affected by rules is basic to morality. This is a purely procedural criterion; for it does not dictate which rules are right and wrong, only how to set about deciding whether a rule is right or wrong."

It can be successfully argued against Benn and Peters, however, that they tended to confuse the procedural principle – the principle of universalisation or impartiality necessary to any rule-following discourse whatever with a substantive principle of impartiality with respect to the interest of all: indeed in *Social Principles and the Democratic State* there is a general tendency to blur this distinction between impartiality of *application* of a principle and the principle of impartial *consideration* of the interest of all others.

This deficiency however has been remedied in Peters more recent work (Peters, 1966) where he suggests that a substantive principle of impartial consideration of interests might be "transcendentally deduced" in the manner previously illustrated. That is, if moral argument is to take place between people seriously interested in resolving difficult problems of conduct then having treated them in *argument* with respect and consideration, it seems inconsistent to ignore their interests or the interests of people like them when one is making moral decisions. Thus, if one engages in moral argument, so it is alleged, one is committed to a general principle of benevolence or tolerance, for example, in virtue of this very fact.

The great difficulty in this argument, however, has always seemed to me that already briefly referred to in querying Popper's original formulation. That is, the recognition of one's immediate moral interlocutors as persons for whom one shows respect does not entail that one ought to respect *all* persons in the same way. No doubt the transcendental argument applies to the cases where one ignores the interests of people one had previously chosen to regard as rational agents whose interests ought to be considered. Clearly, there is some formal inconsistency here. But what is to prevent me from restricting the range of persons whom I regard as rational agents, and whose views and interests I am prepared to consider, to a select few (say members of the Aristotelian Society). The recognition of the interests of members of such a group emphatically does not imply the recognition of an indefinite number of possible rational agents unless I make some tacit moral generalisation that members of the Aristotelian Society deserve respect for their interests and opinions, in virtue of their being human and for no other reason. What the transcendental deduction may show is that I must, to be consistent, treat moral philosophers, or other men whose opinion I respect, with consideration. It does not establish the necessity for *universal* consideration of interests — but that is what is at issue!

There is a second objection to the use of the transcendental argument in relation to moral education. A logically impeccable move from formal, procedural principles to *any* substantive moral rule truly represents a "Copernican revolution" in *ethics*. But the "transcendental deduction" of such substantive principles can only establish such a link (if it can) between procedural principles and substantive principles of a very high order of generality indeed. Moral principles are on this view *ceteris paribus* principles; that is, they pick out the morally relevant features of a situation.

They are not axioms in a deductive system of morality and thus they cannot determine the weighting given to the moral rules which are relevant in any given situation. I may, if the transcendental deduction is valid, assert a *ceteris paribus* principle of liberty or benevolence but the command "Don't interfere with the liberty of others, other things being equal" is relatively empty of content if we are interested primarily in deciding a particular issue or determining a general moral policy. The application of the moral proceduralist view to moral education is thus subject to two principal objections:

First, it is a matter of controversy at the philosophical level as I have tried to demonstrate; and secondly, it is uninformative in moral *substance* at anything but a very high level of generality.

These two objections do not necessarily invalidate the transcendental argument. They do, however, tell strongly against its utilization as a theoretical ground for a particular form of moral education. No doubt we should teach children to be reasonable, kind and tolerant. Possibly we may have "ultimate" grounds for maintaining this. But such matters are marginal to the problems of moral education — for it is what is to count as tolerance, reasonableness and kindness in complex moral and social situations, that argument centres around. A marginally substantive moral proceduralism can say little to us in *this* respect.

It can, however, be argued that the teaching of moral procedures validated by a transcendental deduction at least offers us a framework within which substantive discussion can take place.

That is, the proceduralist may argue for a programme of moral education organised around certain "philosophically-guaranteed" high-level moral principles and certain procedures which are held to be essential to a definition of what it is to make a moral judgement. Into this framework can be fitted, as far as is consistent with a child's or student's development, the fullest possible range of relevant factual data so that he or she may grasp the technique of seeing what is *relevant* in coming to a moral decision. I shall explore the possibility of "defining moral discourse" a little later but for the moment I want merely to note that the proceduralist position is "essentialist" — that is, it is assumed that morality is a logically independent sphere of discourse and action which can be marked off in a determinate way from other spheres. Moral judgements it is implied are arrived at and criticised by sets of procedures which can be conveyed in the same way as the rules of a game like chess. One can, it is believed, teach the *form* of morality without dictating anything but a minimal content, which outlaws so-called "fanatical" views.

6.3. Now it appears to me that these arguments clearly tell against the implementation of a naive traditionalist form of moral education. The advocacy of moral proceduralism is an attempt to insist that all education must incorporate critical, rational standards and to claim that such standards are implicit in moral discourse as well as in particular curriculum subjects. Moral proceduralism thus acts as a useful and very necessary check upon the enthusiasms of the traditionalist or moral innovator. What I object to, however, is the suggestion that it is possible to locate and teach the essential, fully validated, elements of the logic of moral judgements.

Karl Popper has written of the 'sin of essentialism' that it involves the assumption that there is only one "real" or "fully rational" definition of a concept, and it seems to me that much recent work in the philosophy of education on "*the* concept of education" or "*the* concept of morality" has been dangerously close to sin in this respect. I do not believe that one can define what morality (essentially) is. What one can do is to suggest the existence of certain differences whether substantive or procedural, between different or allied discourses, to defend one's distinctions rationally and to base practical recommendations upon one's arguments. But central to such processes is a *judgement of value*. Argument about the definition of the moral is always, so it seems to me, moral argument. In stating our views about what is to count as moral education we are in fact committed to certain substantive beliefs. But these beliefs cannot be guaranteed – they are always open to challenge. Similarly, our views as to the procedures involved in coming to a moral decision are equally challengeable. If we believe that moral activity is rule-governed then our concept of what it is to morally-educate will be radically different from that of an existentialist with his concentration upon the elaboration of the particular.

7. NO PHILOSOPHICAL GUARANTEES

If the foregoing analysis is correct, then, there can be no "philosophically-grounded" final basis for moral education. Nevertheless, it may be argued, educators are involved, whether they like it or not, in the process of moral education at all levels in the educational hierarchy.

And if certain brands of sceptically-minded philosophers refuse to provide the "right kind of basis" then educators might be excused for feeling it necessary to 'shop around' for a more usable product or else object that philosophy is sterile and hairsplitting anyway, leading only to a series of complicated, negative statements which are entirely unhelpful.

Now whilst I can sympathise with these attitudes in some respects I would not for one moment wish to defend them or even tolerate them. I want to maintain most strongly that philosophy, if it is to be of service to educationists, must be true to its own analytic insights. Philosophy cannot provide the guarantees that so many educationists look to it to provide. And no matter how imperative the demands made upon philosophers of education to translate their analyses into recommendations which bear a philosophical seal of approval, they ought, in my view, to be resisted.

What can be done honestly, however, is to separate analysis, as far as is conceptually possible, from the recommendations which individual philosophers might make in virtue of their interest in and concern with educational issues. Such recommendations will, of course, be philosophically informed but they will not be value-free.

Part II. Teaching Moral Understanding

8. THE ADOPTION OF RELATIVISM AS A POLICY

What I have to say about teaching moral understanding does not depend upon the acceptance of a relativist position in a philosophical sense of the word. In any liberal programme of moral education one surely has to take account of *empirical* differences between people on questions of value, irrespective of any commitment to a particular philosophical position.

Let me illustrate this point further: Opinions as to what is involved in understanding a moral judgement may vary according to one's meta-moral position. Such positions may range between moral scepticism and moral absolutism, broadly as follows:

(a)   Moral scepticism: there are no formal or substantive requirements for admittance to the status of the "moral" since all criteria are philosophically suspect. Alternatively, it may be suggested, moral judgements are reducible to judgements within other discourses (e.g. the political or the prudential).

(b)   There are various *formal* criteria for admittance to the status of the moral (e.g. the principle of universalisation; the requirement that ethical principles provide "reasons for action", i.e. they must be both theoretical and practical).

(c)   Moral utterances are merely expressions of emotions and/or commands to others to act in certain ways.

(d)   There are various formal criteria for admittance (as in (b)) together with a number of high level, *ceteris paribus* substantive requirements — principles which operate both within and outside moral discourse. (Such principles are deduced via the "transcendental argument" previously referred to.)

(e)   There is a relation (either of entailment or some less stringent relation) between man's desires, needs, or wants, and his moral judgements. Hence to understand a moral judgement is to understand that morality is based upon the concept of a common human nature.

(f)   There is no way of understanding a moral judgement except in terms of coming to "see" that it qualifies as such via a detailed examination of the *particular* context in which the judgement is made. Here the model is a cognitive one — one comes, as it were, to "recognise" the moral properties inherent in particular actions.

(g)   There are a number of absolute moral propositions or decrees grounded in religious experience or beliefs or by the opinions of the wise tested through time which define morality in clear substantive terms.

For the purposes of instituting a programme for moral education in schools and colleges, however, one need not, fortunately, resolve these complicated problems. For clearly in providing guide-lines for teachers to assess whether individual pupils are in fact coming to see what is involved in moral discourse certain of these positions may be ruled out since they imply the acceptance of substantive judgements which all teachers do not necessarily share. One cannot assume identity of religious belief, coherence of intuition, similar assessment of what are men's needs or wants, identical views of what is natural to man, or common agreement upon what constitutes happiness or the greatest good.

Any programme concerned with fostering an understanding of morality should, as I see it, aim at adumbrating *minimally acceptable* criteria for the definition of the moral, not because these criteria may be philosophically guaranteed but because they have to be offered as a framework to teachers, parents, pupils and students with a wide divergence of actual beliefs. And even if there *was* a high degree of consensus amongst all these groups it might be thought desirable as a part of a liberal education, not to pre-empt the *possibility* of moral divergency by building into a programme of moral education a strong substantive bias.

The attraction of a relativistic framework, combined with the insistence that certain *formal* criteria need to be satisfied for a moral judgement to qualify as such, is clearly that it protects the pupils from the possibility of indoctrination. Clearly, indoctrination will tend to occur on an ad hoc basis. There is however, no need to give philosophical support to such a process; rather the aim should be to protect the pupil via the *tactical* acceptance of a relativistic view of ethics.

Problems, however, do arise if the relativistic framework is adopted in handling the problem of racial prejudice and discrimination. Clearly one wants either to rule out statements of racial antagonism as unacceptable as candidates for the role of moral judgements, or one wants to resist them as being "immoral" and "beyond toleration", in the sense that expressed disagreement over the norms of sexual behaviour are not. A useful philosophical dodge here would be to argue that the racialist point of view is incompatible with the *substantive* principle of universalisation in that it is manifestly contrary to a precondition of serious moral discussion, i.e. the equality of respect for all sources of opinion.

I do not feel inclined to accept this contention. Consistent racism so it seems to me can, though with difficulty, be maintained as a possible moral view. If one wishes to rule this out by introducing a substantive requirement into the definition of morality, then the "flood-gates" question arises with particular force. The use of the transcendental argument, of course, is an attempt to introduce well-defined and minimal substantive requirements within a definition of the moral in order to avoid just this kind of problem.

My personal view, however, is that rather than attach any programme, as it were, to a particular philosophical masthead, it would be better to adopt the relativistic framework whilst making an *ad hoc exception* in the case of racism on the grounds that informed opinion and the existence of legal sanctions rule out the acceptance of this particular viewpoint in schools. One could make the further point that the identification of "racial" minorities in schools would lead to undesirable *practical* consequences for individual children within these groups. Thus, the promulgation of racism might be denied on the basis that it is more than expressed *opinion*.

This recommendation is of course thoroughly unsatisfactory and invites criticism of the abandonment of the ideal of moral neutrality in this particular area. (Why not others? – especially in sexual morality.) Nevertheless, to make a philosophically arbitrary exception on "racial" questions might be better than to accept the necessity to introduce substantive requirements into the definition of the moral.

The point is academic; nevertheless, it seems of critical importance in practice in view of the necessity of safeguarding a stance of moral neutrality.

9. THE IDENTIFICATION OF MORAL DISCOURSE

If the aim of moral education is to widen and deepen moral understanding then one needs to locate an area of language and behaviour which can be properly identified as "moral". I have tried previously to point out the difficulties in any specifically philosophical attempt to define the "essence" of morality, or to chart its conceptual boundaries. In what follows, therefore, I shall try to present a view of the nature of moral discourse which is consistent with the ordinary usage of the term by educated men, leaving aside the problem of identifying or defining this particular class. I do not claim, however, that my analysis is the only possible one consistent with our ordinary beliefs when we seek to appraise human conduct or decide what we ought to do. I want merely to suggest a framework for the teaching of moral understanding which is consistent with a wide range of substantive moral views and so I have tended to concentrate upon suggesting a number of *formal* criteria which enable us to distinguish the moral from other allied fields of discourse.

Perhaps it is necessary to go further and explore the connection between our moral judgements and concepts of welfare, harm happiness or mental health but to do so would in my view invite the kind of substantive controversy which I think ought to be avoided if possible in setting out the definition of the moral. To define the moral, as I have argued previously, is in fact to engage in moral argument even at the procedural level. But to confine oneself to the procedural questions is perhaps more conducive to a maximum degree of consensus within which a thousand substantive blooms may flourish. Whilst admitting then that the setting out of allegedly formal criteria may in fact prove to be influenced by my own broadly liberal values, I propose to enter the arena.

9.1. Using educated common usage as a basis one may certainly distinguish what morality is not; it is not, for example, commonly regarded as being exclusively defined by political, legal, aesthetic or prudential judgements nor by judgements of taste. A political judgement, for example, takes the form of a means – end hypothetical statement of the kind – "If you want end X then pursue means Y", together with an assessment of the appropriate end(s) to be taken as politically given, in terms of a relatively known or unknown system of power-relations. There is no imperative demand within political discourse to give equal weight to all representation of opinion – politics is the art of the possible – where the possibilities envisaged are determined by the relative powerfulness or otherwise of interested parties.

Similarly, legal discourse depends in the last analysis upon the acceptance as binding of a system of authority which promulgates the law or endorses, through its decision in the courts, customary practice. Criticisms of particular laws, within a *strictly* legal context centres around concepts such as validity and legitimation, not those of justice and morality. Thus, the question "Why ought I to do X?" can be answered by the statement "Because the law requires it." The further question "Why ought I to do what the law requires?" can only be taken to mean in a legal context "How do I identify valid laws?" and not "How am I to tell if the laws are just?" Answers to the question "Why ought I to do X?" are, in a strictly legal context, to be answered (and *fully* answered) by quoting the relevant decree together with its source of legitimation. Further, legal rules are both more restricted and wider in their scope than moral rules since they do not apply to all behaviour and yet apply to behaviour which is morally indifferent (e.g. the law sets out procedures whereby a statement is to be regarded technically as a "Will").

Consideration of legal and political discourse raises the question of what role moral judgements play in our language. At least part of their function is to enable one to answer the question "Why do X rather than Y?" without restricting the answers to particular fields of practical reasoning such as the legal, the political and the prudential. We wish to have a form of discourse in which we may be free to quote considerations which over-ride all others.

Now it may be claimed that this function of moral language as providing a means to discuss over-riding reasons for action is not the only one. There is a vocabulary of morals which enables us to speak of the *worth* of an agent in terms of his motives, intentions, and purposes rather than strictly in terms of his behaviour. We sometimes evaluate people as "good" in spite of their actions. Nevertheless, if a man were never to act and give reasons for his action, one could not evaluate him as a moral agent.

Further to assess a man as a purely political animal is usually to criticise him for restricting the scope of his evaluations — which taken over time make him what he is, morally speaking. Moral language permits us *to challenge such a restriction of scope* whether this is done in a particular judgement or whether it is exhibited in a general disposition to ignore certain kinds of considerations as relevant.

I want to assert that moral discourse is distinguishable from other discourses within the genus "practical reason" by insisting that its function is to enable us to challenge the restriction of considerations to such particular factors as power, the law, or self-interest. Nevertheless, I want to argue that appeals to such factors are perfectly permissible within a moral context — the difference being that here one must argue that they are over-riding. Thus, if someone were to be seen to act only upon the basis of self-interest, then he could quite properly be challenged on the grounds that he was restricting his range of considerations too narrowly; nevertheless, he would not logically be precluded from arguing that questions of self-interest were over-riding in considering what one ought to do.

Further, and more centrally, I do not think that it is, in principle, possible or desirable to list those features of moral discourse which constitute the necessary and sufficient conditions governing the identification of moral judgements. I want, however, to go further than Wittgenstein who suggested that particular instances of generic terms bear only "family resemblances" to each other. I shall not be unduly worried, however, if someone produces a particular and valid counter-example to my choice of "over-ridingness" as the main distinguishing feature of moral discourse. I do want to say, however, that there must exist "paradigm cases" of the application of the word moral, which exhibit the features of over-

F *

ridingness, universalisation, and publicity. It may be the case that everything we wish to count as a moral judgement may not satisfy all the possible criteria I am about to discuss, nevertheless, that they must satisfy at least some of the criteria is a condition of their correct (linguistic) application.

9.2. Having made that point, I now wish to argue, in the full knowledge that particular moral judgements are often exceedingly complex and difficult to analyse at a level of generality, that any moral judgement may be governed by principles. That is, I want to claim that moral judgements must have universality or application.

One needs to distinguish, as is customary, two interpretations of *the principle of universalisation – one formal; the other substantive*. Clearly, in any rule-following discourse whatever, one needs to adopt a formal principle of universalisation to safeguard consistency. One is "*logically* obliged to make the same judgement in another situation which is similar in all relevant aspects" – on the pain of a charge of inconsistency. Now clearly each situation is in a certain sense unique in that the configuration of circumstances peculiar to a particular moral judgement is unlikely to recur. Nevertheless, a moral principle or set of principles draws attention to what is regarded as morally relevant circumstances. Thus, via the application of moral principles different situations may be represented as being similar in all *relevant* respects. Part of moral education may be seen as a search for an increasingly subtle range of principles which properly distinguish or assimilate diverse particular situations. Further, universalisation may enable one to see moral dilemmas in terms of evaluating the primacy of one moral consideration over another. Thus, there might emerge a whole category of judgements in which the central problem was to decide about the relative weightings to be given (say) to the principles of equality and freedom.

Thus, the formal principle of universalisation enables one to draw implications from one judgement to another similar in kind. (In my view, literature may operate as a morally-educative form by filling out in a fictional context the general implications of particular moral dilemmas – although it is rarely aesthetically desirable to state these implications formally!)

The substantive version of the universalisation principle, however, is employed to suggest that moral discourse is characterised by the necessary acceptance of certain substantive and highly general principles such as those of freedom, benevolence and equal consideration of interests.

Now it seems clear to me that a distinction between moral discourse and prudential discourse *as examplified in ordinary usage* does require the acceptance of such substantive principles of the kind indicated. Nevertheless, it is possible to maintain that moral judgements may in fact be *reducible* to prudential judgements; that is, judgements about what I ought to do could be answered simply in terms of what is in my own interests without reference to the interests of others. The fact that the substantive principle of universality rules out this possibility *a priori* inclines me to reject it as a *necessary condition* of a definition of the moral. It is merely a contingent fact that most people use the word moral to refer specifically to considerations of the interest of *others*.

One can, I think pretty briefly indicate the relevance of at least two other necessary features of moral discourse – firstly, that moral judgements must rest upon the basis of certain shared linguistic assumptions (i.e. there must be some publicly recognised criteria for what constitutes the moral) and secondly, that an assessment of the behavioural consequences of any proposed course of action is necessary to the proper definition of the moral.

Clearly ineffable, mystical or purely private judgements are, by definition, non-communicable and hence of no assistance in guiding practical conduct. "I saw Eternity the other night" is not a candidate for the status of a moral proposition, since moral judgements can only be made within a "community' : that is, a group of people in which there is a minimal agreement upon the importance of answers to the question "What ought I to do" within the context of a shared symbolic apparatus for expressing answers to such questions.

Finally, the behavioural consequences of action must be relevant to the definition of the moral since omission of such factors renders morality either a purely theoretical set of beliefs or removes it from this world altogether through the postulation of a non-behavioural concept of the "good will".

9.3. Moral discourse cannot be uniquely identified by isolating a distinguishing set of necessary and sufficient conditions. Nevertheless, a range of criteria which taken together constitute a paradigm for the application of moral concepts may be usefully compiled.

These are (or may be) as follows:

(a)   The discourse is a species of the genus "practical reasoning" — the function of moral discourse being to guide action by *providing reasons for choosing one course of action rather than another*. What is to count as a moral reason for action is left open.

(b)   Behavioural consequences are relevant to the definition of the moral.

(c)   In connection with (a) moral terms may be seen as over-riding. Moral language is used to *challenge* the restriction of considerations to (say) such factors as power or self-interest. Such challenges however may be properly resisted.

(d)   Moral judgements are universalisable in a formal sense.

(e)   Moral judgements must be communicable, i.e. subject to analysis and criticism in terms of shared linguistic assumptions and a consensus on the importance of choice in practical conduct.

10. MORALITY AND EDUCATION

Within a community such as a school or a college of education, most of what goes on under the general heading of moral education seems to me to be merely the attempt to show that "morality" (as defined by those in authority in these institutions) *pays*. That is, pupils and students are taught by and large that it is in their own self-interest to accept the codes of conduct prevalent in these institutions. Clearly this is not necessarily a bad thing. Learning to consider one's own interest is just as important in education as learning to read and write. Indeed it might be argued that the rational pursuit of self-interest in a world (hypothetically) governed by a more or less equal distribution of power would very rapidly realise what are now considered to be Utopian social advances. The fact that honesty is very often the best policy is not a morally discreditable reason for recommending people to be honest. Thus, in spite of the remonstrances of idealists, many practising teachers imply by their routine behaviour in the classroom that it *pays* to be fair, kind and honest and to consider the interests of others.

Unfortunately, however, two considerations prevent one from being wholly enthusiastic about the teaching of prudence to the young. The first is that the morality which pays off within an educational institution is likely to be both highly restricted in its content and class-biased — far too concerned with the rules relating to the maintenance of social order. Secondly, not only is the content of morality restricted but the implicit recommendation to do what is in one's own interest tends to reduce the concept of morality too readily to the concept of prudence.

Thus, in my view there needs to be introduced into the curriculum of schools and colleges self-conscious programmes which aim at enlarging the range of moral issues with which the pupil is presented and extending his appreciation of the *variety of evaluations* which exist in the world outside of British educational establishments.

Concomitant with the introduction of range and variety there needs to be some analysis — sometimes at a very simple level — which enables the children and students to distinguish the boundaries of legal, political, prudential, and moral judgements and to examine their inter-relationships according to the analysis I have presented.

No moral judgements can be made on a rational basis, however, without access to the relevant factual background and it is here perhaps that the introduction of courses in the social sciences alongside History and English on a widespread basis in the schools and colleges is of paramount importance.

Finally, any self-conscious programme of moral education ought to incorporate techniques of discussion and ways of presenting relevant information which will protect the pupil from indoctrination.

Such a programme is as I understand it already underway and although its aims are not necessarily wholly akin to my aims, the spirit of tolerance and respect for evidence which informs it seem to me to be wholly admirable. I refer to the Humanities Curriculum Project, under the direction of Lawrence Stenhouse.

10.1. No programme of liberal moral education can be introduced into the schools and colleges overnight. The changes in curriculum structure implied by such far-reaching proposals will inevitably be resisted — and properly resisted if this means that education in such a sensitive area is given time to develop as a properly organised, intellectually coherent activity with appropriate safeguards incorporated to protect the pupil against indoctrination or heavily biased presentation of evidence. But again, inevitably, the introduction of courses aimed at improving moral understanding will have many unintended consequences — for the authority-structure of the schools, for relationships with parents and for the self-consciousness of teachers within their institutions. Clearly, a programme of moral education based upon pluralistic and relativist notions must push our education system in a more open and more egalitarian direction just as a programme based on the transmission of "established" values would tend to reinforce the status quo. Thus, even a recommendation to concentrate upon the teaching of formal criteria for the identification of the moral and to insist upon the availability of as much relevant evidence as possible is to encourage a moral stance which is in itself likely to lead to innovation in both individual beliefs and in the structure and style of educational life.

Nevertheless, I would not want to recommend a programme of moral education as part of a radical or libertarian ideology. I would prefer the declared aim of educators in this field to be as neutral as possible with respect to different substantive moral views, although the aim of "ultimate" neutrality in moral matters seems self-defeating. For the ideal of neutrality in this area, is, as I conceive it consistent with the general intellectual justification for the process of education. That is, a stance of academic neutrality encourages objectivity of judgement based upon rational considerations, and leads to the "improvement of intelligence" both in the sense of clarity of mind and the consideration of relevant information.

References

ARCHAMBAULT, R. D., (ed.) (1965) *Philosophical Analysis and Education.* Routledge & Kegan Paul. Article by R. F. Atkinson, Instruction and indoctrination, pp. 176–82.

AYER, A. J., (1946) *Language, Truth and Logic*, 2nd edition. Gollancz.

BAMBROUGH, R., (1968) *Reason, Truth and God*. Methuen.

BENN, S. I. and PETERS, R. S., (1959) *Social Principles and the Democratic State*. Allen & Unwin.

DIXON, K., (1968) On teaching moral procedures. *British Journal of Educational Studies*, No. 1, Feb. 1968.

GARFORTH, F. W., (1964) Article in *Education for Teaching*.

HARE, R. M., (1952) *The Language of Morals*. Oxford Univ. Press.

HARE, R. M., (1963) *Freedom and Reason*. Oxford Univ. Press.

HOLLAND, R. F., and HARRISON, J. (1967) Moral scepticism. *Proc. Arist. Soc. Supp.* 41, 185–214.

JEFFREYS, M. V. C., (1950) *Glaucon*. Pitman.

LANGFORD, G., (1969) *Philosophy and Education*. MacMillan.

POPPER, K., (1962) *The Open Society and its Enemies* vol. II, ch. 24. Routledge & Kegan Paul. Revised Edition.

RYLE, G., (1954) *Dilemmas*, ch. 7, p. 94. Cambridge University Press.
STENHOUSE, L., (ed.) (1967) *Discipline in Schools*. Pergamon Press. Article by K.
    Dixon, Discipline, freedom and the justification of punishment, pp. 163–93.
STEVENSON, C. L., (1944) *Ethics and Language*. Yale Univ. Press.
STEVENSON, C. L., (1963) *Facts and Values*. Yale Univ. Press.

Further Reading

ATKINSON, R. F., (1969) *Conduct: An Introduction to Moral Philosophy*. Basic
    Books in Education. MacMillan.
PETERS, R. S., (1966) *Ethics and Education*. Allen & Unwin.
PETERS, R. S., (ed.) (1967) *The Concept of Education*. Routledge & Kegan Paul.
WILSON, J., (1969) *Moral Education and the Curriculum*. Pergamon.
WILSON, J., WILLIAMS, N., and SUGARMAN, B., (1967) *Introduction to Moral
    Education*. Penguin Books.

THE EXPLANATION OF LEARNING

ALFRED DAVEY

SOME theory concerning the nature of the human organism and how it learns is central to what teachers do in the classroom Every teacher has a theory about learning even though he may not be able to verbalise it too well or explain how he came by it. Without some theory of why children behave as they do the teacher would find himself presenting his pupils with no more than a series of ad hoc, time filling tasks. Few teachers would be prepared to concede that no purpose informed their classroom practices, that they were directionless and that they entertained no expectations as to their outcomes. A teacher may have a variety of goals, to create a new society, to enrich the lives of the children he teaches, to be better than his colleagues or simply "to fill their empty little heads". Whatever his aims he wants to get things done, he wants to bring about some change. Unless he had some theory, however simple, about the efficacy of his actions in relationship to his goals he would find himself unable to operate. The question which has to be answered however, is how far is his theory of learning tenable? (held, maintained, defended)

Now, the attempt to develop a comprehensive theory of learning has been one of the major areas of activity in psychology since the turn of the century and our understanding of what goes on when a child learns is largely the result of these research endeavours. Nevertheless, it must be admitted from the beginning that there is still no single theory of learning which commands universal support and in its present state learning theory is still a long way from being able to give confident answers to all the questions which professional educators would like to see answered. The major purpose of theory construction is to place the observed facts of learning into a coherent order so that we may understand what learning is and why it works in the way it does, but, as we shall see, the facts of learning have proved to be very difficult to come by It is hoped, however, that an understanding of the problems of constructing an adequate theory

165

of learning and how they have been tackled may help teachers in their own attempts at explaining the phenomenon they witness each day. It may, after all, be of some value to know that no one now imagines that the explanation of learning is going to be a simple matter and that all the problems of education are not going to be solved "if only we had better teachers".

Learned or innate?

Although psychologists may disagree as to what behaviour is learned and what is innate, and certainly disagree as to how a piece of behaviour comes to be learned, none of them question that the principles of learning are the basic conceptual tools in their explanatory armoury. It is not difficult to see why this should be so. From earliest infancy the child is subjected to a training process designed to make him acceptable to his parents and ultimately to society. He is taught when to eat, sleep and defecate. He is taught the language, attitudes and values appropriate to his culture. He is taught how to read, write, calculate and how to earn his living. There appears to be no area of his life into which learning does not enter. Even that most private and intimate part of his being which seems peculiarly his own, his concept of himself, is learned from the reactions of others.

However, the ubiquitous nature of learning does not mean that nothing of importance for the determination of behaviour is inherited, or that the mind can be regarded as John Locke's *tabula rasa*. Few psychologists would now be prepared to subscribe to J.B. Watson's (1930) assertion:

"Give me a dozen healthy infants, well formed and my own special world to bring them up in and I'll guarantee to take any one at random and train him to become any kind of specialist I might select – doctor, lawyer, artist, merchant-chief and, yes, beggarman and thief regardless of his talents, penchants, tendencies, abilities, vocations and the race of his ancestors."

The properties of the organism must be taken into account. Simple native responses and the primary appetitive states of hunger, thirst, and sex are the starting points of learning and the inherited structure of the organism determines its limits. To be sure, the environment acts on the organism but the organism acts on the environment and, in so doing, changes it. This interaction sets a problem of such complexity that considerable experimental sophistication is required to determine the learned and innate components in relatively simple pieces of behaviour. The problem is not solved by cutting the Gordian knot and designating some behaviour as instinctive and other types entirely as learned, although this move has been made by some theorists in the past and the term instinct is still used liberally in everyday explanations of behaviour. It is said, for example, that a mother has an instinct to care for her child, a man to fight and a bird to build a nest. The justification for implying that these vastly different kinds of behaviour are all capable of the same kind of explanation is that it is assumed that they all emerged full blown on the first appropriate occasion without previous training or practice. The concept appears attractive since it postulates an irreducible minimum beyond which no further explanation needs to be sought. As we shall see, it is difficult to define learning with any precision but the enterprise may seem more worth while if we begin by blocking up this bolt hole.

As an explanatory move the concept of instinct suffers from a number of serious defects. It groups together into a single category a wide range of different types of behaviour which share no positive characteristics beyond being arbitrarily excluded from the category "learned", thereby blurring individual differences in adaptation. For example, there is now a considerable body of evidence which suggests that learning accounts for many intra-species differences in courting and mating behaviour which the older theorists universally regarded as instinctive. It has been observed, for example, that sexually inexperienced bulls attempt to mount non-receptive heifers while the experienced bull mounts only those in heat. Other investigators noted that in male apes, as in many human males, effective copulation develops gradually through practice. Female apes often find it necessary to assist their inexperienced consort in their sexual role.

In addition to the problems created by the discordant empirical evidence, the concept is a poor analytical device since it is defined to correspond precisely to the type of activity it seeks to explain. Consequently, there has been a tendency to manufacture particular instincts in an ad hoc fashion to explain any piece of behaviour which resisted other modes of explanation. The position was admirably summarised by Holt (1931)·

"Man is impelled to action by his instincts, it is said. If he goes with his fellows it is the herd instinct which impels him, if he walks alone it is his anti-social instinct. If he fights it is his pugnacity instinct, if he defers to another it is his self abasement instinct. If he twiddles his thumbs it is the thumb-twiddling instinct. Thus everything is explained with the facility of magic — word magic."

The resuscitation of instinct as an explanatory device by the ethologists such as Lorenz and Tinbergen has not fundamentally changed the notion of instinct as action-specific energy which is released and directed by external stimuli. Both Lorenz and Tinbergen are satisfied that instinct is a sensible concept to apply to men but none of their examples provide more than analogies between the behaviour of some men and some animals. Indeed, the concept of instinct as a drive passing through predetermined channels and so taking the organism inexorably towards a particular consummatory act, far from explaining the behaviour of men is hardly adequate for explaining the seemingly spontaneous behaviour of organisms well down the phylogenetic scale. Studies of worker bees, for example, suggest that the tasks carried out by the individual bee are not determined by the bee's physiological condition but by the needs of the colony at a particular time. In the hive, the worker seldom carries out the complete, correct, and uninterrupted sequence of all cell building behaviour. She is capable of doing a task from any part of the sequence of construction as and when required. She may begin a cell with her own wax, put the finishing touches to a cell with wax provided by another bee or with the wax taken from an old cell no longer in use. All this is done between duties of an entirely different kind, storing nectar, feeding larvae or attending to the queen. Such flexible behaviour would require us to postulate alternative drive channels of almost unlimited elaboration.

When applied to human behaviour the crude morphology learned — instinctive is even more artificial. The human infant comes into the world with a number of physiological needs and a few sensory-motor reflexes such as crying, breathing and swallowing as the means of satisfying them. He has, however, a drive to preserve himself and master his environment. He reacts actively to the wealth of visual, auditory and tactile stimuli which impinge upon him and his primary needs and fixed responses rapidly become incorporated into patterns of learned behaviour. Very soon he learns that some of his actions are associated with the alleviation of discomfort and he strives to imitate his previously successful actions. He no longer waits for the onset of stomach contractions before engaging in the appropriate adaptive behaviour. Instead it is cued off by the sight of the bottle, the preparations for feeding, or the mother herself. Increasingly the child's actions become part of a learned goal directed sequence.

When all the theories of instinct are shorn of their speculative physiology we are left with the core concept of the internally motivated drive. If no more were implied by the term it would be innocuous but of little operational value. The problem is not to explain why organisms are active. An organism is always active even when it is asleep. Activity is one of the defining characteristics of life. The reason why organisms are active lies in the properties of living tissue. This may be a question for the biologist but it is not one psychologists need to answer. The psychologist's task is not to explain activity but the patterning of activity, in terms of the state of the organism and a particular environmental situation.

To object to the notion of instinct then is not to maintain that all behaviour is learned. To describe behaviour as learned has no more explanatory value than to say that it is innate. At best this dichotomy can only result in a rough classification with a heterogenous collection of behaviours in each class. The objection is rather that intra-species behaviour appears to be too variable to be accounted for in terms of fixed mechanisms. Some account of how these mechanisms are employed to bring about individual differences in adaptation and response would seem to be a necessary part of any comprehensive theory of behaviour.

Facts and Theories

Perhaps the greatest obstacle to the understanding of learning theory for those outside the magic circle of theorists is not its complexity but its apparent redundancy. All of us have benefitted from some form of learning and most of us have deliberately taught someone something at one time or another without troubling ourselves too much about the nature of the process. There appears to be no need for *theories* about learning when the *facts* about learning have become known through everyday experience. *A priori* notions about learning validated by unaided observation have given some practitioners an enviable certainty.

It is a mistake, however, to regard factual statements as discrete and separable from theoretical statements. When we talk about "getting down to hard facts", we imply that facts are somehow solid and immutable. But tangible objects and observable events are not facts, they are merely objects and events. They remain objects and events until some statement concerning their nature or relationships is made about them. It is not sufficient that we should all see, feel and touch real objects or witness events, we must find a statement about them to which we can give our assent. The facts are the agreed meaning which those objects and events come to have.

Even a simple descriptive statement such as the cat is on the mat involves not only a proposition about the order of things which we usually find it sensible to test but also a considerable degree of abstraction. The statement ignores all sorts of things about the cat, such as its size, colour and posture and concentrates on the essential features which constitute its "cattiness" and the animal's relationships to its immediate environment. Now since we can choose which objects and events shall be the subjects of our statements and moreover, what aspects of those objects and events shall form the basis of our agreed statement it follows that facts are not immutable. What are considered to be *the* facts about a situation can change as those in accord shift or sharpen the focus of their observation, reconsider their methods of validation and re-work their conceptual schemata.

Prior to the publication of Copernicus's *De Revolutionibus Orbium Caelestium* in 1543 it was a fact that the sun revolved around the earth. Moreover, it remained a fact for the Roman Catholic Church for some time after this. Or, to take an example more germane to our present discussion, it was a fact for Victorian educationalists that all children, other than imbeciles and those that were insane, could learn if they wanted to and therefore the amount they learned would be in direct proportion to the amount of effort expended by the teacher. Payment by results was logically contingent on this agreed view of the child's nature.

However, for a statement to achieve the status of a scientific fact there must be an agreement of a particular kind. It is not sufficient that there should be a concordance of opinion or even a concordance of opinion amongst the leading authorities in a particular field of enquiry. As Peters (1959) has pointed out, science is basically anti-authoritarian. A scientist "believes that bodies fall at a certain rate to the ground not because

Galileo or anyone else said so but because experiments can be performed which convince him that what Galileo said was true". In other words, the prior condition for universal agreement is reproducibility. The facts of science have nothing to do with unique occurrences, however many witnesses there may have been to that occurrence. The facts of science are those events that different observers at different times and places can experience as the same if a certain prescription is followed.

For example, if a person is given a mild electric shock he will sweat slightly and the amount he sweats can be measured. If a subject is given a shock every time he reads the word 'cow', after repeated pairings of the word and the shock the subject will come to sweat for the word alone even though no further shocks are received. In reporting such an experiment, the psychologist is not assuming that he is telling you something remarkable either about himself or his subject, he is asserting that this conditioned reflex can be established by anyone with other subjects at anytime under the same conditions. He is assuming that his experiment – the pairing of a conditioned stimulus with an unconditioned stimulus and the resulting new connection between stimulus and response – is a particular instance of a general and repeatable event.

In brief, we can say that the fundamental conditions of agreement in behavioural science, as in any other, are objectivity and reproducibility. The credentials of the data gathering must be presented and the results established to be independent of chance. Of course, this prescription rules out many of the classroom observations and experiences which teachers employ as evidence for their personal theories of learning. The behavioural scientist in his quest for facts tends to mistrust uncontrolled observations because he is aware that we so often see what we expect to see. A teacher, as a result of his success with a new method of teaching a subject, may become convinced that it is superior to the old method. But he may have found the new method more congenial or more in accord with his beliefs. As a result, he now teaches with more enthusiasm, is more lavish in his praise and becomes more tolerant of error. These are excellent reasons why he should continue with the new approach but there is no reason to suppose that he has discovered a new principle of learning. Without fairly elaborate precautions it becomes impossible to separate the differences produced by the new method from the differences produced by the improved quality of the teacher–pupil relationship.

This is not to say that classroom observations cannot become facts and be put to good use in the development of an adequate theory of learning providing that the teacher is prepared to accept the same constraints as the behavioural scientist regarding what he looks at, how he looks and what he records. This is not easy because of the complexity of factors in everyday learning situations. In order to identify the reasons or causes for what he observes the experimenter attempts to hold all factors constant except the one chosen as the *independent variable*. This could be amount of reward. He varies it in a predetermined manner and measures the effect on the *dependent variable*, which could be the speed or correctness of the subject's response. It is unusual to be able to control all the potential sources of variation under classroom conditions so as to obtain un-ambiguous results. But it is precisely this difficulty which can make the informed teacher's observations so valuable. Although laboratory studies of learning have the advantages of control and objectivity they typically concern single variables employed out of context. They can seldom give direct answers as to how the variables orchestrate together in context. The usual context for children's learning is not an isolated laboratory cubicle, but a web of social relationships, parent − child, teacher − child, child − child. Within this web of relationships the learners will be differentially orientated towards learning. Some children will feel happy and secure while others are lonely and frustrated. Most will be more concerned about what Bill or Sue thinks about them than by any desire for technical competence. Teachers are specialists in the transmitting of skills and information in their natural context and their observations and records can be important for originating and setting the problems for scientific enquiry. The very feature which excludes their observations from the realm of scientific fact accounts for their success in providing creative ideas for research. The value of classroom observation lies in the questions it raises.

However, if the teacher's questions and observations are to be pertinent and critical he must be aware of the problem which faces the theorist and the rules of the game which he plays. Nothing is to be gained by complaining about the theorist's pig-headed indifference to the facts of learning if the teacher and theorist are not talking about the same thing. Conversely nothing is to be gained by theorists ignoring the problems of practical men.

Before we consider some of the explanations of learning which theorists have proposed and the differences which exist between them, it must be emphasised that all theorists accept all the facts as we have defined fact. All of them work within the same logic of experimentation, so that although some findings are contested when they are first announced, once their status as facts is established, all accept them however inconvenient for their own particular theory these new facts may be. Unless the predictions can be shown to follow uniquely from the terms of a particular theory, and learning theory has rarely been sufficiently rigorous for this, the fresh evidence is rephrased and incorporated into the language of other theories.

The search for the crucial experiment in learning which would establish one theory as correct and every other theory as wrong has proved quite illusory. Nevertheless, although it is true that with sufficient ingenuity one can transpose one theory into the language of another it might prove to be an extremely clumsy and unconvincing way of saying the same thing. An essential requirement for any theory is that it should conform to the principle of parsimony, sometimes called William of Occam's razor.

Essentially this states that when more than one explanation is possible the simplest is to be preferred. The principle helps to dislodge those theories with insufficient empirical support and acts as a spur to scientific advance. The burden of proof is on those who maintain their more complex theory is necessary. It is up to them to find some evidence which requires it. Established theories are not displaced by contradictory facts but only by superior — and often simpler — theories. If a theory has constantly to be elaborated because of fresh facts produced outside itself there will be a loss of confidence in its usefulness and it will eventually die of neglect. As Hebb (1958) puts it: "What we need from a theory is that it should hold together long enough to lead us to a better one."

What is Learning?

The problem about learning, of course, is that it is not a fact as we have defined fact. Various activities can be denoted as learned such as memorizing a list of words, riding a bicycle, or managing a cocktail party, but there is no agreed statement as to what learning is. What actually happens when an organism learns is not easy to define. Reciting a list of words with fewer and fewer errors or getting better at bicycling, or managing cocktail parties are not learning. These are merely changes in performance. The learning has gone on elsewhere at some other time. The difficulty lies in the fact that whereas performance is observable and empirical, learning is not, learning is an inference from changes in performance. Only confusion can result from a failure to distinguish learning from performance. Factors which disrupt the one may facilitate the other. An actor may not welcome the presence of others when he is learning his lines but an audience will certainly enhance his performance.

Most attempts to define learning take account of the necessity of inferring learning from changes in performance, but they run into difficulties because learning is not the only prior condition which can be inferred from such changes. Performance can change as the subject grows older, because he is fatigued, has lost his motivation or from some temporary indisposition brought about by drugs or illness. Two moves are possible. Either, the theorist can attempt to specify all the changes in behaviour which are not learned and leave learning as a residual effect or, he can attempt to denote those behavioural changes which he desires to be called learned.

If we consider the wide diversity of situations in which organisms can be observed and the number of different responses which can be made, it is obvious that neither of these strategies will be successful unless types of behaviour can be specified which are less numerous than the situations they are designed to explain. Moreover, as we saw from our discussion on the concept of instinct it is no less difficult to state the defining characteristics of non-learned changes in behaviour than those assumed to be learned. In both cases the type of change and their correlated antecedents must be stated.

This places the learning theoriest in an embarrassing position as McGeoch and Irion (1952) point out. He wishes to study the conditions under which learning occurs and to establish functional relationships between the conditions and the learning process but, strictly speaking, he cannot study the learning process at all unless he makes a preliminary statement of the conditions of learning for definitional purposes. By making such a statement he may define away part of his area of study. If, for example, the theorist defines learning as those changes in response which occur when some state of need has been reduced or satisfied he has settled forever the question of whether learning can take place in the absence of reward. If it is subsequently demonstrated that changes in behaviour occur by the mere repetition or contiguity of stimulus and response, he must either deny that the observed changes are learning or believe that some undetected reward followed the response.

Few theorists find the lack of an agreed definition of learning a cause for embarrassment. Quite logically it can be argued that a definition is the terminating point of an enquiry not its beginning. Most of them would agree with Hilgard's (1951) opinion:

"A precise definition of learning is not necessary, so long as we agree that the inference to learning is made from changes in performance that are the result of training or experience, as distinguished from changes such as growth or fatigue and from changes attributable to the temporary state of the learner. The experiments themselves define the field ostensibly."

This is all right, as far as it goes. Learning is, more or less, defined as some state of the organism which intervenes between certain events, such as training, and subsequent changes in performance but plainly the statement leaves a considerable area open to dispute. This is where theory steps in. Learning theories are attempts to specify the environmental conditions, here collectively referred to as training and experience, that determine the changes in behaviour and to formulate the nature if the interrelationship between the two sets of variables.

The issues which divide the various theorists can be subsumed under these two headings, differences concerning the environmental conditions assumed to be necessary for hypothetical learning changes to take place, and differences in intervening variables, or concepts, employed to represent the postulated changes within the organism.

If we follow Spence's (1951) classification and divide the rival theories according to necessary environmental conditions we get three groups. First, there are those which hold that the connection between a particular environmental event, the stimulus, and the subsequent behaviour, the response, has to be reinforced or rewarded for learning to occur. That is, we learn what proves to be satisfying. These can be designated reinforcement or law of effect theorists. Secondly, there are those that believe reinforcement is not necessary for learning, that the mere contiguity of stimulus and response is sufficient. Doing is learning could be said to be the principal view of these contiguity theorists. Finally, there is a third group, the two-factor theorists, who assume that there are basically two different learning processes, one governed by the principle of reinforcement and the other occurring independently of reinforcement.

Alternatively, if we choose to divide the theorists according to which type of intervening variable they favour we get two groups, the stimulus-response theorists and the cognitive theorists. The S—R theorists prefer to explain learning in terms of stimulus-response connections, variously referred to as habits, bonds or associations. The cognitive theorists, on the other hand, freely infer such cognitive processes as intentions, expectancies and insight. However, since as Spence points out, the majority of the cognitive theorists support the non-reinforcement position, or regard reinforcement as only marginally important, and the majority of S—R connectionists accept reinforcement as a basic law of learning, it will be sufficient for our purposes to consider theorists as belonging to either the connectionist or the cognitive groups.

It must be understood that while it is convenient to treat the various theories as belonging to one of these families, the distinction is based on a broad approach to learning problems. Some issues cut across the boundary. It is, for example, impossible for any theorist, whether or not he acknowledges the law of effect, not to make some statement about reinforcement. It cannot be doubted that rewards "work". They are the tools of the pedagogue's trade. How a theorist considers their work depends on his basic orientation. Gutherie, a connectionist, who maintains that the basic condition of learning is the strict temporal contiguity of stimulus and response, sees reward as "safeguarding" the S—R connection. Tolman, a cognitive theorist, considers that learning consists in the formation of hypotheses concerning "what leads to what" and that reward confirms the learner's expectations or hunches.

To understand the more subtle differences between contemporary learning theories one must acquire a greater familiarity with their formal characteristics than can be provided here. We will not be able to examine every aspect of the controversy which divides the theorists but we can become aware of the major questions on which they differ. Many of the disputes between theorists are internal ones and not always important in relation to immediate practical outcomes. Our plan will be to select representative experiments from each group to get an idea of what each has achieved and to attempt to extract principles of learning which can be of some practical value. We will see that while some experiments increase our understanding of successful learning, others are more useful for explaining why some of our learning and teaching goes wrong.

The Connectionist View of Learning

First, let us consider the empirical foundations of the connectionist viewpoint. The essential notions underlying S–R theory can be briefly stated. Whether of the reinforcement or the contiguity type, the aim of S–R theory is to account for learned behaviour in terms of relatively simple mechanical links between inputs at one end and outputs at the other, without recourse to cognitive events such as "desires", "intentions" or "expectations" which are regarded as inaccessible and unverifiable. Instead, changes in performance are accounted for in terms of the increased probability of certain movements occurring, given certain stimuli or distinctive cues.

That is to say, these theories attempt to account for the behaviour both of men and animals in terms of "associations". These associations are not as in the older associationism between ideas and impressions but between stimuli and responses. In the same way that the older associationist tried to explain complex mental events as the compounding of elementary sensory impressions, so the S–R theorist seeks to understand complex behaviour as the mechanical compounding of simple S–R units.

Two major figures in the early development of the S–R position have left an indelible mark both on learning theory and the methods by which the fundamental nature of learning is studied. Thorndike (1932) systematically applied associationist ideas about learning to animals escaping from puzzle boxes. Pavlov (1927) developed the conditioned response paradigm of learning.

The type of theory which Thorndike came to evolve was based on his famous experiments with cats in puzzle boxes. The boxes were constructed so that the door would open when some concealed mechanism was operated by a latch on a loop of string from inside the box. A young, hungry cat was confined in the box and set the problem of reaching the food on view outside. The time he took to secure his release was carefully noted. At first there was a great deal of wild biting and clawing but sooner or later one of these random movements operated the catch. The cat was allowed to eat a little food but was returned to the box while still hungry.

Once the animal had secured his release in this way there was an increasing tendency for the successful action to be repeated. Slowly the time taken to secure release declined until the escape procedure was immediate and stereotyped.

It was this gradualness that suggested to Thorndike that the animal did not understand how he brought about his release but achieved it by a process of trial and error. By dint of repeated attempts the successful movements were stamped in and the unsuccessful ones stamped out. Contained within this relatively simple experimental situation are three of the elements which all S–R theorists have felt compelled to juggle with, motivation, reward and continuity. It is understandable how motivation and reward came to dominate interpretations of findings derived from this type of experimental technique when we consider the important part played by each factor in the situation.

The motivation of the subject (here achieved by food deprivation) appeared to be essential for the production of the repertoire of responses from which the desired ones were ultimately to be selected. Secondly, the consequences of the responses, reward or punishment, success or failure, bears some relationship to the selection process. Satisfying effects strengthen the S–R bond, unsatisfying effects weaken it. Finally most S–R theorists (the notable exception being Guthrie (1935)) have come to favour the principle of continuity since learning appears to involve the slow building up of S–R connections over many trials, whereas the cognitive theoriest alleges there are sharp discontinuities in the pattern of response as the animal shifts *systematically* from one mode of behaviour to another or achieves insight into the problem. We shall have more to say about this when we come to examine the cognitive theorists' position.

Thorndike became convinced, contrary to popular belief at the time, that animal learning was not mediated by knowledge or ideas. Moreover, the data from note memory experiment such as those conducted by Ebbinghaus (1885) led him to believe that the same mechanical compounding of S–R bonds was fundamental to human learning also. Thorndike embodied this view of learning in a number of statements which he considered to be laws; that is to say, statements concerning regular and predictable relationships among empirical phenomena. The most important of these was the Law of Effect which refers to the strengthening or weakening of a connection as a result of its consequences.

When a S–R connection is followed by satisfactory consequences the strength of the connection is said to be increased; if a connection is made and followed by an annoying state of affairs its strength is said to be decreased. In its original form the law was open to the behaviouristic objection that "satisfying" and "annoying" were purely subjective terms since there was no way of establishing from the outside what state the animal was in. In response to his critics Thorndike put his definition in operational terms.

"By a satisfying state of affairs is meant one which the animal does nothing to avoid, often doing things which would maintain or renew it. By an annoying state of affairs is meant one which the animal does nothing to preserve, often doing things which put an end to it."

This does not answer another objection to the Law of Effect that is, that it is circular. Surely we can only tell whether or not a given consequence is satisfying by observing whether or not the animal repeats the response that produced the alleged reward? In effect we are saying an animal likes a food if he comes back for more and we explain the coming back for more by saying that he likes it! However, subscribers to the Law of Effect argue that the circle is not a vicious one since we can easily discover in the first instance what state of affairs are reinforcing by seeing what connections were strengthened and then go on to predict what connections would be strengthened in future. This is a perfectly legitimate move provided we are sufficiently precise in our specification of the state of affairs in question.

The implications of the law, however, reach further than this. Thorndike wished to deny that learning by continuity of stimulus and response was possible Mere repetition achieves little. Practice alone does not make perfect.

"When the law of effect is omitted [he wrote in his *Psychology of Learning* (1913)], when habit formation is reduced to the supposed effect of mere repetition – two results are almost certain. By the resulting theory little in human behaviour can be explained by the law of habit; and by the resulting practice unproductive or extremely wasteful forms of drill are encouraged."

Thorndike is one of the few theorists who make a determined attempt to apply his findings to learning as it occurs in schools, but his insistence that elementary S–R bonds were the foundations of learning and that these were formed by trial and error behaviour without the intervention of ideas had unfortunate consequences in an educational world which was already convinced of the efficacy of mental drill.

On the positive side Thorndike's emphasis on regulated practice and the measurement of its outcome led to a great improvement in the teaching of the basic educational skills in schools. After all, if you believe that learning begins in random behaviour from which the successful actions are selected by a survival of the fittest, it does not follow that you need to stand by and watch the learner thrash around. By analysing complex skills into separated distinguishable and comprehensible parts one can see to it that there are only a limited number of connections or S–R bonds which can be made. Consider, for example, all the complications in the teaching of reading. What is it fundamentally that the child must be taught? Thorndike's answer was simple, "words". But not all words are equally important. The array can be drastically reduced. Thorndike tabulated thousands of printed words from newspapers, magazines and other sources and arranged them according to their frequency of appearance. The most common words were offered to teachers in vocabulary tests, dictionaries and controlled vocabulary readers as the words which, above all, the child most needed to understand. Similarly, the language of arithmetic can be reduced to 390 number bonds involving the four rules and the numbers 0 to 9, thus rendering basic arithmetic amenable to teaching methods based on the law of effect.

Thorndike's matter-of-fact conception of learning provided the teacher with straight forward rules as to what to look for and what to do. However, his emphasis on the mechanical compounding of S–R bonds led to the subordination of understanding to drill, habit and memory in schools. Thorndike did not deny insight to man, but he did regard him primarily as an "associative mechanism", with the result that many teachers came to see their pupils in this way rather than as organisers of their own experiences.

Those behaviouristically inclined psychologists who were impressed with the performance of Thorndike's cats were even more impressed by the behaviour of Pavlov's dogs. Pavlov was fundamentally a connectionist in outlook and his concept of "reflexes in the brain" seem to provide a respectable physiological underpinning to associationist ideas about learning. Watson (1919) saw the conditioned reflex as the basic unit of behaviour and complex acts were considered to be chains of conditioned responses. Although no contemporary theorist would describe himself as a Pavlovian these early experiments have persisted as major points of reference in all later theorising. The basic facts of conditioning are now well known but perhaps a brief description would be in order to introduce the terminology and the concepts.

The basis of Pavlov's experiments was the already well-established phenomenon that certain stimuli regularly produce reflex action. A light flashed into the eyes causes pupillary contraction, a tap on the patella tendon causes the knee to jerk, food in the mouth produces salivation. These natural reflexes are called *unconditioned reflexes* (UR) and the stimuli which evokes them *unconditioned stimuli* (US). Now, if a second stimulus, such as a bell or the beat of a metronome is regularly presented just before or accompanying the US it comes to elicit the response when presented alone. This second stimulus is called the *conditioned stimulus* (CS) and the learned response the *conditioned reflex* (CR). In other words, if a dog sees food its mouth waters. If a metronome is always started just before the food is seen, then after a while the saliva will begin to flow when the metronome is heard even though no food is given. The behaviour which was originally a response to food has become a response to the metronome.

This can be condensed into a simple diagrammatic form:

During training

Metronome (CS) ———————————→ alerting behaviour (UR)
  paired with
Food (US) ———————————→ salivation (UR)

After training

Metronome (CS) ———————————→ salivation (CR)

Thus we now have the following series:

Metronome (CS)→Salivation (CR)→Food (US)→Eating (UR)

In this series the US and the UR are termed the *reinforcement*.

If the conditioned stimulus is repeatedly presented alone and not reinforced the CR weakens and eventually disappears altogether and *extinction* is said to have taken place. Extinction, however, should not be equated with forgetting; it is more like learning not to respond. The conditioned response after a few pairings of the CS with the US will soon revive and in any case will revive if a short rest follows extinction.

Pavlov went on to show how the twin processes, generalisation and discrimination, which are fundamental to all learning can be achieved by this technique. Let us take generalisation first. No two stimuli are precisely alike. The objects which we respond to in our daily lives are all unique relationships of colour, size, shape and other attributes. Even the same object will have its stimulus properties transformed by changes in the lighting conditions or with changes in its spatial relationship to ourselves. But if we live in a constantly changing world, how is it that we are not overwhelmed by the uniqueness of all things? The answer, of course, lies in our ability to generalise, to respond to new stimuli in accordance with the similarities they share with familiar ones. Only because we can perceive that the past has something in common with the present is it possible to learn at all. The ability to generalise lies both behind the young child's response of "Doggy" when any four legged furry object appears and the most sophisticated scientific observations regarding the relationships between social and physical phenomena.

Pavlov found very early in his experiments that a new stimulus not previously reinforced would elicit the conditioned or learned response the first time it was presented, the probability that it would do so increasing with the degree of similarity to the conditioned stimulus that had been reinforced. For example, if a dog has been trained to salivate to a metronome beating a hundred times a minute the dog would also salivate for 90 beats per minute or 110 beats per minute. 80 beats or 120 beats per minute would also produce the conditioned response but of a lesser magnitude.

Conversely, Pavlov discovered that by a process of *differential reinforcement* an animal can be trained to make quite fine discriminations between stimuli. For example, if a dog has been taught to salivate in response to a circle, he will by virtue of stimulus generalisation also salivate for an ellipse. If Pavlov continued to deliver food with the circle but not with the ellipse the dog soon learned to salivate for the circle alone. The dog's discrimination was tested further by making the ellipse more and more circular. The dog continued to discriminate successfully until the ratio between vertical and horizontal axes of the ellipse reached 9:8. At this point the animal became extremely disturbed and excited and responded at random to either the circle or the ellipse. Moreover, the whole of his previous training became disorganised and he appeared to be unable to re-learn even the simplest discriminations.

This condition, brought about by the conflict in the animal over whether or not to respond has since been demonstrated by a number of other experimenters. Masserman (1943) trained cats to eat from a box when a buzzer sounded. When the response to the buzzer was well established the cats began to encounter a sharp blast of air in their faces when they attempted to eat from the box. Frightened by the blast of air and wanting the food, the cats found themselves in an insoluble approach-avoidance situation and exhibited extremely disturbed behaviour. Masserman noted that much of the cats experimentally induced behaviour was similar to the neurotic behaviour of human beings. It was stereotyped and compulsive. At the signal some cats buried their faces in the box, making no attempt to eat, others sought to escape always by the same route even when they had to cross an electrically charged grill. Outside the experimental situation their behaviour was regressive, they mewed like kittens and courted affection. But, as with Pavlov's dogs, the most notable feature of their behaviour was the failure to relearn. Prolonged rest would reduce the fear of the food box on a first trial but fear would return on the next trial even although the cat had suffered no blast of air. Cats starved themselves within sight of an appetising and harmless food box.

There are, of course, differences between the disturbed behaviour of animals in limited experimental situations and the rich variety of neuroses which human beings are capable of producing, the most obvious difference being that people can find conflict in situations far removed from the area of the original experience. Nevertheless, psychologists such as Eysenck (1960) who regard neurotic symptoms as a learned pattern of nonadaptive behaviour which can be understood without reference to unconscious causes, have made extensive use of the Pavlovian paradigm both in their explanations and therapeutic techniques.

The failure to relearn is a feature of all untreated neurotic conditions. It is arguable that the sufferer fails to discriminate between the fear evoking situations in childhood and situations which approximate to them in later life. People who have phobias about cats, dogs, enclosed spaces and other harmless stimuli may have acquired them in the same manner as young

Albert in the now famous demonstration of Watson and Rayner (1920). Albert, a nine-month-old infant, was allowed to become acquainted with a white rat. Later, each time the rat appeared the experimenters made a loud noise behind Albert which made him cry. After pairing the rat with a harsh noise about five times the experimenters found that the sight of the rat alone would cause Albert to cry, Moreover, he cried whenever he saw other furry animals.

If we substitute the Pavlovian terminology as follows:

Rat (CS)→Stroking or (CR)→Noise (US)→Fear (UR) reaching which becomes after conditioning

Rat (CS)→Fear (CR)

we have a model of how any type of phobic anxiety might be acquired. Because conditioned responses generalise in the manner demonstrated by Pavlov, any object or situation which resembles the original fear evoking stimulus will have the power to give rise to anxiety. The sufferer shrinks from such situations and therefore does not give himself the opportunity to learn that the situation is no longer a punishing one. Masserman's cats need never have felt another puff of wind, but they starved within sight of the food box. The neurotic adopts various strategies, rationalisations and functional ailments to keep him out of what he believes to be punishing or fearful situations and these become deeply embedded in his personality structure.

Learning to have a phobia may be regarded as a highly specialised form of learning, but learning by stimulus substitution occurs in the lives of all of us although rarely as the result of deliberate teaching. Usually it occurs because some temporary or permanent regularity in our environmental conditions brings about the repeated pairing of some chance stimulus with another (the unconditioned stimulus) which naturally generates some diffuse emotional response. People who have had many unpleasant injections may become fearful at the sight of a syringe, a particular scent may evoke pleasurable nostalgia independently of the wearer, or the mother's footstep may become the signal for the infant's smile. Many children refuse to go to bed without a particular stuffed toy, a piece of fluffy blanket or some other stray object which by dint of its repeated association with the pleasurable embracing warmth of the bed has itself become a comforter.

Despite the widespread occurrence of conditioned responses in everyday life it is extremely doubtful if we would be justified in regarding the Pavlovian paradigm as the prototype for all learning.

The examples given above have one important characteristic in common, they all concern diffuse, involuntary responses. What Pavlov's experiments essentially demonstrate is the passive establishment, by temporal contiguity, of a connection between an inborn reflexive response and a new stimulus. The animals were not required to co-operate in any way with the proceedings. They were isolated in a sound-proof laboratory and rendered immobile by a harness so that no irrelevant stimuli or random responses should interfere with establishing the unnatural connection. Food appeared at a standard time interval whether or not the dog responded and after many pairings of the metronome and food he began to salivate in anticipation. He had to.

Choice and motivation play no part in reflex responses. The knee jerks, the pupil contracts and glands secrete their juices whenever the appropriate stimuli are present quite independently of the organism's intentions or drives. But it is yet to be convincingly shown that voluntary acts like reading or writing can be conditioned in this way. Habits composed of voluntary movements are not stimulus bound. Going to bed is a much practised and reinforced habit for most of us but we do not undress every time we see a bed.

In essence what Pavlov had discovered was learning by contiguity and repetition, but long before this the associationists had shown that if two elements, A and B, were constantly and contiguously related in the mind the presentation of A would call up the image of B. Pavlov's experiments could be said to be the most elaborate demonstration of learning by contiguity ever staged. However, it is not necessary to accept Pavlov's methods in toto to accept the importance of the principles he characterised. Phenomena such as reinforcement, extinction, generalisation and discrimination which play important parts in learning also show up in the much simpler type of conditioning demonstrated by B. F. Skinner (1938, 1953).

Skinner, unlike a number of other theorists, holds the view that Thorndike's Law of Effect learning and Pavlov's conditioning cannot be reduced to a single set of laws since they are concerned with two different classes of responses. Skinner distinguishes between responses which are elicited by known stimuli, such as a blink to a puff of air or a startled reaction to a loud noise, and those which are not called forth by a stimulus but are spontaneously and randomly emitted. The first class he designates *respondents* and the second group he calls *operants*. It is largely from the second class of response that he believes our habitual pattern of behaviour is fashioned. Respondents he considers to be acquired according to the principles of Pavlovian conditioning whereas operant behaviour is thought to be established on the basis of the Law of Effect. Skinner suggests that the central nervous system (involving more or less voluntary skeletal and muscular movements) is controlled by "effect" learning but that the autonomic nervous system (involving all involuntary and emotional reactions) is controlled by Pavlovian or classical conditioning. This argument is quite plausible and plainly Thorndike had the same distinction in mind when we wrote in 1932:

"Indeed, I venture, though somewhat timorously, the prophecy that the phenomena of the pure conditioned reflex will teach us more about excitability than about learning."

Although Skinner and Thorndike are alike in that they are both connectionists who emphasise the selective rewarding of trial and error behaviour as the basic factor in learning, Skinner's technical ingenuity and experimental sophistication have revealed facts about the behaviour of organisms which could not have been deduced from Thorndike's principles. With the aid of a simple problem box he designed, now universally known as the Skinner box, he has shown that animal behaviour can be shaped into the most intricate patterns simply by the selective use of rewards.

Typically, a Skinner box consists of a small chamber, fitted with transparent walls, in which the animal can move freely. On one wall is mounted a food magazine which automatically delivers food when a bar is pressed in the case of a rat or, when the subject is a pigeon, a small plastic window, termed a key, is pecked. The feeding mechanism can be set so that during training, known technically as operant conditioning, the animal can be rewarded for every bar press or peck, or he can be rewarded according to some predetermined schedule, say every fifth peck. Alternatively the experimenter can control the feeding by a hand switch so that training need not be confined to pecking and pressing. Any response in the animal's repertoire can be reinforced.

Skinner has show that by the careful programming of reinforcements animals can learn the most surprising pieces of behaviour in a very short time. Let us suppose that the experimenter would like a pigeon to turn clockwise. He does not wait for the complete response to occur before reinforcing it as in Thorndike's demonstration of trial and error behaviour. Instead, he rewards any response that contributes to the clockwise movement such as turning the head to the right or stepping forward with the left foot. Reinforcement ensures that the bird repeats this response almost immediately and reward can now be witheld until a more clockwise movement is made. Progressively, the experimenter becomes more demanding, witholding rewards for rough approximations to the behaviour he requires and rewarding only close approximations. Finally, the pigeon is only reinforced after he has turned a complete circle.

Skinner has also demonstrated that quite different behaviour can result from different reward schedules. A naïve animal placed in a Skinner box needs to be rewarded every time he presses the bar or pecks the key, but once the response has been rewarded a high level of performance can be maintained on a few reinforcements.

There are many ways in which reinforcements can be scheduled. The animal can be rewarded after a fixed number of responses (fixed-ratio schedule) or regularly at fixed time intervals (fixed-interval schedule). Alternatively he can be rewarded according to variable ratio or variable interval schedules, i.e. more or less randomly. In everyday life we rarely receive our rewards on a uniform basis. A class teacher cannot reward every individual child's correct responses so the change in performance these schedules bring about is of more than academic interest.

If, for example, a pigeon is rewarded in a random fashion he pecks about as briskly and steadily as the ticking of a watch. Since the probability of reinforcement is equally likely at every peck a rapid rate of response improves his chance of reward. If, however, he is rewarded for every 10th, 20th or 100th peck his behaviour changes. Paradoxically, we find that the more infrequent the reinforcement the more rapid the response. An animal that is rewarded every hundredth time it does something will repeat the action more often than one which is rewarded on every occasion. He is like a man on piece rates, the faster he gets through a unit of work the more he is paid.

When, however, the reward stops altogether the relationship is reversed. The bird who has been rewarded for every peck very soon stops responding but the bird who has been rewarded for every hundredth response will continue working for a much longer period, since he has habituated to producing a great number of unrewarded responses. The pigeon who was sometimes rewarded and sometimes not, in a random manner, goes on pecking and pecking until exhaustion overtakes him. He has no way of determining when the last reward has been given. Like the pathological gambler who has an occasional win, the bird is in the grip of the unpredictable contingencies of reinforcement.

If the principles deducible from Skinner's demonstrations are applied to human learning they suggest that the best technique would be to reward the desired behaviour on every instance which it occurs. Once established the behaviour can be maintained by less frequent reinforcements. These should be given in a regular manner according to some predetermined schedule so that the more frequent the occurrence of the behaviour the more frequent the reward or approval. A child rewarded randomly will lack any clear discriminatory cues by which he can adjust his behaviour and is therefore likely to persist with it in season and out of season.

If this is put to the harrassed class teacher he is likely to retort that this is just the sort of useless perfectionist advice that he has come to expect from learning theorists. Faced with a large class he cannot score and reward responses with anything like the promptness and consistency which Skinner's demonstrations imply is necessary to successful learning. He does his best, he feels, with team points, conduct marks, termly reports, G.C.E. grades. Of course, all these may serve as reinforcers, but there tends to be a gap between the behaviour and the consequences contingent upon it. Moreover, when we use competitive success as a reinforcer we must recognise that someone has to suffer competitive failure.

However, it is not at all certain that we need these elaborate competitive schemes to spur children on. Operant conditioning techniques applied to human learning suggest that behaviour can be influenced by remarkably small results. A smile or a nod at the right moment, the clarification of puzzlement, the successful completion of a task or simply moving on to the next book or work card can all be reinforcing.

Skinner saw clearly that it was impossible for a class teacher to arrange for each child the subtle reinforcement schedules that the shaping of complex behaviour required, but suggested that they could be applied effectively by means of a teaching machine. Teaching machines at times have evoked all kinds of emotive reactions among teachers. Some have seen them as a threat to their professional status, others have complained that they will turn children into regimented robots. Skinner, however, saw programmed learning as nothing more than the translation of attested laboratory results into rules of practical teaching.

Accordingly, Skinner's teaching machines embody the essence of the principles of learning which he has derived from his animal studies. Learning takes place most readily when an act is followed immediately by reward. But behaviour cannot be reinforced until it occurs, therefore a complex piece of behaviour has to be achieved by shaping. In teaching machine terms this means that what is to be taught, say the use of logarithms, needs to be broken down into its component parts, so that each increment of knowledge is very small and the probability of a correct response very high. This is called the programme and no teaching machine is better than the programme fed into it.

With a skilfully constructed programme the learner should be right about 95 per cent of the time. The pigeon is rewarded by food, but the human learner is rewarded by the knowledge that he is right. The machine itself need be little more than a box containing two windows, one for presenting the programmed text, the other for accepting the learner's response. The programme, printed on a folded sheet, is divided into instructional "frames" which can be seen one at a time through the left-hand window. The learner makes his response by writing his answer on the continuous strip of paper in the right-hand window which moves in phase with the text. By operating a lever he moves his answer under a transparent perspex cover and reveals the correct answer and the next item. The function of the box is simply to direct the learner's attention to the relevant stimuli in a prescribed sequence and to get him to make an active response which can be reinforced.

Whatever the teacher may think about the efficacy of Skinner's learning principles it cannot be argued that his teaching machines either eliminate the need for teachers or reduce their status. A machine does not teach. It brings the learner into contact with a set of stimulus conditions in which learning is possible. These conditions are created by the programmer or tutor. Ordering the material to be learned into a developmental sequence, so that a correct response is almost guaranteed at every step, requires great skill on the part of the teacher and a confident grasp of the subject matter.

When he first tries out his programmes the teacher will probably find that in his traditional lessons he has been accustomed to omitting several essential steps, and to presenting many points ambiguously. Unless he is extremely able, he will almost certainly find that he still has something to learn about the presentation of his subject.

However, difficult as good programming is, it has its compensations. One of the greatest sources of controversy in education has been the various attempts to group and segregate children by ability, but a well-designed programme virtually provides the pupil with a private tutor. Like a good tutor the machine sustains a high level of active learning, it only asks him to take the step for which he is ready, it hints and prompts so that the learner comes up with the right answer and every correct response is immediately rewarded. By assigning certain mechanisable aspects of learning to machines the teacher not only ensures that children learn at their own pace but frees himself for more creative functions.

In terms of the theoretical debate as to the nature of learning Skinner's achievement is but a modest extension of Thorndike's Law of Effect. Skinner (1950) has in fact declared himself to be anti-theory. He considers that speculation as to what goes on between the stimulus and the response has generated much useless experimentation. When the theories are overthrown the greater part of the associated research is discarded. The end result of scientific investigation, whether the investigation is descriptive or an attempt to demonstrate an intervening mechanism, is to state a functional relationship between observables. Since the end result is the same Skinner suggests that we see how far we can get without a theory. He recommends that investigations should at this stage of knowledge concern themselves with contingency explanations, i.e. what leads to what? Answers to these kind of questions do not give much understanding as to why a piece of behaviour occurs; they do, however, enable one to make predictions and to have a measure of control over behaviour.

Skinner's antagonism to theory has found its justification in the discovery that his laboratory animals have exhibited complexities and subtleties of behaviour never before reached by members of their species. Moreover, Skinner's techniques have proved extremely helpful in understanding what is required to ensure a steady progression of learning in human subjects. His achievements owe little, if anything, to speculations about the mental or neural events which might form the basis of changes in performance and a practical teacher may well feel that he would be better employed learning how to apply Skinner's concepts of shaping and programming to a variety of classroom situations than engaging in a theoretical debate as to the nature of learning. After all, as Skinner has pointed out, the science of behaviour must eventually deal with manipulable variables and when we say a child has failed to learn it may well be because we have failed in our presentation of the material.

The invitation to stick to observables and to stop worrying about the unseen mechanisms of learning is an attractive one. All that we need to do is to assemble a collection of statements of the kind, "When A occurs B will follow". Unfortunately, all behaviour does not lend itself to rules of this sort. Both animals and men have a habit of coming up with the correct solutions to novel problems. Behaviour which does not fall into regular and invariant sequences presents a considerable problem for Skinner's approach. For example, Skinner does not regard the acquisition of language as qualitatively different from the process by which pigeons learn to obtain food by pecking at an illuminated key. Words are vocal responses conditioned to occur in the presence of the appropriate stimuli.

But the fundamental problem about language acquisition is not our ability to associate sounds with environmental events but our ability to understand a diversity of utterances never heard before and to produce an equal variety of novel utterances. By the age of three or four, children appear to have mastered all the combinatorial possibilities of simple sentences up to a length of ten or eleven words. No careful schedule of rewards appears to have been necessary. It is sufficient that they have grown up in an environment where language was used. Chomsky (1954) in his highly critical review of Skinner's book *Verbal Behaviour* puts the view that conditioning theory is not only inadequate for the explanation of language but totally invalid.

The Cognitive View of Learning

Both humans and animals plainly do learn from the consequences of their actions but it does seem that this principle needs helping out a little when it comes to explaining how problems never met before are solved. The general difficulty for any explanation of novel behaviour derived from the law of effect is that by definition every correct response has a history. That is to say, to understand the learning process at any particular point it is necessary to have a knowledge of the prior course it has taken, as learning is considered to be a continuous modification of stimulus-response relationships. Cognitive theorists, on the other hand, do not have this difficulty when a new, yet correct, action is produced. They conceive of learning largely as a matter of perceiving the relationships between the elements within the contemporary situation. On the cognitive view, learning is not simply a function of compounding actions which have been successful in the past, but is also how the learner sees the situation. Thus learning depends not on blind accident or the fortunate contingencies of response and reward but on the "hypotheses" or "expectancies" that the learner is testing at each attempt. Actions, both in animals and men, are held to occur "for the sake of" what is expected to follow, i.e. they are purposive and goal directed. Moreover, it is held that the organism will act as insightfully as the situation will permit.

This emphasis on the phenomenological visual field, or how the situation is experienced by the learner, led to the re-designing of learning experiments. The traditional problem box was rejected because it was held that since the animal was denied a view of the total situation an intelligent solution and the relationships between them are visible to the learner. In random trial and error behaviour. The basic plan favoured by the cognitive theorists involves presenting the subject with a novel situation in which the direct approach to some desirable goal is blocked but an indirect route is left open. The problem is displayed so that the various parts of the solution and the relaionships between them are visible to the learner. In these situations it has been found that solutions are not always arrived at by the gradual adoption of the correct response. Solutions can be sudden with few pre-solution attempts.

Köhler's (1925) classic work *The Mentality of Apes* contains several examples of this type of approach. In one series of experiments Köhler's chimpanzees were presented with a number of novel problems which involved the use of sticks as tools for their solution. The standard situation for the stick problems was to have the ape in his cage with some fruit in his line of vision but out of reach.

In the simplest problem of this type a stick long enough to reach the fruit was placed between the ape and the fruit. None of the apes had much difficulty with this set of relationships. Not every ape succeeded, however, when the stick was placed at the back of the cage. Success usually came when the ape happened to glance towards the back of the cage soon after staring at the bananas. A more difficult version of the same set of relationships was posed when the ape was placed in a cage without a stick but with a tree from which a branch could be detached. Many passed this test also. The most difficult of the stick problems required the ape to join two sticks together in order to reach the fruit which could not be reached by either stick alone. Only one ape solved this problem and at first the joining of the sticks appeared to be accidental. Once, however, the relationship had been grasped it was repeated over and over again whenever the situation seemed appropriate.

In another series of problems apes were placed in a cage with fruit hanging from the roof. The lure is out of reach but can be obtained by stacking boxes underneath and climbing upon them. These problems often involved not merely fastening on to the relationships between the box and the fruit but also the mastery of a stable two box structure. The relationship was perceived quite quickly but a stable structure was only achieved after considerable effort.

For Köhler, and his successors in the cognitive group of theorists, the behaviour of these apes was plainly indicative of insight learning. That is to say, the solution was not arrived at by chance, nor was it the result of running off old habits carefully built up by some schedule of rewards. Instead the animal was thought to have perceived a set of relationships between himself, the stick and the fruit of which he was previously unaware. He appeared to have a hunch that the box or the stick would help him to the bananas before he ever got them. He had some idea of what led to what and acted purposefully. Even in animals, it would appear, all actions do not occur because they have been rewarded in the past, some appear because it is "foreseen" that they will be rewarded in the future. They are initiated for the sake of achieving something. This apparently predetermined organisation of behaviour is not what would have been predicted on the basis of the Law of Effect but the connectionists do not dispute the fact that it occurs. The problem for the connectionists has been to accommodate the phenomenon of insightful learning within their own account of how learning occurs.

Various explanations have been offered by S–R theorists (see, for example, Hull, 1935, 1952), all in some way designed to show the essential dependence of insight on prior learning of the trial and error type. A much quoted experiment in support of the S—R interpretations is that of Birch (1945). Laboratory reared chimpanzees were placed in cages with food outside beyond reach, as in the Köhler experiments. A rake was perfectly positioned for drawing in the food. Only one of the six animals gave a smooth, purposeful performance; the success of the others had every appearance of chance. Since the purposeful chimp had previously been observed playing with sticks, all the animals were given sticks to play with for the next three days. After this manipulatory experience all the chimps gave insightful solutions not only to the original problem but to several others which were more complex.

On the basis of this kind of evidence the S—R theorists suggest that the learner has a hierarchy of responses determined by past reinforcement experience. Placed in a novel situation the strongest responses will be those that were successful in similar situations. But a variety of responses may seem appropriate according to the aspect of the problem which catches the learner's attention — what Spence, somewhat cumbersomely, calls the learner's "receptor-exposure adjustment", and a period of trial and error behaviour will ensue. If the experimentally determined "correct" solution is high in the response hierarchy and the appropriate aspect fastened upon, the solution can appear to occur quite suddenly. If it is low in the hierarchy then a prolonged period of trial and error ensues. The greater frequency of insightful solutions observed by cognitive theorists is considered to be partly a matter of method. The S—R theorists, as we have seen, have tended to favour the problem box design where the solution is concealed. The cognitive theorists, on the other hand, have a more "open" situation with all the elements of the problem displayed.

This type of evidence, however, fails to meet the cognitive theorists' argument. The importance of past learning is not in question. All cognitive theorists would accept that an experienced learner is more likely to achieve an insightful solution than a naïve one. What is at stake is the role of experience in new learning. It is argued that in the pre-solution period some perceptual restructuring of the elements of the problem, takes place, the stick must be seen as a tool, the tree as composed of detachable sticks, which enables past experience to be combined and related to the solution of the new problem.

This means that the eventual emergence of the correct response is not entirely predicated by past learning, its emergence is also governed by contemporary organisational factors. Whereas, for the S–R theorist, past learning is a sufficient explanation of present performance, for the cognitive theorist it can only provide the necessary conditions. A child cannot gain insight into a geometrical problem, even if it is within his intellectual capacity, unless he has had some experience of say, circles and triangles. Equally, a knowledge of the properties of these figures is of little use to him if he cannot perceptually restructure the figure in front of him so that he can see its relationship to the problem he has been set.

Of course, the cognitive theorists would accept that some experimental arrangements and some teaching situations are more favourable than others for achieving insightful solutions. Unless the learning situation is set up so that all the necessary elements are displayed, deliberate, insightful solutions will be very difficult to achieve. The ape found it more difficult when the stick was behind him instead of between him and the fruit and yet more difficult when it was necessary to reconceptualise a branch overhead as a stick. Learning insightfully is essentially a matter of structural patterning and mental transformations.

It is in these terms that the cognitive theorists would explain the fumbling trial and error behaviour of the cat in the puzzle-box. A cat, imprisoned in a cage with nothing but a loop of string hanging from the roof, can see no obvious means of escape and is prone to try anything. In the course of these "tries" the first escape is achieved almost by chance. A cognitive theorist would say *almost* by chance as he would not conceptualise the cat's "tries" as mere random movements (unless of course the animal panicked in his prison) but as hunches which needed to be tested. A succession of such hunches may have to be tried before the appropriate one is found. On subsequent imprisonments the cat comes to see the situation differently. The parts of the cage are related both to each other and to his goal. He becomes more selective in his hypotheses and his behaviour appears to become more purposive.

Experienced teachers are well aware that it is possible to present the same problem or learning task so that success which can only be achieved with difficulty by one presentation is achieved with comparative ease by another. The favoured approach may employ a variety of techniques; overviews, outlines, analogies, diagrams, but the aim is always the same. It is to set out the problems so that its critical features are seen in a meaningful relationship and the minor features eliminated or subordinated. The learner is, as it were, given a cognitive map and encouraged to solve his problem by perceiving what leads to what. The same learner can be led to a solution on a step by step basis without ever achieving any understanding of how he got there, simply because that without an overview of the route to be travelled there is no opportunity to relate the parts to the whole.

An excellent example of these contrasting approaches is given in Lewin, Lippet and White's (1939) classical study of children's reactions to authoritarian and democratic styles of teaching. The authoritarian teacher not only differed from the democratic teacher in his attitude to the children, he also presented the work quite differently. Whereas the democratic group chose their own task and had the stages to completion sketched out in advance, the authoritarian group had their task thrust upon them and its manner of execution dictated step by step.

The group that had a bird's-eye view of the task became strongly motivated towards its successful completion and worked almost as hard when the teacher was absent as when he was present. By contrast the step-by-step group failed to identify themselves with the task and the time spent in constructive work was more than halved when the teacher was out of the room. The authors attribute this to the appeal of different styles of leadership but since it turns out that many of the boys did not know what they were making it seems more probable that the drop in output was due to the manner of presentation (Davey, 1969).

Connectionist and Cognitive Theories Compared

At this point we might summarise the contrasting points of view as follows. The cognitive theorist assumes that the learner acts as purposefully and intelligently as the situation permits. If the problem is beyond the learner's capacity or some element essential for its solution is witheld, it will be necessary for the learner to try first one hypothesis and then another, leading to behaviour resembling trial and error. The connectionists, on the other hand, regard trial and error as the primary mode of attack and behaviour resembling insight as explicable in terms of prior learning or internal trial and error.

Since it seems possible to find insight in trial and error experiments and trial and error in insight experiments, the question arises whether there is any real difference between the two positions. Could it not be that this is a pseudo-problem arising from a preference for different words to describe the same behaviour? The findings of one group are, after all, as objective and experimentally impeccable as those of the other and there appears to be no crucial set of experiments which can finally differentiate between the two views.

There is, nevertheless, a real and fundamental difference between the two groups and this concerns the manner in which the unseen learning process is conceptualised. What matters to the cognitive theorist is how the learner sees the situation and what he expects will result from his actions with regard to it. What matters to the connectionist is the lawful relationship he assumes obtains between the learner's response history and his manner of responding in the present situation. In other words, the difference is between those who favour a teleological mode of explanation and those who favour causal explanations of human and animal behaviour.

The S–R theorists have staked everying on the study of behaviour becoming a science. The elimination of subjectivity and the accurate measurement of observable and public data have proved to be the key to understanding in the physical sciences and the aim of the connectionists has been to assimilate psychology to the empiricist tradition by isolating measureable units of behaviour which can be described in operational or physical terms. All notions involving intentionality or consciousness have been purged from their explanations as unverifiable, anthropomorphic, introspective or unscientific. Thus they do not speak of the meaning of the situation for the learner but of a stimulus which can be identified as an object or a sensation in a sense organ. On the response side behaviour cannot be characterised by any desire to bring about an end result but simply as movement executed by the organism.

Similarly, the internal conditions of behaviour cannot be described by concepts which imply an intention or a disposition to behave in a certain way as these, according to the connectionist, have no consistent empirical meaning. Instead internal conditions are identified with "need" or "drive state" which refer to physiological states which can be measured by such means as hours of food deprivation. Alternatively, strings of internal S–R units are postulated. The final explanation is in terms of experimentally determined laws linking together these objectively identifiable events. As Hull puts it in his *Principles of Behaviour*:

"An ideally adequate theory even of so-called purposive behaviour ought, therefore, to begin with colourless movement and mere receptor impulses as such, and from these build up step by step both adaptive and maladaptive behaviour."

The injunction to explain behaviour solely in terms of factual relationships has an obvious appeal. If it can be done it should banish bias, ambiguity and subjectivity from psychological accounts of learning.

However, those who favour a purposive explanation would argue that it can only be done if we are prepared to leave out from our explanations a great deal of the behaviour which many people would consider most worth investigating.

Indeed, Peters (1958) argues that we can never give a sufficient explanation of normal behaviour in terms of mere movement or any other antecedent physiological condition. Man's behaviour is usually explicable because his actions are directed towards ends which he pursues in an appropriate manner. We know, for example, why some people spend hours sitting and listening and others spend hours talking in colleges and universities because we know both the function of colleges and the rules of the game. To ask "What is he doing?" or "Why is he doing that?" implies that we are either ignorant of the rule that is relevant to the behaviour in a given situation or that the person is behaving in a very unusual manner. Of course, movement and the functioning of various organs are necessary in order for a person to go to a lecture, but no matter how exhaustively these are specified we cannot distinguish in this way between arriving late for the lecture and arriving on time, or between arriving late by miscalculation and arriving late to annoy the lecturer. A sufficient explanation of such behaviour can only be given in rule-following, purposive terms.

Peters does not wish to say that non-purposive accounts in terms of antecedent conditions are never relevant. Since the existence of certain organs and their freedom from damage is a necessary condition for certain behaviour, it follows that the absence of normal functioning, such as a brain lesion, can be a complete and sufficient explanation for a breakdown in performance. Similarly, obsessions, phobias and other deviations may admit to a causative explanation. But these are all cases where either something has happened to a man or it is appropriate to ask what drove him to do it. Moreover, the fact that such questions can be asked at all presupposes a generally held belief that action is something which is initiated to bring about an end. In effect, Peters' argument is that the normal operation of organisms follows teleological laws, and that causal or non-teleological accounts can only provide a sufficient explanation for unnatural functioning.

Throughout the period of scientific investigation into the nature of learning this teleological-causative controversy has been the basic issue dividing theorists. It is this controversy rather than the day-to-day exigencies facing the teacher which has motivated learning psychologists, influenced their methods and determined their choice of experimental problems. When Thorndike was first promulgating the Law of Effect it so happened that the schools were enthusiastic about rote learning and, for a time, there was a coincident interest in the pure and applied fields. But apart from an occasional foray into the classroom, such as Skinner's, learning psychologists have not been active in seeking their problems in practical contexts and educational techniques have, perforce, developed independently of learning theory and sometimes, of psychology itself. Personal flair, fashion, expediency and politics have done more to influence classroom practice than any advance in psychology.

There is a gap between the learning psychologist and the teacher and there is little to be gained by ignoring it, even though most text book authors have a compulsion to make heroic efforts to bridge it. Learning theory is concerned with the basic issues regarding the nature of the learning process in general rather than with how children learn all manner of things in a variety of situations. This is not to say, however, that theories of learning based largely on laboratory studies are of no value to practical teachers.

First, a great deal can be learned from the design of experiments which are usually directed towards the facilitation of learning. In the classroom, of course, a number of non-laboratory conditions operate to bring about the changes we call learning, such as the quality of the child's home life, his relationship with his teacher and his status among his peers. An understanding of the social context of learning is of the greatest importance for the teacher and he often finds himself performing the combined functions of social worker, therapist and parent's counsellor. But no matter how he sees his role or where he puts his emphasis his ultimate interest is in the response of the learner. The promotion of particular responses under specific circumstances is, of course, a matter on which learning theorists have a great deal to say. They are divided over the nature of the internal

200 PHILOSOPHY OF EDUCATION AND THE CURRICULUM

processes which intervene between the reception of the internal processes which intervene between the reception of the stimulus and the occurrence of the response, but there is little disagreement about what must be done if a particular response is required.

On this issue there is certainly less argument amongst learning theorists than amongst the practitioners of education. If the animals fail to learn, the experimenter has only himself to blame. He cannot, as the teacher can, complain that he has a poor lot this year or that their backgrounds are deplorable. Either there was something wrong with the way he presented his task or it was beyond the animal's capacity. If, when children fail to accept his offerings the teacher always asked himself if he could have presented his material another way, the children would at least be assured of as much consideration as laboratory rats. No one would wish to deny that social factors facilitate or inhibit the classroom performance but these should be taken into account before the task is selected and the manner of presentation devised. Where there is uncertainty about the manner of presentation an opinion based on careful experimentation is more likely to prove reliable than notions derived from staff room folk lore.

Secondly, some acquaintance with the major theories of learning is necessary if the teacher is to be able to evaluate the changes in classroom practice which are frequently urged upon him by advisors, journalists and other entrepreneurs of educational ideas. Sometimes these changes have been validated under very limited conditions or are almost entirely dependent on their originator's charisma for their effect. Not infrequently, new methods assembled on the basis of *a priori* notions contain elements which run contrary to established principles of presentation and learning.

The teacher should know the kind of questions which should be asked before he commits himself to a new technique. What evidence is used to support the new idea? What evidence is still required and how should it be obtained? Is there any independent evidence which bears on the question? What purport to be new ideas in education occur with a suspicious frequency. Without a good working knowledge of what has been established by learning theorists the teacher can find himself the victim of novelty and the prey of every passing fashion.

Thirdly, the teacher should not allow himself to become the technician of the education system, that is, some one who merely carries out the techniques and methods devised by others. He should be an originator of techniques and methods for the transmission of skills and knowledge and conversant with on-going work in his field. Unless the teacher is literate in the ways of others engaged in research on learning he will not be in a position to make a useful contribution and the gap between the laboratory and the classroom will remain needlessly wide.

The difference between pure and applied research should be one of kind not quality. Hunches can be tried out in the laboratory under more carefully controlled conditions than in the classroom, but once generalisations have been established they need to be subjected to careful testing in the schools so that theory can be confirmed or adjusted by practice. Conversely, the learning theorist can benefit enormously from careful research carried out on practical problems in the schools. If it is executed in a professional manner it may not only refute or substantiate theory, but extend it. Without some knowledge of what learning theorists are driving at and the nature of their problems the teacher will be unable to read about current research, much less participate in it.

References

BIRCH, H. G. (1945) The relation of previous experience to insightful problem solving. *J.Comp.Psychol.* **38**, 367–83.
CHOMSKY, N. (1959) Review of Skinner's *Verbal Behaviour. Language*, **35**, 26–58.
DAVEY, A. G. (1969) Leadership in relation to group achievement. *Educ.Res.* **11**, 185–92.
EBBINGHAUS, H. (1893) *Memory.* New York, Teachers' College, Columbia University.
EYSENCK, H. J. (1960) *Behaviour Therapy and Neuroses.* London, Pergamon.
GUTHRIE, E. R. (1935) *The Psychology of Learning.* New York, Harper.
HEBB, D. O. (1958) Alice in Wonderland or psychology among the biological sciences. In: Harlow, H. and Woolsey, C. (eds.) *Biological and Biochemical Bases for Behaviour.* Madison, Univ. of Wisconsin Press.
HILGARD, E. R. (1951) Methods and procedures in the study of learning. In Stevens, S. S. (ed.) *Handbook of Experimental Psychology.* New York, Wiley.
HOLT, E. (1931) *Animal Drive and the Learning Process.* New York, Holt.
HULL, C. L. (1935) Conflicting psychologies of learning – a way out. *Psychol.Rev.* **42**, 491–516.
HULL, C. L. (1943) *Principles of Behaviour.* New York, Appleton-Century Crofts.
HULL, C. L. (1952) *A Behaviour System: an Introduction to Behaviour Theory concerning the Individual Organism.* New Haven, Yale University Press.
KOHLER, W. (1925) *The Mentality of Apes.* New York, Harcourt Brace.
MASSERMAN, J. H. (1943) *Behaviour and Neurosis.* Chicago, University of Chicago Press.

MCGEOCH, J. and IRION, A. (1952) *The Psychology of Human Learning,* 2nd ed., New York, McKay.

LEWIN, K., LIPPET, R. and WHITE, R. (1939) Patterns of aggressive behaviour in experimentally created social climates. *J.Soc.Psych.* **10**, 271–99.

PAVLOV, I. P. (1927) *Conditioned Reflexes.* London, Oxford Univ. Press.

PETERS, R. S. (1958) *Concept of Motivation.* London, Routledge & Kegan Paul.

PETERS, R. S. (1959) *Authority, Responsibility and Education.* London, Allen & Unwin.

SKINNER, B. F. (1938) *The Behaviour of Organisms: an Experimental Analysis.* New York, Appleton-Century Crofts.

SKINNER, B. F. (1950) Are theories of learning necessary? *Psychol.Rev.* **57**, 193–216.

SKINNER, B. F. (1953) *The Science of Behaviour.* New York, Macmillan.

THORNDIKE, E. L. (1913) *The Psychology of Learning.* New York, Teachers' College, Columbia University.

THORNDIKE, E. L. (1932) *The Fundamentals of Learning.* New York, Teachers' College, Columbia University.

WATSON, J. B. (1919) *Psychology from the Standpoint of a Behaviourist.* Philadelphia, Lippincott.

WATSON, J. B. and RAYNER, R. (1920) Conditoned emotional reactions. *J.Exp.Psych.* **3**, 1–14.

WATSON, J. B. (1930) *Behaviourism.* New York, Norton.

INDEX

203

204   INDEX